THE VANISHING GENERATION

THE VANISHING GENERATION

GENERATION

Faith and Uprising in Modern Uzbekistan

Bagila Bukharbayeva

INDIANA UNIVERSITY PRESS

This book is a publication of

Indiana University Press
Office of Scholarly Publishing
Herman B Wells Library 350
1320 East 10th Street
Bloomington, Indiana 47405 USA

iupress.indiana.edu

Manufactured in the United States of America

Library of Congress Cataloging-in-Publication Data

Names: Bukharbayeva, Bagila, author.
Title: The vanishing generation : faith and uprising in modern Uzbekistan /
Bagila Bukharbayeva.
Description: Bloomington : Indiana University Press, 2019. | Includes
bibliographical references.
Identifiers: LCCN 2018049718 (print) | LCCN 2019008936 (ebook) | ISBN
9780253040848 (e-book) | ISBN 9780253040800 (cl : alk. paper) | ISBN
9780253040817 (pb : alk. paper)
Subjects: LCSH: Islam—Uzbekistan—History—21st century. | Islam and
state—Uzbekistan—History—21st century.
Classification: LCC BP63.U9 (ebook) | LCC BP63.U9 B85 2019 (print) | DDC
958.7086—dc23
LC record available at https://lccn.loc.gov/2018049718

1 2 3 4 5   24 23 22 21 20 19

To my late grandmother Fatima.

If you abdicate from your responsibilities as a human being . . . , and your responsibility as a human being is to treat other people as human beings, if you abdicate on that there is no end to the labyrinth, to the abyss in which you can find yourself.

JAMES BALDWIN,
SPEECH AT THE UNIVERSITY OF CHICAGO, MAY 21, 1963

CONTENTS

PREFACE

IT WAS 1999 WHEN I SENT MY RÉSUMÉ to the Associated Press offering to report for them on my home country, Uzbekistan. I'd just completed a master's in journalism in London. The local media in Uzbekistan was not free, and working for independent foreign media seemed the only way to do the kind of journalism I wanted to do—uncensored and honest. It was just a stab in the dark—a message on the off chance that the AP's human resources office in faraway New York would see something in what I had to offer. I was aware that the Western media had almost no interest in Central Asia, so I was quite prepared not to hear from them at all and soon forgot about it.

But my résumé did not get ignored. In autumn 2001, a few weeks after the 9/11 attacks, I received a surprise call from the editor of the AP's Moscow Bureau asking if I was still interested in working for them. The attacks had brought our part of the world into the spotlight as a staging point for US retaliation against the mastermind of the attacks, Osama bin Laden, who was sheltering in neighboring Afghanistan. US military aircraft and personnel were already arriving and settling in at an air base in southern Uzbekistan to take part in the Pentagon's Afghan campaign.

I was then working for the BBC Monitoring Office in Tashkent, which translated and analyzed Central Asian media reports. I wanted to write my own stories, so I jumped at the opportunity offered by the AP. In a few months, after I'd gone for an interview in Moscow and gotten approval for my hiring from the New York headquarters, I started filing my first stories.

*　*　*

Uzbekistan, an ex-Soviet republic, had by then been an independent nation for only ten years. President Islam Karimov—who emerged as leader because he happened to be the top Uzbek communist boss when the Soviet Union ceased to exist—was at the time busy crushing the country's own alleged Islamist radicals. An alliance with a powerful Western nation in fighting international terrorism was highly welcome as indirect legitimization of Karimov's own campaign, which in reality was about creating an atmosphere of terror inside the country, so he and a narrow group of henchmen could stay in power and enrich themselves indefinitely.

Radical Islamists did emerge in Uzbekistan during the Islamic revival in the few years of relative pluralism leading up to the Soviet disintegration—but that pluralism ended as soon as Karimov got down to building his own regime. Those radicals were a small minority. The overwhelming majority of Uzbeks simply wanted to practice Islam, their traditional faith, more openly and freely than was possible under Soviet rule. Some of them were influenced by conservative Islamic teachings, which were new to Central Asia but were not necessarily political or violent.

The few radicals who had utopian ideas about creating an Islamic state in Uzbekistan had been captured or forced to flee the country in the mid- to late 1990s. But the fear of an Islamist force attempting to challenge Karimov's power was already firmly planted in his mind. The security and law-enforcement bodies continued to jail hundreds and hundreds of people, who did not want to go back to the Soviet-style officially controlled religious practice. Their convictions were based on fabricated confessions forced upon them through torture, which many did not survive. The regime also arranged forced disappearances.

* * *

I spent many days as a reporter inside courtrooms watching trials of group after group of "radical Islamists"—pale, subdued, their shaven heads hung low, the defendants would sit on hard, narrow benches in a metal cage. When trials were closed, I would be outside listening to accounts by their distraught family members, usually wives, mothers, and sisters.

From time to time we, a handful of journalists working for foreign news organizations, would hear of yet another death by torture in police custody or jail and meet another family in grief and pain. With the local media under total government control, we were the only ones reporting on all that with the help of a few brave human rights activists. In 2004 I moved to Kazakhstan, partly because I felt emotionally overwhelmed by these stories—it seemed that I was covering one story all the time.

In May 2005 I came to Uzbekistan to do interviews for a few features. A few days later an uprising broke out in the eastern city of Andijan. A few other journalists and I were lucky enough to reach the city before an inevitable government crackdown and witness what happened.

Seeing how the heavily armed military indiscriminately mowed down a mostly defenseless crowd left me shocked and traumatized. (The rebel leaders had guns, but the thousands gathered in the city's main square to support them or to look on were unarmed, and many of them were women, children and elderly.) The hardest thing to reconcile was the impunity with which the government violated its citizens, yet again using "Islamist terrorism" as a universal cover for its own crimes.

The United States condemned the Andijan massacre and joined calls for an international investigation. The short-tempered Karimov responded by ordering the US military to vacate within 180 days the Khanabad air base in the south, which they were using as a major hub for combat and humanitarian operations in Afghanistan. Karimov also expelled foreign journalists and most international organizations.

After covering the Andijan story, I returned to Kazakhstan and did not visit Uzbekistan for the next three years to avoid possible persecution as an "accomplice of terrorism"—an accusation the government made against journalists who'd reported on the Andijan unrest.

* * *

In 2008, now a citizen of Kazakhstan and no longer with the AP or any other news organization, I returned to Tashkent—a home city I was missing. The saleswoman in the Uzbek national airline's office in Moscow (I worked in the AP's Moscow Bureau in 2007–08) who issued me a ticket did not realize how much love I was feeling for her as I watched her routine manipulations.

I was elated to be back, to take in Tashkent's special spring air, delicate and fragrant from blossoming fruit trees, to retrace my childhood steps around our neighborhood, to walk the city's tree-lined alleys, to smell the freshly baked Uzbek flatbread, to enjoy the first strawberries of the season. I wanted to be there not as a journalist but simply as someone for whom this place meant home.

But it was impossible not to notice the signs of Karimov's regime—the tense quietness of people, the sterile cleanliness of the deserted streets, the cocky confidence of the police. The sight of a police van used for transporting defendants or convicts brought back memories of torture stories I had come across as a reporter.

One of the most frightening sights was the president's motorcade. Preparations for its passage would begin well in advance—policemen would line up along the route, with their backs to the road. The motorcade would go at about 150 kilometers per hour—a police car would speed past first and then another; and then the president's big, shiny, black armored car would swoosh past flanked by two black Jeeps, with commandos in black uniforms and balaclavas hanging out of the open windows and holding their automatic guns at the ready, as if about to open fire on people like in Andijan in 2005. The thought that Karimov was still in power and that he and the others responsible for the Andijan violence and other atrocities were unlikely to ever be brought to account was disturbing.

* * *

It is an Uzbek neighborhood tradition that every evening elder residents sit outside on a bench to share family news with one another and discuss local and faraway events and various matters of life. Among the neighborhood elders that I would see every evening sitting outside our nine-story apartment bloc in central Tashkent was Fazlitdin aka. (*Aka*, with the stress on the second *a*, is how you address an older man or elder brother in Uzbek.) A government minister in the Soviet past, now in his eighties, he still had that air of authority about him.

On his face, there was a mark of deep grief. Sometimes I would see him sitting on the bench on his own—in such moments his figure seemed especially tragic and sad. Everyone in the neighborhood knew their family story. His son Rukhitdin was in jail as an alleged radical Islamist leader; one of his sons-in-law had been kidnapped by the authorities for giving private Islamic lessons; and Fazlitdin aka had not seen his youngest son, Usmon, forced to become a refugee in Europe to avoid prosecution at home for alleged Islamism, for eleven years.

I grew up with Fazlitdin aka's children, sharing with them the same playgrounds and going to the same grocery shops. I feel a special bond to them that probably amplifies my feeling of empathy with their dramatic destinies. It is what compelled me to go back to their stories and those of other victims of Karimov's fight against "religious radicalism," trace their journeys, and clear their names.

I felt like Fazlitdin aka's family and all the other Uzbek families that had been violated by the Karimov government were left to face the hurt and trauma from their losses on their own with no hope for any justice. Karimov died in 2016 but according to the US government's 2017 report on religious freedom, there are 13,500 religious and political prisoners still being held in Uzbek jails.

If the stories of these people, arbitrarily jailed, forcibly disappeared, and tortured to death, and of the toll it all took on their families remain untold and do not reach as many people as possible, the real depth and magnitude of what the Uzbeks as a nation went through under Karimov's regime might never be realized and comprehended, the victims might never be rehabilitated, and Uzbek society might never learn lessons from the atrocities perpetrated during his rule. And this requires a narrative that every human being can relate to, a narrative that will show real people behind the terrible but cold and faceless statistics of human rights abuses.

Writing this book, I was also hoping to contribute as much as I could to countering the Islamophobia that the world seems to be sinking deeper into. Mainstream public opinion is shaped by a simplistic narrative (in essence similar to the approach of Karimov's government) that does little or nothing to separate Islam as a faith and spiritual practice from Islamism—various ideologies of hatred and violence that use Islam as a fake moral prop.

The stories of Uzbek Muslims persecuted for nothing but trying to exercise religious freedom (which includes, I believe, exploring and choosing various teachings within their faith—even conservative ones, as long as they are tolerant to others and do not promote and practice violence) are extreme examples of the demonization of a whole group of people based on the actions of a criminal minority. Today many people seem to be in the same way judging and shunning Islam and all its followers, nearly a third of the world's population, based on the actions of several groups and individuals whose real and only "religion" seems to be, sadly for them and for all of us, the manifestation of their murderous and suicidal inclinations.

I do not practice Islam, but it is the main religion practiced in the region I come from; it is part of our history, and it is the religion of my ancestors, my grandparents, my extended Uzbek and Kazakh families, and my many friends and neighbors. Even in the atheist Soviet environment in which I grew up, Islam was always around in a low-key way—in the prayers said at funerals and weddings; in the blessings given to me by my grandparents, other elder relatives, neighbors, or simply kind strangers; in the poetry of Rumi and Hafiz, in the beautiful ancient mosques and madrasahs of Bukhara and Samarkand, and in the design patterns on traditional ceramics and embroidery.

Writing this book was for me a personal journey of learning more about Islam, seeing it as a complex living thing, and accepting its diversity, inner contradictions, and clashing interpretations, which in essence reflect the universal flaws of human nature. All this, naturally, does make grasping the true depth and messages of Islam a challenge for many of its followers.

For me the work on the book was also a journey into the history of Central Asia, which has strengthened and made more meaningful my sense of connectedness to my own people and myself. On an even deeper personal level, I had to write this book to recover from the emotional trauma that I was left with after witnessing so much human tragedy and pain. Only through sharing this pain and bringing it into the open, will I, the people whose stories I tell in this book, and the Uzbeks as a nation be able to heal.

ACKNOWLEDGMENTS

ABOVE ALL, I WOULD LIKE TO EXPRESS HUGE gratitude to everyone who has shared with me their stories for this book or for my journalistic articles. Without their courage to tell me about some of the hardest and most painful moments of their lives, this book would never have happened. I am deeply grateful for their trust.

A special thank-you to my husband, Robert Greenall, for his calm presence and faith in me. He also acted as my first reader and copy editor.

Another special thank-you to Eva-Marie Dubuisson, a true friend and scholar who deeply cares about Central Asia. I had her emotional and moral support throughout this project.

I would like to thank all my former colleagues at the Associated Press, especially at the Moscow Bureau, stringers across Central Asia, and everyone in AP offices in other parts of the former Soviet Union.

A big thank-you to all my friends who at different stages read my draft chapters and encouraged me to continue.

I am very grateful to Indiana University Press for their immediate interest and strong commitment to my book. It gave me much-needed added strength in the last few intense months of preparing the manuscript for publication.

NOTE ON TRANSLITERATION

To make it easier for readers, with known or better known geographical and personal names I've used their most widely used spellings, usually transliterations from how they are said and written in Russian (for example Tashkent, not *Toshkent*; Andijan, not *Andijon*; Islam Karimov, not *Islom Karimov*; Fergana Valley, not *Farghona Valley*).

With lesser-known Uzbek names I have generally transliterated them from their Cyrillic versions in the Uzbek language. (Since 1995 Uzbekistan has used the Latin alphabet, but I grew up with the Cyrillic version and am therefore more familiar with it. In any case the Uzbek Latin alphabet has some obscure pronunciations, and readers might find some Latin spellings of Uzbek words confusing.)

NAMES OF CENTRAL CHARACTERS

Names of central characters and important characters connected to them, as they are referred to in the book, with full name (first name followed by surname) in parentheses.

ZUKHRA (Zukhra Fakhrutdinova)—author's childhood friend and neighbor.

FARRUKH (Farrukh Khaydarov)—Zukhra's husband, has not been heard from since 2004, believed to have been abducted by the authorities for giving independent Islamic lessons.

ABDULLO (Abdullo Khaydarov)—Zukhra and Farrukh's son.

RUKHITDIN (Rukhitdin Fakhrutdinov)—Zukhra's elder brother, an independent preacher jailed by the authorities for alleged extremism.

FAZLITDIN AKA (Fazlitdin Fakhrutdinov)—Zukhra's father.

MANZURA OPA (Manzura Fakhrutdinova)—Zukhra's mother.

USMON (Usmon Fakhrutdinov)—Zukhra's youngest brother, studied Islam in Yemen, where he was jailed without any charges; at home was wanted as an alleged extremist, now a refugee in Sweden.

IMAM NAZAROV or **NAZAROV** (Imam Obidkhon qori Nazarov)— popular dissident preacher, was forced into hiding in 1998; lived in secrecy in Kazakhstan until 2006 when he received asylum in Sweden; in 2012, in Sweden, survived an assassination attempt.

NASRETDINOVA (Munira Nasretdinova)—wife of Imam Nazarov, currently a refugee in Sweden.

ABDUMALIK (Abdumalik Nazarov)—Imam Nazarov's brother, served several years at the notorious Zhaslyk jail, currently a refugee in Sweden.

KHUSNUTDIN (Khusnutdin Nazarov)—Imam Nazarov's son, missing since 2004, believed to have been kidnapped by the authorities.

MIRAKHMAT (Mirakhmat Muminov)—one of Imam Nazarov's students, currently a refugee in the United States.

ERKIN (Erkin Shermurodov)—one of Imam Nazarov's students, currently a refugee in Europe.

DILMUROD (Dilmurod Turopov)—one of Imam Nazarov's students, currently a refugee in Europe.

FARKHOD (asked not to use his family name)—one of Imam Nazarov's students, currently a refugee in Europe.

KARIMOV or **PRESIDENT KARIMOV** (Islam Karimov)—Uzbekistan's leader from 1989 till his death in 2016.

ALMATOV (Zokirjon Almatov)—President Karimov's interior minister, was fired in 2005 after the Andijan revolt.

INOYATOV (Rustam Inoyatov)—powerful head of the National Security Service (known as SNB under Karimov); was fired in January 2018.

KULUMBETOV (Alikhaydar Kulumbetov)—boss of the notorious Zhaslyk jail, where most inmates were alleged religious extremists.

IMAM MIRZAYEV or **MIRZAYEV** (Imam Abduvali qori Mirzayev)—one of the most popular independent imams of the post-Soviet Islamic revival; disappeared in 1995, believed to have been abducted by authorities, who accused him of preaching radicalism.

ABDULQUDDUS (Abdulquddus Mirzayev)—Imam Mirzayev's son, died in a car accident in Saudi Arabia in 2007.

MOHAMMAD YUSUF (Mohammad Yusuf Mohammad Sodiq)—prominent Uzbek Islamic scholar, served as Uzbekistan's chief mufti in 1989–93, was forced to leave because of his centrist position, died of a heart attack in Tashkent in 2015.

HINDUSTANI (Muhammad Rustamov Hindustani)—one of the most authoritative semiunderground Islamic teachers during the Soviet period, moderate, died in 1989.

YULDOSH (Tohir Yuldosh)—leader of the militant Islamic Movement of Uzbekistan, killed in Pakistan in 2009.

NAMANGANI (Juma Namangani)—leader of the militant Islamic Movement of Uzbekistan, killed in Afghanistan in 2001.

YULDOSHEV (Akrom Yuldoshev)—founder of the Islamist group behind the Andijan uprising, had been in jail since 1999, where he reportedly died in 2010.

YODGOROY (Yodgoroy Yuldosheva)—Akrom Yuldoshev's wife.

PARPIYEV (Kabuljon Parpiyev)—one of the leaders of the Andijan uprising; currently in jail.

THE VANISHING GENERATION

1

MAKING CHOICES

THE APARTMENT BLOCK I GREW UP IN, IN a central neighborhood of Tashkent, could be described as a small model of the Soviet Communist Party's declared principles of social equality and internationalism. Some of its inhabitants worked in factories—both as top managers and workers—some were teachers, some musicians, some officials, doctors, and so on, and we all were of various ethnic backgrounds: Uzbek, Kazakh, Tatar, Armenian, Jewish, Korean, Russian.

The long nine-story concrete block in the neighborhood called Ts-1— "Ts" is short for *tsentr*, the Russian word for "center"—stood at the intersection of First of May and Pushkin Streets (as they were called then). The ground floor was taken by Detskiy Mir, or "Children's World," a department store, which was very handy for children in our block, as we could always pop down there for pens, erasers, and small plastic dolls and spend a few more minutes staring at more desirable, more expensive—and in my family's case, unaffordable—bigger dolls with hair, nice dresses, and shoes.

Another nearby landmark was the Hotel Uzbekistan, designated for foreign tourists, who stopped over in Tashkent on their way to see the ancient Islamic architecture of Bukhara and Samarkand. Seventeen stories high and looking like a concrete honeycomb, the hotel was probably meant to symbolize Uzbekistan's modernization under Soviet leadership. But the true symbol of Tashkent and my favorite nearby attraction was the cozy, shady, circular Revolution Park, which the Hotel Uzbekistan looked down on. The park featured tall, old sycamores, wide-branching oaks, well-tended flower beds, and a monument to Karl Marx in the middle. The monument was designed to look like a torch—a granite support shaped like a handle topped with Marx's head, the thick wavy hair and beard on it sculpted like a flame flickering in the wind. The same spot had in the past hosted a monument

Figure 1.1. The circular Amir Timur Park in central Tashkent, 2008. It used to be called Revolution Park and featured a monument to Karl Marx. After independence Marx's monument was replaced with a statue of the medieval conqueror Amir Timur, who we know as Tamerlane. © Author's photo.

to Joseph Stalin. At present, it is occupied by a formidable equine statue mounted by the medieval conqueror Tamerlane. But it was another change to the park that would serve as a more appropriate and accurate metaphor for and monument to the country's first post-Soviet regime: one day—or rather, night—the authorities would have all the trees in the park cut down, leaving the city with a void in the middle and all its residents, current and past alike, with emptiness in their hearts.

Our family lived in a four-bedroom flat on the fifth floor. We had acquired such a big (by Soviet standards) and centrally located flat thanks to my father's writing talent and assertiveness. Housing was provided by the state for free, but you had to wait for it for years unless you could find a way around the waiting list.

My father was a journalist and knew how to write convincing petitions to officials. He also cleverly played the ethnic card: because we were ethnic Kazakhs, he wrote to Dinmukhammed Kunayev, the Communist Party boss at that time in the Soviet Republic of Kazakhstan, saying that he was a promising young Kazakh journalist in Uzbekistan who was going to devote his professional life to writing about the life of the Kazakh minority living in Uzbekistan—about one million people. But, he explained, he had a problem with housing and was forced to live in rented rooms with a wife and, at the time, three young daughters.

Somehow, perhaps because of its eloquent style, his letter got noticed, and a note was sent from the Kazakh Communist Party to the Uzbek Communist Party suggesting that the young Kazakh journalist in Tashkent should be taken care of. We moved into our flat in 1976.

My father was a totally self-made man with a tremendous amount of energy and confidence and an unbending determination to succeed as a writer. After finishing secondary school at the age of sixteen, he had come to Tashkent penniless from his *kolkhoz* (Soviet collective farm), about two hours' bus ride away. He spent a large portion of his first earnings from various manual jobs in the big city on volumes of classical literature, from Balzac to Turgenev.

He went on to study journalism and worked his way up to become the host of a Kazakh-language program on Uzbek television, which made him a celebrity among the Kazakh community of Uzbekistan. Acting both as a journalist and cameraman, equipped with a very basic movie camera, he traveled to various kolkhozes to shoot stories, mainly about cotton growers and sheep breeders. Back home from his reporting trips, he would type away at his program scripts or novels until late into the night on an old, loud green typewriter.

Our home was always full of various Kazakh talents—writers, poets, musicians, singers—whom our father invited to appear on his program. My three sisters and I did not really appreciate their presence in our lives; for us it meant having to help our mother look after what seemed like an endless stream of guests, serving them food, washing dishes, and making their beds.

Father was totally engrossed in his own world, in which there was not much room for us. But when we were young kids, we would impatiently wait every night for a new episode of stories about Zhalmauz Kampir, the "Old Ogress Witch," and Olmes Batyr, the "Immortal Hero," that he would make up for us off the top of his head.

In a flat identical to ours on the third floor lived the family of Fazlitdin Fakhrutdinov, a forestry minister in the Uzbek Soviet government. He, his wife, and their children had moved into their flat four years before us, when he'd gotten his ministerial job.

Fazlitdin aka had eight children—three daughters and five sons. One of his daughters, Zukhra, was the same age as me, and sometimes we played outside together. Our repertoire of games included rope skipping, dolls, hide-and-seek, and chasing butterflies in our neighborhood, which, despite its central location, was full of fruit trees, elms, oaks, wildflowers, and grasses. Zukhra had green eyes, soft features, and short, light-brown, curly hair, and I secretly admired her beauty.

Zukhra's two sisters, Mavlyuda and Mashkhura, the eldest children in the family, were fifteen and thirteen years older than Zukhra, respectively. When they had been married off, Zukhra had still been a child, and she spent most of her childhood with her five brothers—the three older ones (Bakhmitdin, Rukhitdin, and Mukhitdin), her twin brother (Khasan), and the youngest (Usmon). Their mother, Manzura opa (like *aka* for men, *opa* is used to address an older woman), never had a professional career, fully devoting herself to raising the children.

Fazlitdin aka was born in 1930 to a farmer's family in the Parkent District, east of Tashkent. He studied forest irrigation at the Tashkent Agricultural Institute and worked his way up to become the forest management boss for Tashkent and the three regions in the eastern Fergana Valley. In 1972, he was invited to the capital and made chairman of the newly created

Timber Processing Committee in charge of forests, paper mills, and so on, a position equal in status to that of minister.

Because of his senior government job, Fazlitdin aka was the most important person in our apartment block. Every morning an official white Volga car would wait for him by the entrance. He had a notable paunch but was tall; his back was always straight, his head was held high, and he always wore well-ironed white shirts and formal suits. Sometimes he would shake hands and chat with some of the neighbors for a few minutes before getting into his car.

Fazlitdin aka was determined to bring up his children as "good people," educated and with strong moral values. He believed the best way to accomplish this was by instilling discipline and demanding obedience from them. To some extent he continued to act at home like the boss that he was in his office, but by and large he was no different than many other Uzbek fathers who made all the rules at home and all the decisions concerning family matters.

The children were never to answer back to Fazlitdin aka or to disobey his word. They were to be home each day by six o'clock, before his return from work. Every evening, Fazlitdin aka would make the boys do one hour of vigorous exercise—push-ups, sit-ups, jumps, and so on. In addition to having good marks at school, he wanted his sons to be physically strong too. The lone way his children ever showed any resentment was by calling him "the General"—and this only behind his back, of course.

After Zukhra and I went to school in 1979 at the age of seven—to an Uzbek-language school and a Russian-language school, respectively—we began to play less and less often together. Maybe this was because language and cultural barriers began to separate us. Russian was becoming my main language; hers was Uzbek. I was now mixing with my multiethnic classmates—Russians, Tatars, Jews—while Zukhra was in a predominantly Uzbek environment. We were still growing up in the same neighborhood but becoming parts of two different communities.

My three sisters and I went to School No. 50, just a five-minute walk from our home. It specialized in mathematics and physics, which meant extra classes on these two subjects.

My class was a model one at our school because our form mistress, Lyudmila Vladimirovna, who was in her thirties and taught mathematics, seemed to be putting all her energy into us, her pupils. Maybe this was because she had no family of her own—only poodles, whom she adored. She was tall, had blond curls, wore spectacles, and walked quickly and purposefully. She was a nerdy, confident type and also quite a Communist activist. We regularly marched and paraded and sang ideological songs because being a model class meant winning various ideological competitions. But we had lots of fun too, like picnics in the mountains and parties.

Our class was called Plamya (Flame) and was named after the Czech Communist activist and antifascist journalist Julius Fucik. I was so impressed by his story that every time we went to his museum in Tashkent, which we did every week, I felt a strong sense of admiration, mixed with pity, for him and his *Notes from the Gallows*, which he'd written in prison, before being hanged.

Outside school, however, there was the unescapable reality of Soviet life, including the humiliation of standing in queues for butter, sausages, meat, and other food that was not available every day.

One of the neighbors in our apartment block, Parida opa, worked at the Moskva food shop across Pushkin Street. She would tip off our mother and other neighbors she was friendly with when the shop was going to have some rare and sought-after item, telling them what time the shop was going to begin selling it.

Our mother would dispatch at least two of the four of us to stand in the queue, so we could get two or more rations. I did not like doing that, sensing that there was something undignified in having to queue for basic food. I also resented the rude service at the shop, the quick and nervous movement of hands wrapping sausages in thick brownish paper, and the greedy, hungry, and impatient atmosphere around the people standing in the queue.

As a government minister, Fazlitdin aka was on *gos-obespechenie*, which meant "state provision." Every week, a car would bring the family food supplies, including delicacies that were never seen in the shops.

But there were no other signs that the family was living any kind of privileged life, and Fazlitdin aka's children also queued for milk and other things at the Moskva. In Soviet times, the surest signs of a family's wealth and high social status were the foreign-made clothes they could afford to buy and get hold of, like jeans or good quality shoes. Fazlitdin aka's children, however, were dressed modestly, in clothes from regular Soviet shops. He did not think of using his position to spoil his children like that. He believed that they, like most Soviet citizens, had all they needed.

"There was everything in the shops. There was nothing that you could not find. There was good education. Education was open and free, like medical services," Fazlitdin aka told me in a conversation recalling those times. "There was order. If anyone complained about anything, there would always be a response from the authorities. Everything was fair. We did not know that we were living under communism. We understand that only now," he said, reflecting the sense of nostalgia many older former Soviet citizens feel for the good old days and their disappointment with the post-Soviet social turmoil and onset of cutthroat capitalism. But there was a lot more than that to Fazlitdin aka's nostalgia.

* * *

In Zukhra's memory, her and her siblings' childhood was unclouded and happy, though in parts too strictly overseen by Fazlitdin aka.

Without her father's knowledge, Zukhra went to a dancing school—the famous Bakhor (Spring) dance company—where she learned traditional Uzbek dance and the dances of other ethnic groups living in the Soviet Union, the company's specialty. Fazlitdin aka, who considered dancing too frivolous an occupation for a proper girl, was unaware of her classes for all the eight years that she took them.

Zukhra and her siblings read books and discussed them all together. They took turns cleaning the house, divided into "teams." Zukhra was on one team with Rukhitdin, the fourth child in the family, and they would use their pocket money that was given as a reward for the cleaning to buy books and visit museums, unlike the others, who would spend the money on ice cream and the cinema.

Rukhitdin, born in 1967, was his parents' most promising child, always well behaved and keen to study, exactly how Fazlitdin aka wanted his children to be. According to one family story, when seven-year-old Rukhitdin started attending school the family would always miss him in the morning. By the time they got up between six and seven, he would already be gone, having caught one of the first trams of the day, with his bag full of textbooks. The school caretaker would say to his parents that he felt so sorry for this little boy every time he saw him sitting in the dark by the school door, waiting for it to open.

Rukhitdin was the pride of the school and his teachers' favorite. When he was in the eighth or ninth grade, he made a pyrographic portrait of Lenin in wood, and it was the spitting image of the former Soviet leader,

Zukhra told me. His work was sent to Moscow to be judged in a Soviet-wide children's competition. With his father so highly placed, Rukhitdin's future was mapped out for him.

Rukhitdin graduated from secondary school in 1984 with a Golden Medal, awarded for excellence in all subjects throughout the ten years of his education there—the school specialized in French. The same year, he entered the prestigious Oriental Studies Department of Tashkent State University (TashGU)—one of only a few schools in the USSR that trained specialists in oriental languages, like Persian, Urdu, Pashto, and Arabic. The school was second only to the Soviet Union's main academic center and school of Oriental studies in Leningrad (now St. Petersburg). The Tashkent Oriental Studies Department, known as Vostfak (an abbreviation of the Russian Vostochnyy Fakultet, or "Oriental Department"), was famous for its Pashto program, the language of Afghanistan's largest ethnic group—an important one for Russian diplomats, military, and KGB because of the Soviet Union's military intervention in that country. The school's Arabic program, which Rukhitdin chose as his main subject, also had an excellent reputation.

Everyone knew that to get into Vostfak you had to be either exceptionally brilliant or from a family with good connections. It was also prestigious to study there because the department's students got sent abroad—an extremely rare opportunity for Soviet citizens—to practice the languages they studied.

Zukhra and I finished secondary school in 1989. She wanted to become a doctor, but competition to get a seat at the Tashkent Medical Institute (TashMI) was always tough, and even though she had private tutors preparing her for entrance exams, she could not find the courage to try. Rukhitdin advised her to try TashGU's Romance and Germanic Languages Faculty to study French.

By then, Rukhitdin was a star at the Oriental Studies Department because of his excellent academic performance. He was also made leader of the department's Komsomol—the Communist Party's youth branch.

"Are you Rukhitdin Fakhrutdinov's sister?" the TashGU rector asked Zukhra when she was sitting for her entrance exam.

"Yes," Zukhra replied.

"OK, we'll give you a five [the highest mark]. You look like your brother, and you're as smart as him."

Zukhra's department was in the same building as Rukhitdin's, and soon she learned how popular her brother was. Many students sought to make friends with her in hopes of getting introduced to her brother.

"He was so respected that when he walked down the corridor, students would spill out of all the classrooms to stare at him. Everyone wanted to talk to him," Zukhra recalled.

Rukhitdin, already in the final years of his course, did not have many lectures to attend and would mostly come to the department only to hand in his assignments and to sit for tests and exams, so his every appearance was "like a sensation."

My decision to go for a journalistic career was influenced by Mikhail Gorbachev's perestroika—the liberal reforms he announced in 1985—though my parents said I had been saying that I would be a journalist since I was three years old. I was finishing school at the peak of perestroika. One of the central elements of the reforms was the glasnost, or openness, policy—that is, access to information and freedom of speech. The press and television suddenly obtained a new voice and became interesting, examining previously taboo subjects concerning both the Soviet Union's past and present. Our family, like many other Soviet families at the time, subscribed to a dozen or so newspapers and magazines and read each of them from cover to cover. Inspired by all that, I applied for a place at Tashkent University's Journalism Department.

By 1989, perestroika was already beyond the control of its architect, and the Soviet Union was into its last days. But the Soviet state machine was still running, and it provided one last, fateful service to Rukhitdin: he was selected by the TashGU administration to be sent to study for one year in an Arabic country to improve his language skills as part of an established Soviet practice of training experts on the Middle East. Rukhitdin was offered a choice between Syria, Egypt, and Kuwait. He asked his father which country to pick.

"If you want to go, then it's better to go to Kuwait because it's a rich country, and they have the best teachers. I think you'll be fine there," Fazlitdin aka said. He personally saw his son off, flying with Rukhitdin to Moscow, from where the select pupil could take a flight to Kuwait. In Kuwait Rukhitdin and four other students on the same program, three from Moscow and one from Armenia, lived at the Soviet Embassy.

Another crucial event that would later determine Zukhra's future took place in December of the same year. On that day, Zukhra was reading in her department's library, sitting in the last row. She noticed that a young man sitting in the first row kept turning back and looking at her. Zukhra was struck by how much he looked like Rukhitdin, who at the time was in

Kuwait. His name, she later learned from fellow students, was Farrukh; and he was Zukhra's future husband. Zukhra also learned that Farrukh was taking the same Arabic course as her brother but was a few years his junior. After a few more chance encounters in the library, Farrukh came up to Zukhra and introduced himself. After the New Year's holidays, they began to see each other every day at the university.

Farrukh came from a professional Tashkent family. His father, a gentle, intelligent man, worked for state television. His mother, a domineering woman who was the boss in the house, taught in a primary school. One of Farrukh's two elder brothers was a soccer player, and the other, a businessman. His only sister was a musician.

* * *

Fazlitdin aka's successful official career meant he was a committed Communist and by default an atheist. God was never mentioned in the house, and there was never any talk of religion. Zukhra's mother, Manzura opa, did perform regular prayers, but she would never mention Islam to her children.

It was the same in my family—no talk of God or the existence of any religions. The only way we came in contact with religion was seeing our maternal grandmother, Fatima, who was Uzbek, pray when she visited or seeing other elderly relatives pray when we visited them in their village. I cannot remember exactly how often or regularly our grandmother prayed. She would use a scarf as a prayer mat, placing it in front of her on the floor. After carefully smoothing the scarf down with her hands, she would sit down, eyes closed, and begin her prayer. As if it were something too insignificant, no one explained to us the meaning of that ritual of sitting in a corner, whispering, and then prostrating oneself several times on the floor.

* * *

Rukhitdin had started performing *namoz*, Islamic prayer, before going to Kuwait, but no one in the family, in my later interviews with them, could say exactly when or why. It is probable that Rukhitdin's interest in Islam was awakened by students from Arab countries studying at TashGU. As part of the Soviet Union's ideological contest with the West, every year the Soviet government offered thousands of scholarships to students from dozens of Moscow-leaning countries in Asia, Africa, and the Middle East.

Tashkent was the fourth-largest city in the Soviet Union and had many academic institutions, and these received a fair share of those foreign students. It was natural for the local students studying Arabic to seek contact with students from Arabic-speaking countries to get language practice. Of course, you cannot really study a foreign language without studying the culture of the people who speak it. The culture and mind-set that comes with Arabic is centered on Islam.

Thus, inevitably, future Uzbek Arabists' contacts with their Arab peers could involve, depending on the degree of interest and preparedness on both sides, an introduction to Islam. Some of the Arab students saw it as helping their Uzbek Muslim brothers who had lost touch with their religion under Russian subjugation. And these students from Syria, Lebanon, and elsewhere took it as their duty to tell fellow Uzbek students what it meant to be a Muslim and how to practice Islam; they would also bring them books to read when they went home for the holidays.

In Kuwait, Rukhitdin completed the language course within three months and spent the rest of his time there studying Islam. After a year in Kuwait, he became a devout Muslim. He returned home in "those clothes," said Fazlitdin aka, referring to his son's white *shalwar kameez*—the loose cotton pants and long, wide shirt worn by men in Arab countries—and with a beard.

For the inhabitants of our apartment block, that was a sensation. The building was designed so every flat had windows or balconies looking onto both the street and the courtyard. If someone spotted Rukhitdin crossing First of May Street, the broad boulevard that our block faced, he or she would alert others: "Rukhitdin is coming!" Gluing themselves to the windows, the whole family would stare at him until he turned the corner. Then the watchers would run to the windows facing the courtyard to watch him reappear again and follow him with their eyes until he entered the block. There he was, probably aware of the stir he was causing, walking slowly, with a big freely growing beard that, in keeping with his religious ideas, he did not trim and gave no shape to—again at the center of attention, like when he was a star student.

We all felt a certain primitive curiosity about Rukhitdin's exotic new looks. And there was even some jealousy mixed in, toward someone who had been abroad and picked up new fashions. It got even more intriguing when Rukhitdin got married, and then married a second time, and began to show up in the neighborhood with his two wives walking behind him, both covered from head to toe in wide, black, cloak-like clothes.

The neighbors continued to watch the procession out of their windows with the same curiosity, but there was something alien and controversial about the women's black garb and in Rukhitdin's openly having two wives, one of whom was only sixteen years old. It was no longer only a difference in fashion—behind it there was some ideology unknown to us that seemed to challenge our society's established way of life.

For Zukhra, Rukhitdin was "a different man" now, following a new etiquette regarding women. "He would not even look me in the eye and would not talk at all," she said.

Fazlitdin aka did not like Rukhitdin's new looks, especially the beard. When Islam came to be marginalized under the Communist regime in Central Asia, the beard came to be seen as an attribute of the community elders and the wisdom that comes with old age. So Rukhitdin's growing a beard could be seen as his jumping ahead of his father and, in a way, claiming to be more knowledgeable and respectable than him.

"I am your father and do not have a beard. How come you, my son, do?" he said to Rukhitdin. "It won't do here. Trim it," he said, which Rukhitdin did.

Rukhitdin also began to share his new faith and knowledge with his family. "Rukhitdin explained everything [about Islam] so beautifully," said Zukhra. "When we sat all together at home, he would always talk about God, tell us *hadiths* [accounts of the Prophet Muhammad's sayings and actions] and tell us about the Prophet's life, what he did and what he said. Gradually we began to like his talks."

* * *

Upon his return from Kuwait in 1991, Rukhitdin got a job as an Arabic teacher in a secondary school in the Tashkent *mahallya* (neighborhood) called Samarkand Darvoza (Samarkand Gate).

Some six months after starting the job, Rukhitdin asked for his father's blessing to accept a proposal from the neighborhood elders to become an imam at the local mosque.

Fazlitdin aka did not like the idea as he envisioned a different future for his son, in academia. "You should become a famous scholar," he said. Rukhitdin did not argue and said that that would be his response to the elders.

But a week later, the bell rang in Fazlitdin aka's home. At the door, there were four bearded men. The two older ones wore white skullcaps, which meant they were *qozha*—someone who has been on pilgrimage to Mecca—and the two younger ones wore traditional black Uzbek skullcaps.

Fazlitdin aka guessed at once that they were the Samarkand Darvoza neighborhood elders. The four men were invited inside and seated in the living room.

"What brings you here?" Fazlitdin aka asked them.

Following the traditional etiquette, the visitors approached the subject in a roundabout way. One of the men started by introducing himself as someone who had been in charge of public utilities in their mahallya for the past thirty-five years. Finally, he approached the matter at hand.

"Our mahallya has never been so peaceful and orderly as it has become since your son began to teach at our school. He has had a great influence on all of us. We asked him to become our imam, but you would not let him. We went to (Chief) Mufti Mohammad Sodiq (Mohammad Yusuf), and he advised us to come to you with our request and pass on to you his words."

The mufti's message went as follows: "We [Uzbekistan] are independent now. New mosques are being built everywhere. Old ones are being refurbished, fitted with electricity and telephone lines; plumbing and carpets are being donated to them. It's no good if he [Fazlitdin aka] does not let his son serve religion."

At that moment Rukhitdin came home from work. When he sat down with everyone else, the four men briefly repeated the purpose of their visit.

"If you allow me, Father, I will accept the offer, but I have two conditions," Rukhitdin said. "First, I do not want to be paid anything. Second, I will only lead the Friday prayer and will not work on the other days."

Rukhitdin was at the time already living the busy life of an independent preacher and teacher of Arabic, knowledge of which was in high demand with the surge of interest in Islam. As someone with a privileged background, he was well known and popular as a religious authority among some richer Uzbeks, who were keen to become more observant Muslims. Rukhitdin would be invited by them to perform Islamic rituals at family events, like weddings and funerals, and to give Islamic lessons.

The visitors were happy with the conditions, and Fazlitdin aka gave his blessing. "If it won't get in the way of your other commitments, you may do this. Maybe it will be a temporary thing," he said.

The official muftiyat also gave its approval.

In an increasingly pluralist climate, in 1991—the year of the Soviet collapse—Zukhra's fiancé, Farrukh, in a group of twenty Arabic students,

Figure 1.2. Children returning home with groceries in a typical *mahallya* (neighborhood) in the old part of Tashkent, 2016. © Alexey Volosevich.

was sent on a government scholarship to Saudi Arabia for a course at the Islamic University, which would transform him, like Rukhitdin, into a devout Muslim. When Farrukh left, he was "modern" and "a long way from religion," according to Zukhra. After the first year of his studies in Saudi Arabia, "he turned 180 degrees." He came home for a holiday with a long beard and boasting that he knew by heart the entire Koran and numerous hadiths and was keen to share his new knowledge with everyone he met.

"He explained everything [in Islam] so passionately, citing two or three hadiths at once to support his every point," Zukhra said. "Because my brother was already like that [religious], I already liked it a little. I thought it meant that Farrukh would have good moral principles and would not hurt other people."

Zukhra and Farrukh married in the summer of 1994. Farrukh had three more years to complete his course in Saudi Arabia. His letters from Medina were full of references to Allah and showed that he was fully engrossed in his intense studies of Islam.

"In whose hands is our future, our happiness and our destinies as a whole? In your hands, in my hands or in the hands of the government?

What human being can figure out and decide his future and fate? Does anyone ever think about anyone who isn't born yet? No. But Allah Ta'ala [the Highest], who has created man, has already written everyone's destiny, and knows already when someone is still in his mother's womb if he is going to be happy or unhappy," said one of his letters sent in 1994.

"I've hardly found time to write a letter. There is so little time, I sleep three-four hours a day and even when I am eating my eyes are on a book," Farrukh wrote in another letter in December 1994.

* * *

For Uzbekistan's Communist leadership, the 1980s (the years leading to the republic's independence from Russia) were turbulent years as the Kremlin subjected it to a massive anticorruption purge. There is one theory that the 1982–84 Soviet leader Yuri Andropov, a hardline former KGB chief, wanted to use investigations against Uzbek officials to shake up the entire thoroughly corrupt Soviet bureaucratic machine. The corruption probes launched by the Kremlin against Uzbek officials, from top to bottom, were dubbed Khlopkovoye Delo, or "the Cotton Case."

The special investigators sent from Moscow to Uzbekistan revealed that under the pressure of ever-rising and unrealistic cotton harvest targets set by the Moscow economic planners, local officials had developed a brazen practice of inflating figures to please the Kremlin—the scheme rested on a bribery chain from collective farm directors to district and then to regional and then republican officials. Eventually the inflated reports were sent, along with hefty bribes, to the supervising officials in Moscow—hence, Andropov's plan for a broader purge.

The purges brought down Uzbekistan's longtime Communist boss Sharaf Rashidov, forcing him allegedly to commit suicide in 1983 after twenty-four years on the job. Rashidov was replaced by Inomjon Usmankhodjayev, who also, five years later, faced corruption charges and was jailed over the ongoing Cotton Case.

In the perestroika years the inquiry was criticized for breaches of "socialist justice," meaning various abuses in the course of the investigations, and was eventually closed in 1989. More than 2,600 officials in Moscow and Uzbekistan went to jail as a result, and a number of others committed suicide.

At its peak in the mid-1980s, the Cotton Case was broadly covered by the Soviet media for propaganda purposes. In Uzbekistan, understandably, it was taken as humiliating, the parading of their particular ethnic group before the entire country as backward and corrupt.

It further spurred the growing nationalist sentiment among many Uzbeks and contributed to the rise of the Birlik movement, which involved mainly the intelligentsia most active in the capital, Tashkent. They campaigned for Uzbek to be made the republic's main language, instead of Russian. They were also against sending Uzbek conscripts to serve in other parts of the Soviet Union, to save them from bullying on ethnic grounds, which was rampant in the Soviet army. A split within the movement later produced the Erk (Freedom) Party, led by the writer Mohammad Solih.

A cruder kind of nationalism was arising in the overpopulated, ethnically mixed eastern Fergana Valley as a consequence of the Soviet government's ethnic policies and as an outlet for the many public frustrations and insecurities. In June 1989 it erupted into violence against an ethnic minority, the Meskhetian Turks, accompanied with slogans saying that they, the Russians, and other non-Uzbeks should "get out." About two hundred Meskhetian Turks were killed, and tens of thousands were forced to leave Uzbekistan.

Meskhetian Turks are ethnic Turks from Georgia's Meskheti region, which borders on Turkey. Stalin deported more than 115,000 of them to Central Asia, mostly to Uzbekistan, in 1944 when the Soviet Union was considering expansion into Turkey, over which it had territorial claims.

Usmankhodjayev's successor, Rafik Nishanov, a career diplomat, was made to resign days after the Fergana riots, after just one year on the job. Gorbachev invited him to Moscow to become speaker of the Soviet parliament's Sovyet Natsionalnostey, or "Council of Ethnic Groups."

Since December 1986, when the appointment of an ethnic Russian as Kazakhstan's new Communist leader had sparked massive protests, Gorbachev was faced with mounting nationalist sentiment and ethnic unrest across the Soviet Union. Azerbaijan and Armenia were locked in a conflict over Nagornyy Karabakh, an ethnic Armenian enclave within Azerbaijan; there was a growing push for independence in the Baltic republics; movements for greater self-rule were strengthening in Ukraine, Moldova, Georgia, and Central Asia; the Crimean Tatars, deported by Stalin from Crimea to other parts of the USSR as "unreliable" after World War II, were rallying to demand to be allowed back.

After initial attempts to suppress nationalist protests by force, Gorbachev decided to try "a uniform democratic approach," hoping to save the territorial integrity of the Soviet Union through political and economic re-forms. Perhaps that's what he meant to signal by giving the job of head of the Sovyet Natsionalnostey to a non-Russian.[1]

There are various versions of how the next leader of Uzbekistan, Islam Karimov, was selected. Some say he had been eyeing the position himself and managed to find an ally—an influential official in the Kremlin with access to Gorbachev—to put in a word for him at the right time, when it was decided to move Nishanov to Moscow; others say that as a native of Samarkand, Karimov had been pushed through by Ismoil Jurabekov, the leader of the Samarkand clan; still others say the deciding factor for the Kremlin, busy with managing various crises all over the crumbling empire, was that the little-known boss of the backward southern Uzbek Qashqadarya Region had a firm management style and a relatively clean background, unmarred by corruption scandals, and this was how he was introduced by whoever acted as his referee. Karimov was appointed to the job on June 23, 1989.

The volatile Fergana Valley provided the first major crisis for Karimov as the Uzbek republic's leader. It was another outbreak of ethnic bloodshed, this time between Uzbeks and Kyrgyz. The focal points of the June 1990 violence were the predominantly Uzbek-populated towns of Osh and Uzgen in a part of the valley belonging to the Kyrgyz Soviet republic.

The Central Asians had been divided into five main ethnic groups and respective republics within the Soviet Union during a national delimitation process that was completed in 1936. The first to emerge between 1920 and 1924 were Uzbekistan, Kazakhstan, and Turkmenistan, and later Tajikistan and Kyrgyzstan. The division was "to a great extent artificial, a result of efforts by historians and statisticians, bureaucrats and politicians," according to the Russian historian and ethnologist Sergey Abashin.[2] It effectively erased many subethnic groups that existed in the region, but at the same time it was a logical culmination of a process of national self-identification and formation of the region's main distinct ethnic groups (with their own languages and cultural elite) that had already been under way since before the 1917 Russian Revolution.

The densely populated Fergana Valley was probably the most challenging place for drawing ethnic borders. Just several years earlier, the Russian tsarist government's statisticians were struggling to count the populations of the valley's many ethnic groups. The surveys published for several years starting in the early 1900s showed great fluctuations, which Abashin puts down to the absence of a clear definition of each ethnic group and "the absence of a clear idea of who they were on the part of the Fergana inhabitants themselves."

Nevertheless, the Fergana Valley ended up being divided between the Uzbek, Kyrgyz, and Tajik Soviet republics, with each getting minority enclaves on their territories. But the Soviet borders existed only on maps, and the valley continued to live, as it always had done, as a single melting pot.

Because of its arable soil and favourable climate, the Fergana Valley—stretching for 170 kilometers from north to south and 330 kilometers from east to west and surrounded by mountain ridges, sources of the rivers that feed the valley's farming lands—is the most densely populated and most heavily cultivated piece of land in Central Asia. Tightly packed with towns and villages, surrounded by fruit orchards and fields under various crops, it is a crucial agricultural oasis for all three republics that share it—the rest of both Kyrgyzstan and Tajikistan is covered by mountains, while Uzbekistan's territories to the west are mainly desert.

The valley has traditionally had a high birth rate, which in the last decades of the Soviet Union was further encouraged by relative economic stability, ensuring a steady population growth and consequently a high proportion of young and unemployed, which made the question of distribution of resources even more acute. The conflict between Uzbeks and Kyrgyz was not so much about ethnic hatred but rather rooted in the centuries-long competition for resources between the region's settled and nomadic peoples. Identification along ethnic lines, from a historical perspective, is a recent thing—up until the Soviet delimitation, Central Asians saw themselves as Muslims of Turkestan.

The settled Uzbeks, traditionally skilled traders and farmers, tend to be better off than the nomadic Kyrgyz. The 1990 unrest was sparked by Kyrgyz anger over the perceived unfair distribution of land, which they believed was in favor of Uzbeks and the cause of their less advantageous economic situation. Hundreds were killed and thousands wounded in several days of deadly rampages by Uzbek and Kyrgyz mobs armed mostly with knives, metal rods, and sticks. The unrest only ended with the arrival of Soviet troops and the establishment of their heavy presence on the streets of Osh and Uzgen.

Official Uzbek propaganda would later credit Karimov with preventing the violence from flaring up further by allegedly arriving on horseback and stopping Uzbeks from the Uzbek side of the valley from going to Osh to aid their kin. Whatever his role was, Karimov would have to make a mental note about the Fergana Valley as a source of more trouble in the future.

* * *

In August 1991 a coup by Communist hardliners against Gorbachev's reforms set in motion his demise as leader, along with that of the entire Union of Soviet Socialist Republics.

The fifty-three-year-old Karimov was left to lead Uzbekistan on his own. He had a very shaky start. The Soviet collapse gave a powerful boost to all the political and social forces that perestroika had inspired and galvanized—the nationalists, Islamists, and a few liberals. They all saw Karimov as a representative of the outgoing regime.

With only two years at the helm, Karimov had no clout within the Uzbek political elite either. And they too were eager to take advantage of the new uncertain political situation. Already in September, Karimov came in for scathing criticism for authoritarianism from a group of parliament members led by Vice President Shukurullo Mirsaidov, an influential Tashkent clan member. Karimov would later describe the attack as a "conspiracy and coup attempt."[3] It was the very parliament that had elected him president in 1990.

Seeing that he could no longer rely on the MPs' backing, Karimov needed to get stronger validation of his presidential status, which he intended to do at presidential elections scheduled for December 29, 1991. Karimov's only challenger was Mohammad Solih, the secretary of the Union of Writers and leader of the Erk Party, popular among the politically active university lecturers and students and in his western home region of Khorezm. But the source of a greater political challenge to Karimov lay again in the Fergana Valley, where, despite the seventy years of Soviet rule, people's ideas about morality and how society should be organized remained deeply rooted in Islam.

Divided from the rest of the country by the Chatkal mountains and accessible only through the narrow Kamchik pass, and now with the restrictions on practicing Islam gone, the valley was going through its own outbreak of public activism, shaped and commanded by new self-proclaimed Islamic leaders. Unlike nationalists, they blamed all the social problems and ills, like crime, on the infidel communists and generally on secular rule. In Namangan, one of the valley's three largest cities, vigilante groups set out to impose what they believed to be Islamic Sharia law, catching thieves and publicly punishing them by beating them up and filming the process to serve as a lesson to others.

"Police would come to take them [captured thieves] in, but people would not want to let them go. They didn't believe that the state would punish them accordingly," a witness who lived in Namangan at the time and is now living in Europe told me in a conversation in 2009.

"You only take bribes and let criminals go!" the people would say to the police.

The groups, among them Adolat (Justice) and Iman (Faith), were made up of street youths, many with a background in sports. The most outstanding figure among them was Tohir Yuldosh. A native of Namangan in his early twenties, Yuldosh possessed striking self-confidence and was a fiery orator. He was said to have had contacts with and probably been influenced, for a time, by the Namangan *qazi*, or Islamic judge, at the time, Umarkhon qori Namangani, before going completely his own way.[4] Yuldosh was easily accepted as their leader by many of the local wayward youth who had hardly any knowledge of Islam. He set out to organize in his own way the unruly vigilante groups, setting up his own Islom Lashkarlari (Warriors of Islam).

At the frequent rallies in those days, Yuldosh delivered his messages in a belligerent tone as if castigating his listeners for straying off "the true path," bludgeoning them into submission to his "moral" and "religious" leadership. Those rallies and the bold new ideas about "rights and wrongs" struck a chord with the town's youth, and it was something different to nationalism. "The entire city was reeling," according to the same former resident of Namangan.

Karimov was meanwhile preparing for the December 29 presidential poll. He came to Namangan several days before polling day to meet local officials as part of his election campaign. When he left, the Islamist youth, angered because he didn't find time to meet them and listen to their demands, started a massive rally in the city center, seizing the city administration building, previously the headquarters of the Communist Party's city branch. They were led by Yuldosh and had fifteen demands, including that Uzbekistan be declared an Islamic state, the Koran be taught in schools, Friday be made a day off, and all food be halal. Karimov was forced to return to Namangan and face the protesters.[5]

A green Islamic flag was hoisted on the city administration building. The crowd filling the building and the square in front of it was jubilant. The president and the officials accompanying him were invited to the hall inside the building that had once been used for Communist meetings. Now it was packed with thousands of men believing that they wanted Islamic rule. Emotions were running high, and for a few minutes even Yuldosh, who was running the show, was unable to calm down his followers.

Slim, in a tall, black fake-fur winter hat and traditional cotton-padded robe over a dark blue tracksuit, a microphone in his hand, Yuldosh repeatedly called for order, raising his index finger and then making a calming gesture with his hand—to no avail. But when he brought the microphone closer to his mouth and started chanting in Arabic—perhaps in praise of Allah and the Prophet—the crowd, as if hypnotized, immediately went quiet, and everyone fell to their knees. Karimov, in a similar black winter hat and a long dark coat, had no choice but to kneel down too, beside Yuldosh, who remained standing.

Yuldosh first berated the crowd for the earlier disorder, telling them they were not "children of Marx" but of the Prophet Muhammad, so they must behave. He went on to accuse the Namangan authorities for their economic failures, neglect of the ordinary people, and in general for their "un-Muslim" ways. When Karimov attempted to take over the microphone, Yuldosh said he was going to speak first; then "the presidential candidate" would be given his chance.

The crowd in the hall and on the balconies around the perimeter received Yuldosh's words with shouts of approval and waved their fists in the air. When Karimov was allowed to speak, he apologized profusely for his "mistake" of not meeting the Namangan Muslims. "I am ready to get down on my knees. Next time I come I will first meet you," he said to the approving shouts from the crowd. "I was wrong. . . . They say that only God is beyond any reproach," he went on to say. And the crowd chanted, "Allah Akbar!" (God is great). "I was wrong, so I admit my mistake, looking in your faces, your eyes. Forgive me," Karimov said. Throughout his speech Karimov maintained an apologetic and humble tone, trying to keep at bay the hostile crowd by repeating again and again the words "do not get me wrong."

But the crowd remained unfriendly. When Karimov said that all his decisions as Uzbekistan's top leader had been to the advantage of the ordinary people and asked the crowd if anyone could deny that, voices in the crowd shouted yes. When Karimov turned to his foreign policy efforts, Tohir Yuldosh, who had been standing next to him all along, snatched the

Figure 1.3. President Karimov and the future militant leader Tohir Yuldosh address protesters demanding a greater role for Islam in the eastern city of Namangan, December 1991. © YouTube screenshot. https://www.youtube.com/watch?v=HKhoDL1QQT4.

microphone from his hands and demanded that he instead address people's more immediate concerns, like the price of meat.

"You stand still; let me speak," Karimov told Yuldosh, trying to save face. "When you were talking, we listened, so let me say what I have to say," he added with a note of cold annoyance.

Karimov went on to pledge to "never denounce my Muslim identity" and to allow an Islamic state if "a majority" voted for it. "If everyone votes for it, why would I be against? . . . I promise you I will personally raise this issue in Parliament," he said, to approving chants of "Allah Akbar!"

"If Parliament unanimously, with participation of your Namangan representatives, decides to declare an Islamic state, so be it," Karimov said.

Yuldosh grabbed the microphone again and said: "He is deceiving us." Then, probably with everyone sensing that the crowd was on the brink of getting out of control, it was decided that Karimov would meet the rally leaders face-to-face instead of speaking to the crowd.

Karimov tried to use the more private meeting with Yuldosh and a few of his associates to get their backing in the coming elections and to further push his message that Parliament was the only obstacle to proclaiming an Islamic state. "If the Supreme Council does not vote for it, does not decide on this issue, I as president cannot declare it by myself," he said. "But if you elect me president, I need just one provision giving me authority to dissolve Parliament. Then my word will have a different weight." Despite Karimov's diplomatic efforts, the thousands-strong crowd remained inside and outside the city government building and did not look any friendlier. Effectively, Karimov and the official who'd accompanied him on the trip to Namangan were trapped inside.

On that day Karimov also encountered for the first time Abduvali qori Mirzayev, the imam of the central mosque of the biggest city in the valley, Andijan, and one of the most influential and crucial figures in Uzbekistan's post-Soviet Islamic revival. Imam Mirzayev, according to his son, pacified the people and "helped the president" by telling Yuldosh to disperse his followers, as it was damaging to "the Shari'a and the Muslims." According to him, Imam Mirzayev also made Interior Minister Zokirjon Almatov, who was among the accompanying officials, write an undertaking not to prosecute any of the people involved in the seizure of the government building.[6]

Karimov was boiling with anger as he left Namangan.

"He went back after being made to feel worthless," said a witness of the events. "A twenty-three-year-old man [Yuldosh] shouted at him publicly," he said. "When he left, Karimov swore at the Namangan governor: 'Who is the governor here, you or that boy?'" For Karimov this was firsthand experience of the influence and control the new Islamic leaders had over people's minds.

Some witnesses deny that Yuldosh grabbed the microphone from Karimov—according to some accounts twice, to others once—during his Namangan speech. Perhaps, as with any turning points in history, with time the public memory has dramatized and mythologized that fateful face-to-face showdown between Karimov and Yuldosh. Nevertheless, Karimov's future relentless, brutal campaign against any Islamic practice outside his government's control was probably conceived in those minutes when Yuldosh—a young nobody from a provincial town—publicly humiliated him, if not by grabbing the microphone, then certainly by making him kneel at his feet as he sang praise to Allah.

* * *

The political events in Uzbekistan in the late 1980s and early 1990s passed me personally by. One of the reasons was that I was part of an ethnic minority and lived in the bubble of the capital's Russian-speaking community. The momentous events of those days were mostly driven by nationalistic or religious feelings. It was becoming clear that with the Soviet collapse, we had lost our connection to the political changes—still liberal at the time—that were happening in Moscow because it was no longer our center, and the winds of change that originated there were not going to be blowing our way anymore. Changes in Uzbekistan were inevitable too, but we now had to begin from some other starting point. What that point could be was not for me, a young girl who'd grown up in the Soviet cocoon, to understand.

In the early 1990s I was enrolled in a journalism course at Tashkent University. The curriculum, teaching methods, books, and the teachers' mentalities were still Soviet. Everyone, including the teachers themselves, knew everything was out of date. So the course seemed pointless, and the idea of becoming a journalist was turning into an increasingly distant and unrealistic dream.

Also, following the January 1992 students' riots on our university grounds against increased food prices, the authorities introduced free attendance, which meant that lectures were not compulsory and students were only required to show up for tests and exams—the idea was to reduce students' political activism by preventing them from seeing each other regularly and discussing any sensitive issues. As a result, only a few students, and even lecturers, turned up for classes. I remember spending more time in the glassed atrium, sitting with fellow students on a thick heating pipe, than in classrooms. There was a feeling of boredom and an acute sense of uncertainty about the future.

With so much free time on my hands, I started learning English. That choice would later allow me to get a scholarship to study in the United Kingdom and then bring me to writing this book.

Notes

The story of the Fakhrutdinov family throughout the book is based on interviews with family members, Tashkent, 2008–09.

1. Mikhail Gorbachev, *Memoirs* (London: Doubleday, 1996), 339.

2. Sergei Abashin, *Ferganskaya dolina: etnichnost, etnicheskiye protsessy, etnicheskiye konflikty* (Moscow: Nauka, 2004), 65, 90.

3. Mir Kaligulayev, *Doroga k smerti bolshe chem smert* (Wolverhampton, UK: Black Quadrat, 2005), 30.

4. Martha Brill Olcott, "The Roots of Radical Islam in Central Asia," Carnegie Endowment for International Peace, 35–38, http://carnegieendowment.org/files/olcottroots.pdf.

5. The episode in Namangan is based on Kaligulayev, *Doroga k smerti*, 25–30; author interview with a former official who requested anonymity, Tashkent, 2008; two YouTube videos supposedly made by Yuldosh followers, uploaded August 11, 2011, https://www.youtube.com/watch?v=xwVS8CQg2s4, and October 28, 2010, https://www.youtube.com/watch?v=xwKyf8PMlK4; Radio Liberty Uzbek Service, August 19, 2010, http://www.ozodlik.org/a/2131950.html.

6. Abdulquddus Mirzayev, interview with the now defunct uznews.net website, October 3, 2007.

2

BACK TO ISLAM

MY MATERNAL GRANDMOTHER, WHOSE INCONSPICUOUS PRAYING ritual I used to watch and not understand as a child, was a daughter of a wealthy mullah. Their family belonged to the Qurama subethnic group, also known as "mountain Uzbeks." They lived in the village of Dukent in the Katartal Mountains, part of the range that separates the Fergana Valley from the rest of the country. Great-grandfather Rysqul owned lands in Layly, now the town of Yangiabad, with adjacent territories that he used as a winter pasture for his livestock. His piety can be seen from the names he gave his children, of which he had nine. Four of his sons were called Ismail (Ishamel), Israil (Israel), Yusuf (Joseph), and Imamali (Imam Ali). My grandmother's name, Fatima, was the name of the Prophet Muhammad's daughter.

After the 1917 Russian Revolution all that the family had was taken away by the Bolshevik authorities when they set about destroying both religion and private property. My great-grandfather died in the famine that followed. His sons left or fled, each their own way, trying to survive and escape arrest. With one of the brothers went my grandmother's twin sister, Zukhra. The girls would find each other again several years later.

Grandmother Fatima, who was fifteen at the time, stayed and married a young man from their village, but her husband was soon killed in the violence going on at the time (armed resistance to the Bolsheviks went on into the late 1920s)—one day he was found dead in a field where he was sowing wheat. His face was covered with a white cloth, probably by some passer-by.

My grandmother, still only a teenager, was left with no home and nobody to turn to for help. She and her sister-in-law, Qunduz, who was also left alone along with her three young sons, set off on foot in the direction of

Tashkent. As they walked they exchanged their jewelry for bread. When the jewelry ran out, they starved. Two of Qunduz's boys died of hunger.

The rest of them survived because an old butcher gave them shelter and let them have blood from the animals he slaughtered. They would cook the blood until it became hard "like liver" (as my mum, who told me my grandmother's story, said) and eat it.

Eventually they ended up in the Kazakh village of Zhantak, where they made a living by cleaning and doing laundry for others. When an older Kazakh man called Zholdasbek, who was childless, proposed to my grandmother, hoping she would give him children, she agreed. In her circumstances that was her best option for a future.

The future would prove not to hold much good for Grandmother Fatima though. Her new husband died leaving her with a baby boy. His relatives made her marry another man from their village so that she would not go back to her Uzbek family, taking along her "Kazakh child" and "turning him Uzbek." By her third husband she had a daughter, my mother. But she left him while she was still pregnant, angered and humiliated by his failure to defend her when a kolkhoz supervisor swore at her and kicked her in front of him for not turning up to pick cotton. I guess that was the last straw. Men had let her down too many times, and she was finally taking her life into her own hands, even if it meant condemning herself and her two children to extreme poverty. Until the end of her life, her opinion of men would remain quite low.

Both my parents were born in the 1940s—my father in 1941, the year the Soviet Union entered World War II, and my mother in the spring of 1945, weeks before the war ended. Both grew up in rural poverty, like almost everyone around them in those days, but the overall postwar atmosphere was relatively positive—the war had been won, and it was time to rebuild.

The hardships of war also in a way overshadowed and dimmed the memory of the Bolshevik terror of the 1920s and Stalin's purges of the 1930s (which wiped out Central Asia's entire prerevolutionary and early Soviet intellectual and political elites for being suspected enemies of the Soviet system). World War II forced the Communist Party to rethink and soften its line on religion. It had to recognize that religion, or God, was what most citizens were turning to for moral strength to endure wartime suffering. Instead of being completely eradicated, religion was now to be allowed a restricted and controlled presence.

Figure 2.1. Author's grandmother Fatima posing for a picture at a sanatorium in Uzbekistan, 1980. © Family archive.

For Central Asia's Muslims that policy readjustment manifested in the creation in 1943 of the Spiritual Board of the Muslims of Central Asia and Kazakhstan, based in Tashkent. Two years later, Bukhara's sixteenth-century Mir Arab Madrasah began to produce official imams, who would also be trained in socialist ideology. The situation with religious freedom started to look better, but understandably, the official Islamic institutions did not have much credibility on the ground.

On the ground Islamic practice never stopped, only adjusted to the new times by retreating from public into private, family, and community spaces. Weddings (in parallel with state registration), funerals, and circumcisions, which would continue to be an almost universal practice, took place according to Islamic and pre-Islamic tradition and involved a mullah. Only a small number of urbanized Central Asians or those who had become particularly staunch Communists (i.e., atheists) would begin to move away from those traditions.

Some independent Islamic training continued, too, through a semiunderground system of classes given by community mullahs one on one or in small groups. The system, called *hujra*, relied on the limited pool of knowledge that had survived the Bolshevik crackdown. Nevertheless, it worked as a way of preserving some form of independent Islam. The KGB kept an eye on it but let it be, since the new government policy on religion was not eradication but control. Some hujra students would even go on to become official imams—the main priority was survival, and that required flexibility. Still it would be the hujra system from which would emerge the main figures of the post-Soviet Islamic revival. Everywhere outside those small niches of spiritual tradition, Central Asian society continued to be put through sweeping secularization.

For my parents' generation, Soviet rule and its antireligious narrative were already a reality they had to live with and within. They went to secular state schools; as teenagers they joined the Komsomol, the Communist Party's youth wing; and even though neither of them became members of the Communist Party, in their workplaces they were watched and guided by local party committees and were obliged to join in various ideological activities. They watched Soviet films and television and read Soviet newspapers; their lives were segmented into periods between Communist Party congresses measured, according to official reports, by the successful implementation of industrial and other development plans adopted by those congresses. My father avoided the two-year compulsory army service—there were some loopholes for working students like him—but the majority of Central Asian young men would go through it, and for them it would be another strong secularizing experience, as observing any religious practices there would be out of question.

My father had no problem with letting old traditions go. When he married my mother in 1969, he went for a "Komsomol wedding," without a mullah and against the will of his father, who thought it was "wrong and shameful." They had a heated argument over it, which ended with Father, who was quite bad-tempered, throwing a tea bowl at Grandfather. The bowl missed, hitting the wall behind him and smashing into pieces.

For Father, who was at the time studying journalism in Almaty, Kazakhstan, and trying to get his foot in the door of the Kazakh writers' community, it was far more important to get two known Kazakh writers to his wedding as VIP guests—probably he wanted to impress them with his modern ways. So important was it for him to make the writers happy that he himself hardly sat at the wedding table, which was set up in the courtyard of his parents' house. Instead he was busy making sure his special guests were looked after and got enough to eat and drink. So my mother, who also had no problem with breaking with tradition and was wearing a white "European" above-the-knee, short-sleeved beaded dress and a 1960s-style high bun hairdo, ended up being entertained for much of the evening by those writers.

But the next morning, like any traditional bride, Mother would put on a headscarf and a loose long dress over cotton trousers and begin to shoulder much of the domestic work in her in-laws' house. My parents followed some other old marriage rituals too, like dowry and *betashar*—a ceremony in which the bride's face is revealed to the groom's family. In fact, Father's family was too poor to honor those traditions fully, so to save face before guests, they only pretended to. The groom's family was supposed to present the bride with a whole new wardrobe of dresses, coats, cardigans, scarves, and the like, which were to be hung on the walls of her new home for all the guests to see. Instead of buying all those things, Father's family borrowed some from neighbors. Mother did not realize this and was quite surprised when the real owners of those dresses that she thought were presents for her started to show up to collect them.

In any case, my parents' wedding was the first Komsomol wedding in their district, so there were curious uninvited guests from all over trying to get a peek.

* * *

Figure 2.2. Author's mother, Manzura, standing in the middle, pictured with relatives soon after marrying author's father in 1969. © Family archive.

Being citizens of a superpower state tightly locked in a standoff with another superpower and being constantly reminded of that, the Soviet people had a heightened interest in international affairs. The main source of international news on Soviet television was the weekly analytical program *Mezhdunarodnaya Panorama* (International panorama). In the 1960s and 1970s, in the thick of the Cold War, the presenter would often open the program or sign off with the slightly unnerving statement that "the international situation remains tense." Viewers would be updated on the ongoing and new *ochagi napryazhennosti* (hotbeds of tension)—one of the favorite clichés of Soviet journalism used to describe unrest and conflicts around the world. At some point during the program the presenter would often deliver another unnerving piece of news, or rather a reminder, that the hostile imperialist West was continuing its buildup of armaments and predatory behavior toward poor nations. Meanwhile, the Soviet Union, the presenter would say, was continuing to support oppressed peoples and work toward international disarmament.

This was an extremely significant period in the history of political Islamism: it saw the conception by Sayyid Qutb, an imprisoned member of Egypt's Muslim Brotherhood, of what is seen as the founding manifesto of Sunni political radical Islamism (Qutb was executed in 1966 after twelve years of imprisonment); the Arab defeat by Israel in the 1967 Six-Day War triggered a wave of religious revival throughout the Middle East; and in 1979 the world witnessed the first Islamic revolution, which deposed the US-backed shah of Iran.

The Soviet media had to maintain a certain sensitive "balance" in covering what was going on in the Middle East. The focus would be on the anticolonial side of events, but the fact that the movements opposing Western subjugation drew much inspiration from Islam was not to be mentioned, lest Soviet Muslims followed suit. Soviet propagandists worked to portray Islam as a source of social and political problems and violence. For example, one of the books about Islam published at the time featured photographs of a Saudi beheading, with a caption describing it as fidelity to Islam; it also carried photos of armed Islamic revolutionaries, pictures of an airplane hijacking, hostage-taking, and children hiding behind sandbags, with a caption saying that hundreds of thousands of children in various Muslim countries have known only war.[1]

Attempts at a more objective approach were blocked. In 1967 the Russian writer Vera Panova began writing a book about the Prophet Muhammad. The idea was that it would become part of the hugely popular series of biographical books Zhizn Zamechatelnykh Lyudey (Lives of remarkable people), known as ZhZL. Offering her idea to the series' editor, Panova wrote that she hoped the book she had in mind would be both "interesting and useful" to readers as it would "inform them about the essence of Islam at the moment of its inception and its connections to other religions." She wrote, "I hope to be able to combine my author's atheistic position with full respect and tactfulness towards the personality of Magomet [Muhammad] and his followers' convictions, and make sure that the book does not insult the feelings of Muslims (both our countrymen and those abroad)."[2] The book was approved and submitted for publication in 1970 but failed to get a final official green light. Panova died in 1973. Her book *Zhizn Mukhammeda* (The life of Muhammad) would finally be published in 1990.

The government's task of keeping a lid on Central Asians' religious feelings became more pressing when in 1979 the Soviet Union began its military intervention in Afghanistan—a Muslim country, bordering on three of the five Soviet republics of Central Asia, and a home to minorities representing all of Central Asia's main ethnic groups (many of them children and grandchildren of hundreds of thousands of Central Asians who had fled to Afghanistan during the Bolshevik takeover after 1917).

The Soviet military leadership deployed many Central Asian conscripts to Afghanistan, trying to use them as a thin disguise for the real—geopolitical—reasons for the intervention. But some of these eighteen- to twenty-year-old conscripts would switch loyalties after encountering the Afghan mujahideen (those struggling on the path of jihad), who looked like them and many of whom spoke the same languages as them and whose war, which they saw as Islamic jihad, was clearly more justifiable morally than that of the Soviet army.

By coincidence the Afghan campaign started the year I went to school and ended ten years later in 1989 when I left. In one of my senior years at school, as a budding journalist I did an internship with a youth paper and was assigned to write an article about a soldier killed in Afghanistan. I visited his typically Soviet school in one of Tashkent's neighborhoods, where they had installed a plaque in his memory. I talked to his former teachers, walked the corridors that he had once walked, and went into classrooms where he had once studied.

I can't remember what I asked, what answers I got, or what story I produced. It was already perestroika time, and voices criticizing the war and calling for its end were getting stronger—maybe that's why I got assigned the story. But being fifteen or sixteen years old, I was not prepared and not expected to go into the political side of things. I understood I had to, and wanted to, write a human story. Simply telling the story of someone's death in war felt like a heavy responsibility—death and war were then abstract but dark and frightening ideas for me. Visiting the soldier's school was especially sad, because school meant childhood, so it felt like he'd had to step into war straight out of childhood.

However much the Soviet propaganda machine tried to present the Afghan war as an act of friendship, calling the servicemen sent there *voiny internatsionalisty*, or "warrior-internationalists," the truth—about the falsehood of the pretext for the campaign, its disastrous failings, and the human toll it was taking—even if not publicly spoken, seeped through and penetrated Soviet society pretty much from the beginning. And the more the war dragged on, the more it contributed to the moral erosion of the entire Soviet system and its eventual collapse.

* * *

This sense of approaching doom may have increased Soviet citizens' hunger for alternative information and news about the world. Many people in the 1980s would keenly listen to foreign radio broadcasts, which had their own political agendas.

My father would go to bed with his old transistor radio, trying to tune in to his favorite programs on the BBC World Service, Voice of America, or Radio Liberty deep into the night, but much of the time he only got crackling and hissing as the Soviet government consistently tried to jam them.

Others preferred to get their news from the Islamic world. Iran's new revolutionary government launched special radio broadcasts in Tajik and Turkmen from areas close to the Soviet borders, with some programs calling on Soviet Muslims to revolt against their "godless oppressors." It was also possible to tune in to broadcasts from Arabic countries, Afghanistan, and other Muslim countries. And among their listeners were some active hujra students.

One of the most learned and prominent hujra teachers, Muhammad Hindustani Rustamov, enthusiastically kept up with developments. He listened to Arabic, Iranian, and Afghan radio stations, often together with his students, which gave them "the feeling of exploring a wider world," the former BBC correspondent in Central Asia Monica Whitlock writes in her book *Beyond the Oxus: The Central Asians*, citing one of Hindustani's students.[3]

Hindustani was a moderate who throughout his life remained true to the traditional to Central Asia Hanafi school of Sunni Islam. The four main schools, or madhhab(s), of Sunni Islam are Maliki, Hanafi, Shafi'i, and Hanbali, named after their founding imams, and each has its own established traditions and techniques for interpreting and resolving contradictions in the Koran and the hadiths (sayings attributed to the Prophet Mohammad and other major early Islamic figures). Some historians divide Sunni Islam into three madhhabs; others into eight. Some sects reject all madhhabs, saying the only right way to practice Islam is by referring directly to the words of the Prophet and Sunnah (his way of living). The Hanafi school, founded by Imam Abu Hanifa (d. 767), is seen as one of the most liberal schools since it says that Islamic laws should be based on what is generally good for Muslims in a given context. This flexible approach was especially appealing to non-Arabs as it allowed them to preserve their own customs. Currently Hanafism is followed mainly in Central Asia, India, Turkey and some parts of the Arab Middle East.

Hindustani was born in the Fergana Valley town of Kokand in 1892. His religious training, which he received in Bukhara, Afghanistan, and India, was extensive and comprehensive. When Stalin died in 1953, Hindustani was serving a twenty-five-year sentence for anti-Soviet propaganda—a default charge used against any dissenters. He was amnestied a year later.[4]

Hindustani was one of the most active founders of hujra, and he was at odds with the official muftiyat, the Spiritual Board of the Muslims of Central Asia—and notably with its chief, Ziyautdin qori Babakhanov, who headed the muftiyat from 1957 until his death in 1982. Babakhanov leaned toward stricter observance of the scriptures—stricter than that prescribed by the Hanafi school—and some researchers describe his position as fundamentalist. Hindustani was opposed to Babakhanov's slant toward purism but kept quiet, probably realizing that internal disputes could do no good to the already weak state of the Soviet *ummah*, or Islamic community. Babakhanov was apparently aware of his dissent and sent him to serve in a mosque in Dushanbe, the capital of Tajikistan, where Hindustani would live till his death in 1989.

While Hindustani himself remained loyal to the traditional Central Asian Islam, in the 1970s some of his students got inspired by new ideas. They rebelled against their teacher, beginning to conduct the daily prayer in the manner of the Hanbali school and arguing for ritual purism (i.e., doing away with pre-Islamic rituals still followed by Uzbeks), and they also harbored anti-Soviet ideas. The students called themselves *mujaddidiya* (*mujaddids*), the "renovators," while calling their opponents *mushriklar*, "polytheists."

One of the mujaddids, Rahmatulla Alloma, wrote a brief manuscript, "Musulmonobod," describing a country where Islam flourishes, everyone is equal, and Muslims "bow only to God, and not to any party, not to living or dead leaders."[5] He and other like-minded mullahs, including Abduvali qori Mirzayev, who during perestroika would emerge as one of the most popular independent preachers, started underground classes based on their own take on Islam. In 1981, Alloma, at the age of thirty-one, would be killed in a car accident allegedly staged by the KGB. He is still remembered in the Fergana Valley as being exceptionally talented.

In the declining years of the Soviet Union, the Uzbek Soviet government's chief ideologist, Rano Abdullayeva, referred to by some as the Iron Lady, carried out the last Communist antireligious campaign in the republic. The crackdown in 1982–89 involved raids on mosques and churches, greater pressure on dissident mullahs, and the tearing of scarves off women's heads. Nevertheless, an official study conducted in the late 1980s by the prominent Russian ethnographer Sergei Polyakov found that the mosques, official and unofficial alike, in Uzbekistan and other Central Asian republics remained "a powerful social institution" that "in many ways" regulated community and family daily life.[6]

When with the start of perestroika Moscow began to send liberal signals, those preserved Islamic traditions quickly became openly political and anti-Soviet. Gorbachev writes in his memoirs that the top Communist leadership was aware that unofficial religious communities, "especially Islamic," were opposed to the established order. His government was divided about what to do about them—some opposed encouraging religious practices, while others said that the ban only stimulated clandestine worship, Gorbachev wrote.

* * *

But it was no longer in the Soviet government's power to control religious matters. Every Uzbek mahallya wanted its own mosque, now openly. Some started to shun secular clothes, like ties and suits; women put on the hijab. Religious holidays were celebrated with special excitement.

With the official clergy tainted with their link to the Communist authorities, the masses eagerly wanted new teachers. This demand brought onto the scene "new, strong, talented, young preachers"—with varying degrees of formal and informal training or none at all—and with them "the entire palette" of Islamic views, from moderate to extreme, according to an Uzbek researcher on Islam who requested anonymity.[7] The pluralism of ideas split the Uzbek Muslim community into those sticking to the old traditions but wanting to preach independently, the young mullahs who rejected the old traditions altogether, and the official clergy still loyal to the state.

Some of the young mullahs demonstrated a fresh and bold independence from the authorities and an inspiring religious passion. Unlike the official clergy, they seemed more attuned to people's everyday concerns, and in no time they won enthusiastic popular support and began to challenge old mullahs' teachings.

The details of ritual became points of disagreement between the new and old mullahs about what was the right way for a "true" Muslim to worship. Divisive questions included the following: Can you, while reading the

Koran, dedicate your reading to anyone? Should you greet a respected person by standing up or remaining seated? Should you, when praying, say "Amen" out loud after the opening *sura* (Koranic verse)? Should you raise your hands high while taking a bow during prayer? Should you rub your neck while doing the ablution ritual before prayer?[8] These questions arose from dogmatic differences between the Islamic madhhabs. And for those involved in the heated disputes, they seemed of paramount importance, even though some of those arguing probably did not know about the existence of the different madhhabs at all.

The essential and polarizing question behind these clashes over ritual issues concerned what role Islam should play in the Uzbeks' political and social life. Ideas ranged from an Islamic state to just an end to state interference in religious affairs, and others still wanted to keep things as they were in the Soviet times—a secular government and state-controlled religious practice.

In 1989 the Spiritual Board of the Muslims of Central Asia and Kazakhstan came to be headed by one of the most authoritative representatives of the Uzbek Islamic clergy of the time, Sheikh Mohammad Sodiq Mohammad Yusuf. In the same year, he was also elected as a member of the Soviet parliament, the Supreme Soviet, showing how big the political shift toward religion was during Gorbachev's reforms.

Mohammad Yusuf was from the Fergana Valley. In addition to his hujra training, he went through the official system of Islamic education, the Mir Arab Madrasah, and the Tashkent Islamic Institute. As a promising young scholar, in 1976 he was sent to Libya for four years of further theological studies. As chief mufti, Mohammad Yusuf tried to ease state control over religion and mosques. Under him, every community was allowed to choose their own imam. He was the one who backed my childhood neighbor Rukhitdin's bid to become imam of the Samarkand Darvoza neighborhood in Tashkent in 1991.

Rukhitdin's investiture happened in a civilized manner. But elsewhere in the country, especially in the valley, the liberty to choose individual imams triggered vicious battles for control over mosques, involving physical violence and kidnappings.

The most important mosque was the *jami* mosque—the central one in each town or city used as a venue for communal Friday prayers. Winning a mosque meant getting legitimate access to a public tribune and, consequently, an expanded audience, influence, and political weight.

In the fight for the jami mosque of the Fergana Valley town of Kokand in February 1989, a mullah of the old Soviet tradition was outmaneuvered by his own disciple. In a bitter letter, Nasriddin Domulla Toychiyev described the takeover by his student as "meanness" and "a plot against the teacher." He wrote that his student Mohammad Rajab had made him believe that the local Muslims wanted to see Toychiyev as their jami mosque imam. But at the gathering convened to elect the imam, Toychiyev came under a barrage of criticism as being not suitable for the job, and the congregation elected his student Rajab.

"Young people don't like your speeches," Toychiyev was told.

Toychiyev accused Rajab of orchestrating his downfall and public humiliation by bringing hundreds of his supporters to the gathering. "You broke my spirit, you killed me," Toychiyev wrote in his letter in 1990. The Soviet mullah was ill and soon died.[9]

* * *

The central mosque of the Fergana Valley's biggest city, Andijan, was in 1989 won by one of Hindustani's rebellious former students, Abduvali qori Mirzayev. Round-faced, with a long, bushy black beard, the thirty-nine-year-old imam had been on the KGB's radar since the 1970s and had been regularly called in for ideological correction. In 1982, a year after the suspicious death of his close associate Rahmatullah Alloma in a road accident, Mirzayev was taken in for suspected illegal religious activity but released five days later.

Now Mirzayev was free to reveal with full force his potential as preacher. He was well trained, knew Arabic, and was confident enough to offer his own interpretations of Koranic verses and issue his own edicts on various current issues. His following was rapidly increasing. Tapes with his sermons were becoming popular beyond the valley.

When he became the Andijan central mosque imam, he started to run it in a new way. Unlike in other mosques, he and the staff were unpaid, and he would not take payment from people for officiating at their marriages, funerals, and other ceremonies, saying religious service was "a duty, not a paid job." This contempt for money could not but impress the ordinary people and boost his popularity, given the general distrust of the Soviet imams, who were seen as greedy, corrupt, and serving the Communist authorities, and therefore hypocritical and insincere in their service to God.

Figure 2.3. Imam Abduvali qori Mirzayev. © YouTube video screenshot. https://www
.youtube.com/watch?v=CPSceZc9tAM.

Mirzayev also established several businesses to maintain his mosque
and subsidize meat and bread for the needy. He set up canteens at his
mosque, "so people can eat halal food," he told Andijan TV in 1989. His son,
Abdulquddus, would say in a later media interview that his father's mosque
"worked on reforming society and improving its morals" and reeducated
many people, including criminals.

Mirzayev also wanted his mosque to be fully independent from the state
and its interference. He was determined to discard the Soviet government's
practice of making imams promote state policies through their sermons.
"Religion is separate from state in our country. This means that we have the
right not to allow government policies to be discussed in mosques. Only
the policy of Allah should be discussed here, and nothing else," Mirzayev
said, according to his son.[10]

* * *

The deep split between the old and new mullahs became especially evident when Hindustani denounced his dissident former students, including Imam Mirzayev, as followers of *Wahhabism*. Wahhabism is the Saudi name for Salafism, an ultra-conservative ideology that rejects the entire Islamic theology and jurisprudence, and calls for a return to the "pure" Islam of the time of the Prophet Mohammad and the use as reference only of the Koran and hadiths. Wahhabism is so called after its founder Abd al Wahhab (d. 1792), who was expelled from his native Iraq but found popularity with Saudi Arabian tribes. He supported the Saudi royal family's coming to power and they in exchange made his ideas official ideology. The Salafis find the term Wahhabi derogatory as it links them not to the Prophet but to a mortal human.

Hindustani argued with the new mullahs, saying that the Islam they preached was a product of different cultures, social and political systems, and contexts. They, in their turn, accused Hindustani of conformism and cooperation with the secular authorities. One of his opponents likened Hindustani to "a blind man carrying a torch" or "a donkey loaded with books," apparently ridiculing his reputation as a learned theologian.

In a letter in response to the unnamed accuser, Hindustani warned him against calling for jihad and causing "innocent" deaths. "You blindly call for jihad, for war with axes. Do not, like Dukchi Ishon, cause your own death and the deaths of innocent others!" Hindustani said, referring to the 1898 uprising against Russian rule in Andijan.

"You praise the Afghan mojaheddin, saying that they are waging real jihad. However, their jihad is the demolition of Muslims' mosques, the murder of those who pray, robbery, killings of women and children, extortion of money from unbelievers. . . . Is that jihad?" Hindustani said in the letter, written in 1988, one year before his death.[11]

Chief Mufti Mohammad Yusuf, who was also a former student of Hindustani's, held a centrist position in the flaring disputes and tried to reconcile the various antagonistic Islamic groups. In 1990 he initiated an assembly of representatives from various sides, and they issued a "peace fatwa."

In 1992 neighboring Tajikistan plunged into civil war. The war between the United Tajik Opposition and the Moscow-backed government quickly came to be seen and is still generally seen as a clash between an Islamic opposition and a secular government. However, it was not a religious war but a regional war for power—between the southern Kulob and Hisor clans, who had traditionally held power during the Soviet time, on the one side, and those of the Gharm and Pamir regions, who after the Soviet collapse sought to change the unfair power balance, on the other.[12]

One of the groups within the opposition coalition was the Islamic Rebirth Party. Its leaders, "neither in their ideology nor in their conduct," had much in common with Islamists in the rest of the Muslim world, according to the historian Adeeb Khalid. "Islamization was not a central issue of the war," he says, but it took place in an environment when the country was going through "a form of re-Islamization."[13]

The IRP leaders, however, got branded Wahhabis as it was the easiest way for the remnants of the Moscow-backed old regime to demonize them. One of the IRP leaders, Akbar Turajonzoda, one of Tajikistan's senior Islamic officials from 1988 to 1993, like other leading Islamic opposition figures, had Sufi connections—Wahhabism rejects Sufism as a deviation from "true" Islam. The historian Muriel Atkin describes Turajonzoda as a modernist who advocated a political system combining democratic institutions with Islamic teachings and who cooperated with secular reformists and called for ethnic and religious tolerance.[14]

Still, the Tajik war did come as a source of inspiration for some Uzbeks. It is said that secret aid, in cash and food supplies, was organized for the Tajik opposition from the Fergana Valley.

Karimov, by then an elected president, was also watching the violence in Tajikistan, which left up to a hundred thousand dead and forced about half a million Tajiks to flee to Afghanistan, and it only strengthened him in his resolve to eliminate any form of independent Islam on his watch. First of all he needed to regain control of the official muftiyat. Mohammad Yusuf's centrist position did not suit the president's new course, and the chief mufti was forced to leave in 1993.

* * *

Two years after resigning as chief mufti, Mohammad Yusuf issued an article, "On Disagreements," which he had begun to write in 1990, to make sense of the chaos and disunity within the Muslim community, which he described as "abnormal" and "disgusting." Mohammad Yusuf said the endemic study of Islam in the 1980s and early 1990s was "completely sporadic," based on "low-grade literature" and delivered by uneducated mullahs and "imams with dubious knowledge." He wrote, "There were many students but no books. There were mosques but no imams." Things were made worse, he said, by visiting "half-educated" foreign Muslims who criticized the Hanafi madhhab as harmful, reducing religion to senseless argument over trivialities about ritual. Mohammad Yusuf warned that the situation had already led to "serious consequences" but said there was nobody to blame, only general ignorance.[15]

After his forced resignation Mohammad Yusuf lived in Saudi Arabia, Libya, and Turkey. It appeared to be some form of exile, either self-imposed or the result of a quiet deal with the authorities. It ended in 1999 when he returned to Tashkent and after that was able to freely travel in and out of the country. Inside Uzbekistan, Mohammad Yusuf kept a low profile, focusing on research and writing. He wrote his own comments on the Koran in Uzbek and in 2002 finished a 39-volume work *Hadith va Khayot* (Hadith and life), his comments on a selection of the Prophet Mohammad's sayings. He died of a heart attack in Tashkent in March 2015, aged sixty-seven. Many thousands of Uzbeks came to pay tribute to him at his funeral in a remarkable and bold show of respect for a religious leader, who till the end had stayed independent of President Karimov's regime.

It is difficult, if even possible, to pinpoint what exact teachings of Islam or Islamism, from the academic point of view, those new Uzbek mullahs followed and preached. Some of them themselves had little or no idea what, from the theological point of view, they were preaching—all they wanted was change, driven by a desire to practice their religion without restriction and official control, at last. As Mohammad Yusuf puts it, it was a time when people were proclaiming themselves mullahs "after reading just one book."

There was clarity at least about one new Islamist ideology introduced to Uzbek Muslims in those days because it is an established organization with its own wide international network of followers and set methods of recruitment and expansion. It was the teaching of Hizb ut-Tahrir, the Party of Liberation, which was founded by a Palestinian in Jerusalem in 1953. It calls for an Islamic state through a quiet revolution, spreading its ideas through small secretive cells and gradually penetrating government institutions. The researcher Emmanuel Karagiannis suggests that Hizb ut-Tahrir ideas came to Uzbekistan with Jordanian missionaries, and the party had active cells by the mid-1990s. But because of the secretive nature of the organization, their Uzbek leaders and recruits were not among those who were attracting crowds and competing for mosques at the time.

The official Spiritual Board was unprepared to make judgments about and foresee the possible impact of the wave of new teachings and influences pouring into the country through wide-open gates. The official clergy were themselves enthusiastically establishing contacts with various Islamic institutions abroad, including in Saudi Arabia, where Wahhabism is an official ideology.

In 1990, the Saudi government sent a hundred thousand copies of the Koran and other religious literature to the Soviet Union to help it meet the increased demand. It also covered pilgrims' expenses and provided university places to students from the Soviet Union. Foreign Muslim organizations also funded the publication of religious material in Russian and languages of other Soviet peoples, and all kinds of missionaries arrived in Central Asia.[16] Adeeb Khalid, in his book *Islam after Communism*, says that in 2004 in Kazakhstan he found Russian translations of works by Sayyid Qutb, by the Indian thinker of political Islam Sayyid Abdul Ala Maududi, and by Iran's Ayatollah Khomeini, published by foreign Islamic foundations around the time of the Soviet collapse.

One former resident of Tashkent, now a refugee in Europe, recalled that religious assistance coming from Saudi Arabia was particularly noticeable in 1993–94. "Arabs from Saudi Arabia gave lessons, helped build mosques, and met local theologians. They brought books, including the Koran, and distributed them. It was done through the Spiritual Board; everything was official; all the content was checked. This is the way our children learned Arabic," she said. There were also Saudis who bypassed the authorities, "coming independently and conducting interviews to select young men to study [Islam in Saudi Arabia]," she said.

Later, when the authorities launched their crackdown on unofficial Islam, they would stop accepting Saudi Arabia's assistance. One important watershed was the 1996 Taliban takeover of the Afghan capital, Kabul, after which the authorities would recall Uzbek students studying in Saudi Arabia and brand all the deviations from state-controlled Islam as Wahhabism. Imam Mirzayev would be proclaimed to be "the father" of the Uzbek Wahhabis.

Some researchers of the Uzbek Islamic revival and its main figures confirm Mirzayev's alleged adherence to Wahhabism. Ashirbek Muminov (a Kazakh scholar who used to live in Uzbekistan), Martha Brill Olcott of the US Carnegie Endowment, and the prominent Uzbek expert on Islam Bakhtiyar Babajanov say that in the 1970s Mirzayev had regularly attended meetings with foreign Muslim students in Tashkent. Through such contacts he, among others, came across books by Sayyid Qutb, who called for a violent jihad against any oppressive rule because such rule is un-Islamic. They say that Mirzayev came to believe in the "degradation" of the Hanafi traditions, and in his sermons he questioned the authority of Sunni madhhabs. The researchers also say that his interpretations of some Koranic verses were more radical and inflammatory than those by traditional theologians. It is also said that Mirzayev organized aid to the Tajik opposition in its war against the ex-Communist government and blessed his students leaving to join the Tajik war.

Mirzayev himself, until his disappearance in 1995, denied being Wahhabi. His son, Abdulquddus, also (until his own death in a car crash in 2007) would maintain that Mirzayev followed the Hanafi tradition and that the Wahhabi accusation was slander. One Uzbek scholar has told me privately that because the period of Mirzayev's activity was brief, his views remain little studied, and therefore no conclusive academic judgment is possible.

* * *

To try to draw a relatively objective picture of the controversies around Islam in the Soviet and post-Soviet context, and indeed outside of it, it is important to have clarity about the terms "Wahhabi" and "fundamentalist." For a majority of post-Soviet people and others, they are probably nothing but abstract—nevertheless sinister-sounding—labels. To complicate things more, in Soviet and post-Soviet rhetoric the two terms were often used as synonyms, as the historian Muriel Atkin has noted in her article "The Rhetoric of Islamophobia."

The term "fundamentalism" was first used in the West to describe certain forms of American Protestantism in the early twentieth century.

In the late twentieth century it began to be applied to trends within Islam, eventually coming to be generally understood as "Islamic" and referring to "political activism, extremism, fanaticism, terrorism, and anti-Americanism," according to the Islamic scholar John Esposito of Georgetown University, who completely rejects the term on these grounds.[17]

Atkin and other scholars describe Islamic fundamentalism as a response by some Muslims to major social and cultural change (foreign subjugation, forced rapid modernization, and others) that they fear threatens their Islamic identity. But also it can be and often is a response to their own autocratic rulers and economic deprivation as a search for a just and moral society.

Fundamentalist concepts tend to seek refuge and answers in the idealized past, the time of the Prophet Muhammad, when, they believe, Islam was true and pure. And all the things going wrong today are doing so because that original "pure" faith has become "corrupted," they believe—hence their opposition to, among other things, local traditions that Muslims around the world, in places far away from the birthplace of Islam, have kept alongside adopting Islam as their religion.

Islamic fundamentalism has many forms. Some—like the Muslim Brotherhood of Egypt, Syria, and Sudan; Mu'ammar Gaddhafi's regime in Libya; or certain factions in Iran—focus on social and economic issues. Others, including other factions in Iran and the Saudi government, are more conservative. Some are highly political, but one of the largest, the Tablighi Jamaat, which began on the Indian subcontinent, is apolitical by choice as it sees politics as a morally corrupting field. Some are militant; others reject violence. Still other Muslims respond to the same challenges not by trying to entrench themselves in the "romanticized" past or in the scriptures, but through modernism, like the Tatar and Central Asian Jadids.

During perestroika and the post-Soviet period, probably with the KGB's help, "Wahhabi" became a label for any unauthorized new expressions of Islam, no matter whether they were in any way linked to the concept of Wahhabism in the wider Islamic world. The "official clergy" (post-Babakhanov) also used it for anyone who criticized them. The Uzbek authorities ended up defining Wahhabis as "fanatically devoted to the canons of Islam," which basically means anyone who is seen as being too pious, according to Atkin. [18]

Going back to Mirzayev, the journalist Monica Whitlock says that "according to his friends he never joined any sort of religious revival party, maintaining that politics and faith must always be kept separate." He said, "Otherwise religion will become corrupted." And Muslims "would become puppets." [19] The only thing that can be said for sure about Mirzayev is that he was hugely popular in the valley, that his views were different from those of the traditional and official mullahs, and that he opposed government control over his activities.

Another obvious thing is that President Karimov saw him as a source of trouble and a threat to his regime. Mirzayev disappeared in 1995 (more on this in the next chapter), following which the authorities at once launched a massive campaign against all dissident Muslims, with Mirzayev's students

Figure 2.4. Tohir Yuldosh, the leader of the militant Islamic Movement of Uzbekistan. © YouTube video screenshot. https://www.youtube.com/watch?v=PXOjL33xEOw.

and associates becoming prime targets. The clampdown gave a strong impetus to the serious radicalization of many young Uzbek Muslims, who were in essence given a choice between getting arrested, tortured, and thrown into jail for many years or fleeing to Tajikistan and fighting on the side of the Tajik opposition.

Among them were Tohir Yuldosh (the one who would in 1991 confront President Karimov) and his associate Juma Namangani, who went to fight in the Tajik war and set up their own militant Islamic Movement of Uzbekistan (the IMU). After the end of the Tajik war in 1997, the IMU would relocate to Afghanistan and fight alongside the Taliban against the US-led invasion, eventually turning into one of al-Qaeda's fighting forces with bases in Pakistan's Waziristan and expanding its recruitment base beyond Central Asia, becoming part of the global Islamist jihad. Namangani would be killed in US bombings in Afghanistan in 2001. Tohir Yuldosh would be killed in a US drone attack in Pakistan in 2009. With the emergence of the Islamic State (IS) group, however, the IMU would be replaced as the main inspirer and recruiter of regional jihadists. The IMU would swear allegiance to Islamic State, joining the war in Syria and Iraq. Reports would emerge in 2016 that the IMU had been practically annihilated by the Taliban as a group because it had switched sides to IS.[20]

Tohir Yuldosh and many IMU fighters named Mirzayev as their teacher. But it is not clear whether that meant getting "jihadist" lessons from him or just attending his mosque. For years after Mirzayev's disappearance, the Uzbek authorities continued to prosecute people just for listening to his recorded sermons. At trials of alleged Islamic extremists and terrorists, whose testimonies were routinely extracted or rather imposed on them through torture, almost everyone named him as one of their spiritual guides.

Notes

1. Muriel Atkin, "The Rhetoric of Islamophobia," *Central Asia and the Caucasus* 1 (2000), http://www.ca-c.org/journal/2000/journal_eng/eng01_2000/16.atkin.shtml.
2. Vera Panova and Yuriy Vakhtin, *Zhizn Muhammada* (Moscow: Politizdat, 1990), 5–7.
3. Monica Whitlock, *Beyond the Oxus: The Central Asians* (London: John Murray, 2002), 115–16.
4. Bakhtiyar Babajanov, Ashirbek Muminov, and Martha Brill Olcott, "Muhammad Hindustani (1892–1989) and the Religious Environment of his Time (Preliminary Thoughts on the Formation of 'Soviet Islam' in Central Asia)," *Vostok (Oriens)* 5 (2004), 43–59.
5. Adeeb Khalid, *Islam after Communism* (Berkeley: University of California Press, 2007), 144–46.
6. Emmanuel Karagiannis, "Political Islam in Uzbekistan: Hizb ut-Tahrir al-Islami," *Europe-Asia Studies* 58, no. 2 (2006): 261–80.
7. Interview in Almaty, Kazakhstan, 2006.
8. Sheikh Mohammad Sadyk Mohammad Yusuf, "On Disagreements" (1995), trans. and with comments by Bakhtiyar Babajanov, in *Disputy Musulmanskikh religioznykh avtoritetov v tsentralsnoy Azii v 20 veke*, ed. Babajanov, Muminov, and von Kugelgen, 191–249 (Almaty: Daik-Press, 2007).
9. Babajanov, Muminov, and von Kugelgen, *Disputy Musulmanskikh religioznykh avtoritetov*, 158–76.
10. Abdulquddus Mirzayev, interview with the now defunct uznews.net website, October 3, 2007; Martha Brill Olcott, "The Roots of Radical Islam in Central Asia" (Carnegie Endowment Papers, 77, January 2007), http://carnegieendowment.org/files/olcottroots.pdf; Imam Mirzayev, interview with Andijan regional TV station, 1989, an abridged transcript in Russian, uznews.net website, October 11, 2007.
11. Babajanov, Muminov, and von Kugelgen, *Disputy Musulmanskikh religioznykh avtoritetov*, 97–112.
12. Kirill Nourzhanov and Christian Bleuer, *Tajikistan: A Political and Social History* (Canberra: Australian National University Press, 2013), 329.
13. Khalid, *Islam after Communism*, 149–51.
14. Atkin, "The Rhetoric of Islamophobia."
15. Mohammad Yusuf, "On Disagreements," 199, 202–3.
16. Karagiannis, "Political Islam in Uzbekistan," 263; Khalid, *Islam after Communism*, 122–23, 136.

17. Atkin, "The Rhetoric of Islamophobia."
18. Atkin, "The Rhetoric of Islamophobia."
19. Whitlock, *Beyond the Oxus*, 204.
20. Syed Manzar Abbas Zaidi, "Uzbek Militancy in Pakistan" (Centre for International and Strategic Analysis Report no. 1, 2013); Radio Liberty Uzbek Service, January 21, 2016; Afghan media reports.

3

STUDENTS' IMAM

IN 1990 A NEW THIRTY-TWO-YEAR-OLD IMAM WAS APPOINTED to lead prayers at a small mosque in Tashkent's Eski Juva, or Old Tower, neighborhood. Soon Tokhtaboy Mosque was unable to accommodate the thousands of people coming for the traditional communal Friday prayers led by Imam Obidkhon qori Nazarov and his discourses on religious issues and beyond. Traffic would come to a standstill on Fridays in the streets leading to the mosque, which was located near Tashkent's largest bazaar, the Chorsu bazaar. The crowds heading to listen to Nazarov could swell to up to five thousand people.

Slight of figure, Nazarov was "a brilliant speaker" who "knew how to energize the public," according to a researcher on Islam who lived in Tashkent in the 1990s (who requested anonymity to be able to continue research in Uzbekistan). "Bazaar vendors, hooligans, and drunkards all came to listen to his sermons. Even the mafia accepted him as imam. He won their hearts," he said.

Nazarov was a new kind of imam. He was not afraid to criticize President Karimov and his officials; he spoke as if speaking on behalf of some higher authority. For his congregation, emerging out of an imposed foreign ideology, he embodied exactly what they wanted—a bearer and staunch defender of their lost-and-found faith.

To them the young imam's instructions—no vodka, no dating girls outside marriage, no stealing or other offenses "because a criminal first and foremost does harm to himself, his family and society"—sounded like spiritual revelations. His followers say the power of Nazarov's moral authority reformed many pickpockets and other petty criminals from the Chorsu bazaar. Others might have considered his emotional way of preaching to be bordering on inflammatory.

Figure 3.1. Imam Obidkhon qori Nazarov giving a sermon in Tashkent, 1995. © YouTube video screenshot. https://www.youtube.com/watch?v=JlKKj4_BzjA.

"The Muslims have nothing at their disposal [to enforce their faith]. Do the Muslims have jails? Do the Muslims have courts and prosecutors? The Muslims have no jails," Nazarov said in one of his discourses. "They [who deviate from Islam] are only treated according to their words. If they repent we accept them into the ranks of Muslims. But, the most humiliating and frightening thing is what happens tomorrow in the presence of Allah."

In another speech, he said, "If a girl wants to wear a headscarf of her own accord, the believers should cry tears of joy about that. How much longer do we have to put up with the shame of half-naked girls?" However, he also added that no girls should be forced to "cover themselves."[1]

Another thing that boosted Nazarov's popularity was that he would not shy away from speaking his mind on political, social, and economic issues of the day. He would challenge government control over religion and criticize other official policies. Once, when asked whether President Karimov was ruling "like a good Muslim," Imam Nazarov said: "No, he is a *kafir* [infidel]." Such bravery was unheard of. His sermons were recorded and sold or passed on to friends and family.

Nazarov's mosque was especially popular among students. "All students in Tashkent knew it," and they made up 90 percent of the congregation, in his own words. They were discovering Islam for the first time in their lives, and Nazarov became their reference point on everything: from questions like the meaning of life and death to social justice.

"It is hard to describe the sensation that I experienced that day in the mosque," one of those students, Farkhod, said about his first visit to Tokhtaboy Mosque in 1994, which turned him into a devout Muslim.

He'd had a Russian-language education and upbringing and had no contact with Islam before. He'd struggled to make sense of his existence and "so much injustice around." For him seeing thousands of people praying together was "like being given a new lease of life," he said. Nazarov's mosque became "a source of truth" for him.

The students' loyalty to Nazarov strengthened when he stood by them as the authorities began to expel female students for wearing hijab and close down prayer rooms at academic institutions.

For Erkin Shermurodov, another Tashkent student who attended Nazarov's mosque, it meant that Nazarov, "unlike others who initially spoke the truth but then under government pressure changed their line," did practice what he preached—"he always stayed on the path."

* * *

Nazarov came from the Fergana Valley city of Namangan. At the age of nine, his parents, who were devout Muslims—his mother was a respected preacher among women and spoke literary Arabic—entrusted him to the care of the hujra system of underground Islamic teaching. The classes were presumed to be secret, although everyone knew about them—neighbors, official mullahs, the KGB, and even his teachers in the usual secular Soviet school that he was attending at the same time.

The official policy was to let them be. "They just watched, so things didn't go too far," Nazarov told me in a conversation.

A desire to pursue the religious path came to him on a school sightseeing excursion to Bukhara. Nazarov was so amazed by the beauty and grandeur of the ancient Mir Arab Madrasah that he decided to go there after school to study Islam.

But the family had no money to send him to Mir Arab when he finished secondary school, and he went to work at a textile factory. Three years later, in 1979, his father, through a friend who knew some muftis in the capital, arranged a meeting for Nazarov with Chief Mufti Ziyautdin qori Babakhanov, so he could get his blessing and patronage to pursue religious studies. Babakhanov promised him a place at the Tashkent Islamic Institute the following year. Until then Nazarov would stay in Tashkent as an assistant in a mosque.

In 1985, the year when Mikhail Gorbachev became the general secretary of the Soviet Communist Party, Nazarov, having just completed the four-year course at the Islamic Institute, was appointed an assistant imam at Tilla Sheikh Mosque in Tashkent. Although perestroika brought some freedom and openness, Nazarov said, the KGB would not ease its control over the clergy, and he, like every imam and religious student, continued to be called in by the KGB for regular conversations. Apparently, at the time, the KGB were happy with Nazarov's ideological loyalty, and in 1988 he was among only twenty-one people from the entire Soviet Union picked to be sent to Saudi Arabia for hajj. The trip to Saudi Arabia was a turning point for Nazarov.

The performance of hajj—one of the pillars of Islam—came as a powerful spiritual experience, as it is designed to be. The hajj rites—circling seven times around the cube-shaped Kabah shrine in Mecca and kissing its Black Stone, followed by prayers, a night vigil, and animal sacrifice—are full of religious symbolism. When performed by millions of pilgrims at the same time, they awaken a sense of belonging to the *ummah*, the entire Muslim community. Every male pilgrim wears nothing but two sheets of white cloth, one to wrap around the torso, another around the waist—the dress is called *ihram*, which is meant to raise the believer above the material world, above their ego, and remind them that everyone is equal before Allah.

It was Nazarov's first ever foreign trip, and what he saw in Saudi Arabia—a rigid state system based on an ultraconservative Islamic ideology—he took to be "democracy and freedom." In his words, during that visit to Saudi Arabia, he "got a deeper awareness of human and Muslims' rights."

On his return, in February of that same year Gorbachev started to pull Soviet troops out of Afghanistan, and in April he visited Tashkent and made respectful remarks about Islam. In the encouraging atmosphere of perestroika, Nazarov for the first time started to get into arguments with his KGB interviewers. "I began to express our demands," he said, which meant more religious rights. And when Nazarov was appointed imam of Tokhtaboy Mosque, he took it as "an opportunity to preach independently" and "speak the truth."

"Every Friday I was free to choose a subject for my sermon, free to reject things, to criticize. I chose common subjects: what Islam calls for—being faithful, following the Prophet, how we should live, what shortcomings we as human beings have, that we should respect our parents, that there should be both religious and secular education, and young people should be good Muslims. I criticized those who opposed religion, who were against Islam spreading among more people. I openly condemned the ban on headscarves in offices and schools when the government imposed harsh restrictions on beards, hijabs, and prayer. But they took it as interference in state policies," Nazarov told me.

Soon enough Nazarov, still a member of the official Spiritual Board of the Muslims, started to get warnings from his colleagues that his way of running his mosque and preaching could land him in trouble.

"Don't believe that there is democracy. You say too much, be quieter," Deputy Chief Mufti Yusufkhon Shokirov said to him.

Nazarov stood his ground, insisting, "Islam has its own separate way; the government has its own."

Defying Central Asian Islamic traditions, Nazarov opened his mosque to women. In Soviet times, there had been only one mosque in Uzbekistan, in Tashkent, with allocated space for women. Arranged for the wives of official visitors from Arab countries, in case they wanted to pray, it would fit fifty female worshippers.

Mufti Shokirov told Nazarov to "get the women out."

"How come? It's allowed by the Koran," Nazarov argued. "I cannot expel them."

"Don't tell me about human rights. Get them out. Let them go wherever they want," the mufti said and reported Nazarov's disobedience to the Spiritual Board leadership.

As was expected, the matter was passed on to the KGB. After the Soviet collapse, the Uzbek KGB was renamed the SNB (the National Security Service). Nazarov's mosque began to be frequented by SNB agents. During the Friday prayers, there would be government agents filming worshippers—official files were being compiled on all regular visitors to the Tokhtaboy Mosque. Nazarov continued his discourses and did not close his mosque's doors to women, but he did begin to watch his words.

The year 1992 was marked by the first disappearance of a new-wave Islamic leader. Abdulla Otayev vanished from Tashkent in December, soon after he had created an Islamic party. The event went off largely unnoticed—the Islamic revival was at its peak, and its participants were too fired up to take the disappearance as a warning about trouble ahead. And Otayev's family were too scared to make any "noise" about his disappearance through rights activists or to make any demands from the authorities.[2]

The next year, when the authorities replaced the centrist chief mufti Mohammad Yusuf with Mukhtor-Qozhi Abdullayev, the muftiyat immediately set about getting rid of "Wahhabi" clerics. My neighbor Rukhitdin's brief career as official imam ended—he and the imams of nine other mosques were accused of Wahhabism and fired. He went back to giving independent Arabic and Islamic lessons. Fazlitdin aka warned him that his lessons were illegal. Rukhitdin would not argue with his father but quietly carried on with his classes.

Also in 1993 several graves were vandalized at the Muslim cemetery in Tashkent. Following the incident, the new chief mufti gathered all Tashkent imams for a meeting with officials of the state religious committee and an Interior Ministry official, Kutbutdin Burkhonov.

Burkhonov angrily harangued the imams for allowing "Wahhabis" to do "such things." "If you have no influence [over radicals], then let us deal with such things by ourselves!" Burkhonov fumed, according to Nazarov, who was at the meeting.

Some Islamic teachings, including Salafi (Wahhabi), say that worshipping the dead by visiting graves, marking them, and decorating them with stones amounts to idolatry or polytheism. Nazarov said he and many other imams suspected that the vandalism at the cemetery had been staged by the authorities themselves in order to have something to blame on the clergy. "People said they saw two buses with military that arrived that night at the cemetery," Nazarov said.

* * *

Until 1995 SNB officers continued to visit Nazarov or invite him for talks to give him warnings and try to make him cooperate with them by providing written reports on who visited the mosque, with observations on each worshipper.

"It's none of my business who comes to the mosque," Nazarov said to them. "I do not want you to give me any instructions or make any demands. This is my homeland, my people. We want to live peacefully but according to Islam."

Another SNB demand was that in his sermons Nazarov denounce militant Islamic groups, namely, the Islamic Movement of Uzbekistan (IMU) and the Tajik Islamic Rebirth (IRP) party, which was at the time part of an opposition coalition fighting against the Moscow-backed Tajik government. The Spiritual Board also asked him to write an undertaking that he would not join the IRP. Nazarov knew one of the IRP leaders, Abdullo Otto Nuri, and had good relations with him. Nazarov wrote and signed the undertaking but refused to preach against the IRP and the IMU.

"I wanted the freedom to speak about everyone and everything, not only about the things they tell me. Otherwise there would be no point," Nazarov said.

The growing standoff between the dissident clergy and Karimov's government took a sinister turn with the disappearance in August 1995 of the famous Andijan imam Abduvali qori Mirzayev. Mirzayev was last seen on August 29, 1995, at the Tashkent airport as he checked in for a flight to Moscow.

"He went through all the necessary checks, including passport control. But when he was boarding, SNB officers approached him and took him away for additional checks. No one has seen him since then," Mirzayev's son Abdulquddus said in an interview with the website uznews.net in 2007. "We have grounds to say that he was kidnapped."

In September, after Karimov's visit to the United States, Tashkent hosted a conference on human rights organized by the Organization for Security and Cooperation in Europe. Abdulquddus was one of the speakers. He asked the audience to look at Nazarov, who was also attending: "Have a look at him. You may never see him again. There is no guarantee that tomorrow he will not be found with drugs and guns in his pockets," he said.

When Nazarov's turn to speak came, he said: "You must understand that here Islam is a burning issue. I spoke out once and I have suffered for my words. Now, I would like to ask you, our guests, what do you think of what is happening here in Uzbekistan?"[3]

Mirzayev's disappearance shook the entire Fergana Valley—some were angry, but most people were frightened. "Abduvali was perhaps the last of the great imams," one of his friends said. "Many people in Fergana are worried. They are afraid and insulted."

A group of elders traveled from the Fergana Valley to Tashkent bringing a petition to the UN office asking for help with finding Mirzayev. They tried in vain for three days to get a meeting with presidential adminis-tration officials. Thousands of people attended the first Friday prayers after the elders' departure to Tashkent; women gathered in a courtyard nearby cried.[4]

Abdulquddus alleged that his father had been secretly imprisoned by the authorities and at the time of the interview was still alive and behind bars. "As far as we know Abduvali qori is currently being kept in Tash-kent Region. His health has deteriorated and he was seriously ill four or five years ago, but he recovered after doctors treated him," Abdulquddus said in the uznews.net interview.

Abdulquddus's interview was published a few days after his death in a car accident in Saudi Arabia, where he went for hajj. The accident, on September 26, 2007, also claimed the lives of his mother, Sharifa, and his little son, Abdulvadid. He lived the last year of his life as a refugee in Kyrgyzstan, where he had fled after briefly being arrested in his hometown, Andijan, following an antigovernment uprising there in May 2005.

The authorities put Mirzayev on the list of missing people. His family was subjected to repeated interrogations and house searches.

* * *

Nazarov was angered by Mirzayev's disappearance and used his mosque as a tribune to challenge the authorities over it.

"People did not used to go missing like this in Soviet times. Why is it hap-pening now?" Nazarov would say, addressing his congregation, he told me.

The authorities' reaction was swift. Nazarov was summoned to the Tashkent prosecutor's office to see Prosecutor Ergash Jurayev. Jurayev be-gan shouting as soon as Nazarov walked through the door.

"So you think you're such a hero?" he shouted, according to Nazarov.

Nazarov was taken aback by such a harsh welcome. He did not say anything. Then an SNB officer, Tokhir Ibrakhimov, came in with a file on Nazarov. He opened the file and began to read various reports about his "antigovernment speeches and interference in politics."

Nazarov said he only answered people's questions. "Even in Stalin's times things were not as bad as this," he added.

"Let those who have brains and a head on their shoulders speak, but not you. Stupid people should not interfere [in politics]," the prosecutor Jurayev shouted. "I will lock you up; you will rot in jail. I've already locked up many like you," he went on.

Nazarov was made to write a written undertaking that he would not interfere in state affairs. A few days later the SNB sent a car after him for another talk. Nazarov purposely put on his white scullcap and a festive robe that he used for wedding ceremonies—he wanted to be noticeable so that in case something happened some witnesses would be able to remember seeing him.

This time the SNB officers demanded that Nazarov cooperate with them and wanted him to give a written consent to do that. According to Nazarov, he agreed to cooperate "for the sake of peace in the country," but said he wouldn't give a written consent. The officers continued to press, "both nicely and nastily," for a written statement. "We've promised our General—our God—that we would get it from you," one of them said, according to Nazarov.

Nazarov continued to refuse.

"OK, then we are going to be seeing more of each other, aren't we? But don't come dressed like this anymore," said the SNB officer, Rykhsivoy Dekhkonboyev.

After some more attempts to recruit Nazarov as a government agent, the SNB stopped contacting him. At the same time, the Spiritual Board became openly hostile to Nazarov. They demanded that he close his mosque to women and stop criticizing the official policy of banning hijab and prayer at schools.

In winter 1995 the government started to tighten control over mosques and made imams sit exams to filter out the unreliable ones. Mirzayev's mosque in Andijan was closed down; his tapes disappeared from bazaars.

In January 1996 the authorities demolished Nazarov's house that was adjacent to his Tokhtaboy Mosque to make way for a new road construction project. The family were given two flats in compensation and ordered to move out within three days. The same year, Nazarov was fired as imam. That provoked a standoff between his followers and the police outside his mosque, with the followers attempting to protest Nazarov's firing and the police cordoning it off. The standoff ended peacefully.

* * *

By the end of 1996 Nazarov was under constant official surveillance. He continued to give Islamic lessons at home to his most loyal students. They too would often be followed by government agents after their visits to the imam.

Figure 3.2. Tashkent's Tokhtaboy Mosque, where Imam Nazarov used to preach, 2017. © Alexey Volosevich.

"Once I left Imam's house and took a minibus," said his student Farkhod. "Two men got out of a car parked outside and got into the minibus after me. I realized that they were from the police and got off before my stop. They followed. I began to zigzag and managed to lose them. That was the first time I noticed that I was being shadowed."

At the same time, the authorities tightened control over the practice of Islam among students, ordering academic institutions to close down prayer rooms on their premises and ensure stricter enforcement of the ban on beards and hijab.

When Erkin, who studied at the Oriental Studies Institute, returned to school after summer holidays in 1996, he found that their prayer hall had been closed and turned into a classroom. The big prayer hall, divided into two sections with a curtain to segregate males and females, was very popular. The students took turns and prayed in three shifts.

After the closure of the prayer hall, the students started to pray in the corridor, on steps, in empty classrooms. Students also wrote a collective letter to the rector asking him to reopen the prayer room. It was signed by 123 students. Erkin's signature was first on the list.

In two days the dean of Erkin's faculty called him in to say: "The letter is not going to be considered, and there will be no prayer room."

The students continued to defy the school administration. They found some empty space in the basement, put a few carpets there, and began to use it as a new prayer room. In a few days they found it padlocked. When Erkin and a few other students went to the dean, he said the order came from "the government."

"If the SNB finds out [that we allow a prayer room] we will be sacked. Please understand us," the dean pleaded.

* * *

In 1997 things got quite ugly in the Fergana Valley. Several police officers, a government official, and a community leader were murdered, some of them beheaded, in Namangan. The authorities blamed the attacks on "Wahhabis" and launched sweeping arrests among Mirzayev's and Nazarov's followers.

Human Rights Watch issued its report "Creating Enemies of the State" in March 2004:

> At least several hundred, and possibly more than a thousand, independent Muslims in Namangan and Andijan provinces in the Fergana Valley were arrested during the first four months following the murders. The police now targeted people even loosely affiliated with imams Nazarov or Mirzayev, or other religious leaders who had fallen out of favor with the authorities, as well as those who had sided with Nazarov at the time of his removal from the Tokhtaboy Mosque. They placed those who had attended Nazarov's mosque, years before, on special police registers, and subsequently arrested them. Hundreds of young men, labelled "Wahhabis" by the police, were arrested and convicted on falsified charges of possessing narcotics or bullets. Hundreds of others were detained and forced to shave their beards or were placed in administrative custody for 10 to 15 days on false charges and threatened with future arrest. [5]

The police established a heavy visible presence in Namangan with round-the-clock patrolling of all neighborhoods, a Namangan resident remembered. She lived in the same neighborhood as one of the murdered police officers—his severed head was left hanging outside his house. Another murder, of a collective-farm director, was similarly atrocious—as if intended to shock and terrify. Before being killed, he was tortured with a hot iron.

Many people in Namangan were suspicious of the official theory that pointed the finger at "Wahhabis," the Namangan resident said. They believed the police officer had been murdered by his own "enemies."

However, the attacks on policemen were in line with the Islamist vigilante groups' self-proclaimed mission to replace the corrupt police service. Tohir Yuldosh, who had led such vigilante groups before creating the Islamic Movement of Uzbekistan, boasted in a 1992 interview of "punishing many policemen."[6]

The 1997 murders gave the authorities grounds for a broad clampdown on suspected Islamists in the valley. The arrested were carried out in a fashion designed to instill fear. "They would kick open your doors and enter, dressed like ninjas, wielding automatic guns. They used to come in the evening or night. 'We work twenty-four hours a day,' they would say," said the resident who used to live in the neighborhood where the police murders had happened.

Nazarov's family in Namangan kept their gates shut. His father would hide on the roof, in case they came after him.

Bearded men and women wearing hijab were picked up off the street, so many preferred to stay in. Local neighborhood committees made women write written undertakings not to wear hijab.

Around that time persistent rumors started within Tashkent's dissident Muslim community about Nazarov's imminent arrest. By spring 1998 there would be two or three surveillance cars near Nazarov's house every day, and he would be followed everywhere he went.

With Mirzayev gone, Nazarov became, at the time, the country's most influential independent Islamic leader. More flamboyant than Nazarov and based in the more religious Fergana Valley, Mirzayev was from the outset seen by the authorities as a threat, hence his early and willful removal from the scene. With Nazarov, the authorities chose steady pressure.

On March 4, 1998, Nazarov was summoned to the district police office. No reason was given. Nazarov chose not to go. Instead, he and several friends gathered at his home to put their heads together and decide what to do. Everyone agreed that he should go into hiding.

At about four a.m. on March 5, they all left Nazarov's house—they came out at the same time, two of them going one way, another two another way, and Nazarov going a third way. They noticed no surveillance, which they found surprising. They walked on; no one seemed to follow.

They would learn later, according to Nazarov, from friends with connections inside the security services that the reason why there was no surveillance outside his house that night was a late football match that the four officers on duty were unable to resist.

At around nine o'clock the next morning, police and security forces arrived in about fifteen cars and cordoned off the entire neighborhood.

"Where is he? If he's home, let him come out by himself. Let's do everything peacefully without making a fuss," a district police chief told Nazarov's wife, Munira Nasretdinova. They turned everything upside down in their flat. In another flat of Nazarov's, one floor up, where he used to give lessons, they smashed down the door and took away his books and tapes.

For the next year their home was under round-the-clock surveillance. A bold neighbor once asked one of the officers on watch: "Why are you sitting here?"

"We're protecting Imam [Nazarov] from Americans," he replied.

* * *

My childhood friend Zukhra's brother Rukhitdin too found himself under close watch in 1998. The security service and police began to regularly call him in for questions about his preaching activity. One day Rukhitdin came to his father and asked him for permission to leave "for an Arab country."

"Control is tightening here; they are not leaving me alone," he told his father. Fazlitdin aka gave his blessing, and Rukhitdin left. A few weeks later Rukhitdin's photo was published in the official police newspaper *Na Postu* (which means "on duty"), with a note that he was wanted as the Tashkent leader of the "Wahhabis."

Zukhra and her husband, Farrukh, were at the time living in the Kazakh capital, Astana, where Farrukh was teaching Arabic at the Institute of Arabic Language and Oriental Culture. He had been invited there upon his return from Saudi Arabia in 1997.

* * *

In those days in Tashkent, any young men with beards or young women wearing hijab came to be treated by the police as suspected religious extremists, which gave the police unlimited opportunities for abuse and extortion. Imam Nazarov's student Erkin, who had a beard, often got stopped on the street by police. He would usually get away by paying them some money. But when he got stopped again in May 1998, he had religious booklets and a prayer book on him. He was handcuffed and taken to a district police station and beaten up. Erkin, he told me in an interview, demanded a lawyer.

"Where do you think you are, America? We are your lawyers," he was told.

Erkin was interrogated by the head of the antiterrorism department, who judging by his uniform was a major. Then other officers would come in and ask who Erkin was—perhaps out of idle curiosity.

"A *Vovchik*," the antiterror chief would say, calling him the diminutive and demeaning version of the Russian name Vladimir, used by the Uzbek police as a derogatory name for alleged Wahhabis. (*Ninja* was what they called women wearing hijab.) They would hit Erkin several times before leaving. Perhaps they could not help it—it was a professional reflex.

Then a big man entered the room. Like the others, he asked: "Who is this?"

"Ask him," the major replied.

"I will only answer to your boss; I'm not going to talk to you," Erkin said.

"This is our deputy district police chief," the major said.

"Why should I care?" Erkin said.

"We should do away with such scum without trial and investigation. Plant bullets on him and send him to Tashtyurma [Tashkent prison]," the deputy chief said. He swore and left.

After hearing that, Erkin made a last-ditch attempt to get away. An eloquent speaker, for some thirty minutes he pleaded with the major's conscience.

"You can jail me for nothing, but think about your parents, your family, who pray like me. I am just like them. You claim that we are different, that we do bad things. Think what your parents would say about what you are doing to religious people."

The major let him go.

* * *

After leaving home before light on March 17, 1998, for the next two years Nazarov secretly lived in various rented flats in Tashkent with the help of his followers. They rented places not far from his home in neighborhoods around Tashkent State University and the Medical Institute's new compound in the northwestern part of the city—an unattractive mass of gray concrete apartment blocks and student hostels.

Nazarov's followers visited him and brought him food and sometimes his own youngest children for him to see and spend time with. For up to a year, they kept his whereabouts secret from his wife—she was under particularly close watch by authorities, and it was safer if she did not visit Nazarov and did not even know where he was, in case she was arrested and tortured or pressured in other ways.

In those two years, Nazarov at least three times narrowly escaped capture—with the help of Allah, he believes. "I prayed every morning and evening asking him for protection," Nazarov said.

Once he moved from a flat just before it was raided by police on a tip-off from a detained follower, who was involved in supporting Nazarov in his underground life. Another time, the police got a tip-off from a woman who sold sunflower seeds in the neighborhood and at the same time acted as the eyes and ears of the police. She reported that women in headscarves frequently visited the apartment block where Nazarov lived at the time.

"One evening I walked up to the window, looked out carefully from behind the curtain, and saw a Nexia car driving up from the left. It stopped, and four men got out. I ran to the door and a minute later saw the four men coming out of the lift and walking straight to my door. They pressed the bell; it was not working—between ourselves we used special knocks as a password. They started knocking. They were in civilian clothes. I turned off the lights and the fridge," Nazarov said.

Nazarov had his own two young children with him that day and a student, Khusan. Nazarov told the children, eight-year-old Madhiya and five-year-old Nuritdin: "Be quiet, be quiet. It's the police."

After getting no response, the four men knocked on the door opposite and asked the man who opened it about Nazarov's flat. The neighbor said all he knew was that there was a tenant living there. Officially the place was rented by a friend of Nazarov's who sometimes showed up, so neighbors would see him. He would also bring food for Nazarov. The four men then went to look for the house supervisor—someone elected by the residents of an apartment block as an administrator to deal with various maintenance issues.

Meanwhile, Nazarov and Khusan began to call their friends, using special code words to inform them of what was going on. They also started to pack up everything in the house—books, documents, tapes, putting them into boxes—and emptied the computer of all files and disks. They decided the place was no longer safe, and they needed to leave.

Several followers came to help Nazarov escape. They checked all the streets and entrances to the apartment block for suspicious people who could be government agents. Then they signaled to Nazarov that there was only one suspicious guy hanging around.

Praying the whole time, they waited till evening. First they sent out Nazarov's daughter Madhiya alone with a laptop in her bag. She was to go down and then turn right, and there one of Nazarov's students would meet her. Then they sent his son Nuritdin out in the same manner.

Then Nazarov, who had shaved off his beard, walked out alone and empty-handed. The suspicious guy who was hanging around near the block glanced at him but paid no attention.

* * *

In those two years that Imam Nazarov spent in hiding, a young Tashkent resident named Iskandar Khudayberganov was taking a cameraman course at the State Institute of Art and Culture, commonly known by its old name the Theatre Institute. He had been born in 1974 and grew up in Sebzar, one of the four historical parts of old Tashkent, where whitewashed walls and the tall locked gates of traditional Uzbek houses along narrow winding streets create something like a labyrinth and seem to take you back in time.

Iskandar's father was a journalist with the state broadcasting corporation, and his mother was a doctor. As a child Iskandar was a big fan of Bruce Lee—he watched all his films, and the walls in his room were covered with photos and posters of the movie star, his sister Dilobar told me. Iskandar dreamed of mastering karate like Bruce Lee, but he had a kidney problem, and doctors prohibited him from any physically demanding sports.

One day, in his teenage years, he acquired an old camera and started experimenting with photography. He liked taking spontaneous, natural shots, without staging, and was very proud of his pictures. That led to an interest in video cameras and filming—he started making short videos and decided to become a cameraman and shoot feature films.

At school Iskandar, along with Dilobar and their elder brother, studied Arabic as a foreign language. Iskandar was keen on languages, and he also learned Turkish.

Their house was near a jami mosque named after the tenth-century Sufi master Al-Hakim at-Termizi. When Iskandar was a child, his father, who regularly attended Friday communal prayers, would sometimes take him and his brother along. At the same time, to help Iskandar cope better with his health issue, his mother told him that if he believed sincerely in Allah and prayed for good health, he would certainly get well. Iskandar started praying regularly after that, mostly at home.

When in the early 1990s the government started encouraging Islamic revival and expanding contacts with Muslim countries, the mosque in Iskandar's family's neighborhood started receiving frequent foreign visitors. The imam would sometimes ask Iskandar to help him as an interpreter during such visits.

"Nobody could imagine what helping the imam and the mosque would lead to," said Dilobar, remembering those times. "It seemed life was going on as it should. We were all either working or studying, and the brothers got married and had their first children. It seemed we were all getting what we wanted from life."

That normal life in which everything made sense, in which there seemed to be certainty about the future—Iskandar had just started working as an assistant cameraman at Uzbek TV—collapsed on February 16, 1999, when Tashkent was hit by several explosions near government buildings. They killed sixteen people and injured dozens more.

"Like all Tashkent residents, we were shocked," Dilobar said. "Over the family dinner that day, Iskandar was emotionally saying that people couldn't commit such crimes and kill innocent people."

The next evening Iskandar had a call from his friend Toir, who told him about arrests among their fellow students and also at the mosques. Iskandar took the news calmly, saying that there was no need to worry because there was nothing they could be prosecuted for.

"Two days later the whole of Tashkent was engulfed with arrests," Dilobar said. "We started hearing from friends, neighbors, and relatives about arbitrary arrests and about those arrested being tortured in the MVD [Ministry of the Interior] and SNB basements. The whole of Tashkent was at the mercy of the police. There were policemen all over, and the entire city was gripped with fear."

Arrests among Iskandar's friends meant the authorities would certainly be coming after him soon. He decided to go into hiding.

Iskandar was arrested in Tajikistan on August 24, 2001, as an alleged "Uzbek spy." Relations between Uzbekistan and Tajikistan had been quite hostile since the Islamic Movement of Uzbekistan had set up a base there in the mid-1990s during the Tajik civil war. After six months in Tajik police custody, during which he was interrogated and tortured, he was handed over to the Uzbek authorities.

His trial at Tashkent City Court began in August 2002. It was one of many similar ones going on at the time in the aftermath of the February

1999 blasts. When the first trials began, my neighbor Rukhitdin, who was in hiding, emerged in suspects' "confessions" as one of Uzbekistan's top militant Islamist leaders. According to their "testimonies," Rukhitdin and other "leaders," including IMU founder Tohir Yuldosh, had gathered in Istanbul in 1997 and decided to unite all Uzbek Islamist forces into one organization, that they allegedly called the Islamic Rebirth Movement of Uzbekistan, which would train its future fighters in Chechnya and Tajikistan. Their alleged goal was jihad against President Karimov, and the blasts were the beginning of that jihad.[7]

The IMU would never claim responsibility for the 1999 attacks. By the unwritten rules of terror activity, terrorist groups admit to their attacks since that's what they exist for. (The IMU would claim responsibility for failed incursions into Uzbekistan from the Kyrgyz and Tajik parts of the Fergana Valley in August 1999 and 2000.)

Iskandar stood trial along with several other defendants facing the same charges. Thanks to his sister Dilobar's tireless activism, the hearings attracted the attention of journalists (including myself), rights activists, and foreign diplomats.

The charges against the defendants included membership in the Islamic Movement of Uzbekistan, robbery, murder, training in terror camps in Chechnya, plotting to kill President Karimov, and even personal contacts with Osama bin Laden. The prosecutors had no evidence or witnesses to support the charges. All they had were the defendants' confessions.

A few weeks into the trial, Iskandar managed to pass on a letter to his family. It read:

> *Assalomu Alaykum [peace be with you] my dear mother and little sister Dilobar.*
>
> *I hope that this letter reaches you. I know you are very worried about me and your hearts must be very heavy with pain. But please believe me, I never wanted to cause your souls any pain. If only you could know how frustrated I am because of not being able to sit down with you and talk and tell you the entire truth.*
>
> *Dear mother, please believe me that I have done nothing wrong. I have been putting up with so much suffering in the hope that the trial would be fair. But you can see for yourselves what kind of trial it is turning out to be.*
>
> *Everyone can see that there is no evidence to support the accusations against me. But what could I do? Under all the pressure I was forced to sign up to the charges.*
>
> *At the MVD I suffered all sorts of violence. They said they would tell my family where I was, only if I confessed to everything, otherwise you are going to*

die here [they said], but I toughed it out. When they tied my hands behind my back, beat me with clubs, with chairs, kicked my kidneys nonstop, hit me against the walls till my head was bleeding, I toughed it out. They did not let me sleep at all at night. They kept me hungry for weeks. When they kicked me between the legs, when they kicked my head, I still toughed it out.

Even if I die, I have never killed anyone, I have never broken into anyone's house, I am not going to sign up to all that. The only thing I did was go on the run because I had been praying and was afraid [of prosecution for that]. But I have never seen Juma Namangani [one of the IMU leaders], I do not know how to make bombs at all, I told them.

After they had hit my head with a tube, I started to hear noises in my head. My heart nearly stops when I remember all that torture. I am telling you this, not to make you pity me but so that you know the truth.

At the MVD there was no sign of any lawyer. Those who did everything [interrogations] in the basement—investigators, or operatives—are all very physically fit, with very short hair, aged between 30 and 35. Now any slightest thing makes my heart pound with fear. I endured everything.

What I was not able to cope with was their threat to go after my mother, wife and sister—think about them, otherwise it is going to get nasty [they said] . . . How could I bear such words?

Please understand me. I am sorry. The most important thing for me is that now you know the truth. I was never involved in any of those things.

I will write again if I get a chance. Your son Iskandar.

Twenty sixth day of the ninth month of two thousand and two.

Dear mother, everything written in this letter is true.

In court the defendants denied the charges and said they had signed confession papers under duress. They said they had been tortured during the investigations. They showed torture marks on their bodies and gave exact details about when, how, and by whom they had been tortured. Judge Nizam Rustamov's response to that was "You weren't in a sanatorium."

Iskandar's family and lawyer provided a document from the Theatre Institute that demonstrated that in 1997–98, when the prosecutors said he was getting terror training in Chechnya, he was actually attending a cameraman's course at the institute. During that period, he also had his first child.

Through his secretary, Judge Nizamov asked Iskandar's family for twenty thousand dollars in exchange for dropping the case against him. The family would not have been able to collect that much even if they sold their house.

"They did not even try to pretend that they were acting under the law," Dilobar told me. "The words law, justice, and criminal code began to seem like fiction to me. The only things that the system was able to understand at the time were torture and money. People's fates were decided just like that. Justice could only be bought for money."

On November 28, 2002, Iskandar was given the death penalty.

In Uzbekistan the death penalty is carried out without giving the family any notice. Iskandar's family had kept the UN High Commissioner on Human Rights informed about his case throughout the trial, which helped to make sure that on the day after the verdict, the UN formally requested that the Uzbek authorities hold off on the execution until they had considered the allegations of foul play during the proceedings.

It took several more requests before on December 11, 2003, the government finally said the execution was on hold, pending a UN decision. After its investigation the UN recommended that the Uzbek authorities overturn the death penalty and carry out a new investigation. It took five years for the Uzbek government to drop the death penalty, but instead of a new investigation they replaced Iskandar's sentence with twenty years in jail, where he remains to this day.

Because of Dilobar's active efforts to save her brother—she had spent all her days camping on the doorsteps of various organizations, local and foreign, carrying in her bag a heap of documents about her brother's case—she and the entire family came under official pressure. Dilobar was excluded from the literature course she was attending at Tashkent State University. The family decided to seek asylum abroad, and in 2009 Dilobar, her parents, and another brother with his family moved to Sweden.

Iskandar is being held in Uzbekistan's most notorious prison, Zhaslyk. Dilobar sends him letters but is not sure if he is getting them. She has approached Red Cross representatives in Uzbekistan with a request to visit her brother at Zhaslyk to get some news about him, but they have failed to get government permission.

"It's very painful," Dilobar said to me in an interview in 2017. "He has been in jail for almost eighteen years, and I still have no answers to my questions—why and for what?"

* * *

The February 1999 blasts had direct consequences for Imam Nazarov, his family, and his followers too. Immediately after the attacks, Nazarov's family home in Tashkent was raided by eight masked police commandos, armed with automatic guns. Nazarov's scared grandchildren cried as the police searched the house, going through all the books and tapes. They left giving a summons to Nazarov's wife, Nasretdinova, to come to the police station the following day.

She did not turn up at the appointed time, and the police came after her, saying they would only ask her some questions and would let her go after fifteen minutes. They held her for ten days, moving her from one cell to another four times, all filled over their capacity, so the detainees had to take turns to sleep on metal bunk beds.

She was threatened that if she did not tell them Nazarov's whereabouts, they would lock her up, and her children would go to an orphanage, or they would hand her over to "other guys" who would do "whatever they want" with her.

"You are going to bleed from your mouth," they said.

She denied knowing anything.

Nazarov's students also came under much more severe official pressure after the February attacks. In May Erkin and his friend were called to the rector's office and given a sealed envelope.

"Take this to the SNB, ask to see Major Ravshan, and say that you are from the Oriental Institute," the rector told them.

Erkin thought they were going to be locked up when they came to the SNB. They thought long and hard what to do. "Are they calling us for an interrogation or to jail us?" they wondered. "If we run away, they will put us on a wanted list and search for us." Finally, they said a prayer together and decided to go.

At the SNB Major Ravshan led both of them into a room on one of the upper floors.

"It was a room for informers—a big room where informers and officers had their meetings. There were people everywhere, sitting at about ten round tables with from two to four chairs around each one," Erkin said.

The major began to question Erkin and his friend.

"We have information that you are Hizb ut-Tahrir members," he started.

"No," they replied.

"Then you are Wahhabis."

"No."

"Then who are you?"

"We are ordinary Muslims; we simply pray. If someone prays, does he have to be either a Hizb ut-Tahrir [member] or a Wahhabi?" Erkin said.

Then the major told them each to write a statement addressed to the SNB chief Rustam Inoyatov, pledging allegiance and love for the constitution and President Karimov and vowing never to seek to overthrow the current constitutional order. The two did so and were let go.

* * *

About six months later, in January 2000, when Erkin came to the institute, he was approached by a stranger who flashed his police ID at him, told him to stretch out his arms, and handcuffed him.

"We are going to the MVD," the man said.

"In what capacity? As a witness, a suspect? I need a lawyer," Erkin said and started to shout, trying to attract attention: "You have no right to do this! You will answer for this!"

The man started hitting Erkin and pushed him, sending him tumbling down the steps. The man punched and kicked Erkin, forcing him outside, where there were riot police with automatic guns and a black Nexia without a number plate waiting for them.

On the way to the Interior Ministry, they continued to beat Erkin. At the ministry he was taken to the fourth floor, the department for fighting terrorism. They continued to beat him there, without saying anything.

"I could not comprehend that: one beater would have been enough, because I was thin. They were all big and tall; two held me, and another beat me in the head and kicked me in the kidneys. I lost consciousness after one of the blows, but they continued to beat me. I came to after they sprinkled some water on me."

Erkin was told they were going to search him. Among the things they took out of Erkin's pockets, there was something wrapped in foil.

"What have you got in that foil?" one of the interrogators said, unwrapping it and revealing some white substance.

"It is not mine," Erkin replied.

"Oh! You've got heroin. That's it; consider yourself jailed."

Erkin asked them to let him say a prayer, and they did, but after that they played Russian roulette with him. One of the officers took a revolver, took out of it all but one bullet and began to fire, aiming at Erkin's legs.

He was sitting in a chair, with his hands cuffed behind it. He lifted his feet as fast as he could from the floor every time the officer fired a shot.

"They were laughing; they were having fun," Erkin said.

Erkin spent the next five days in the MVD basement cells notorious for being torture chambers.

"They would take you to the basement in a lift. They would tell you to turn away when they pressed the button of a level they wanted to take you to," Erkin said.

Before being led to his cell, number 20, Erkin was stripped naked and searched in a small room next to the lift. Then he was given a pillow and a "very thin" mattress.

To the left of the duty officer's glass booth on his level, there was a door with metal bars leading into a corridor with four or five interrogation rooms alongside. Another metal door straight from the duty officer opened into another corridor with cells, about eight on each side.

Erkin was held in cell number 20 for five days; he was unable to sleep the first two nights because of long interrogations. His cellmate was a *lokhmach* (literally"mop-headed"; in Russian prison jargon an inmate who cooperates with prison administration), who looked like someone who had spent a long time in prison.

He advised Erkin to talk "nicely" to his interrogators and "do what they tell you to do." But lokhmach himself did not always talk nicely. One day he threatened to rape Erkin.

"Do you think I will let you? I have teeth, and when you fall asleep, I'll tear at your throat," Erkin responded, trying to sound as aggressive as he could. Inside he knew he would not be able to even hit him.

The good-cop-bad-cop routine was practiced on Erkin as well. Once, after another beating Erkin was taken to the office of the MVD's antiterrorism chief at the time, Botir Tursunov. Tursunov stroked his head and gave him a piece of bread. "Sonny, are you hungry? I will tell them not to beat you anymore. Just admit everything," he said.

On the morning of his third day in detention, Erkin was taken for more questioning. Before the interrogator could begin, his mobile phone rang, and he was asked to go somewhere. The officer left, locking Erkin up in the interrogation room and telling him "to stay put."

Erkin was left alone with his case file on the desk in front of him. He wanted to know what he had to be prepared for. He was handcuffed and afraid to be caught reading it, so he stayed in his chair and read the open pages upside down. According to the file, the authorities were charging him with drug use, on the basis of the heroin planted on him. The religious extremism accusations against Erkin were based on testimony given by Toir Abdusamatov. According to the file, Abdusamatov admitted to being a follower of Imam Nazarov and helping him distribute "extremist literature" and also having intentions to go to Tajikistan or Chechnya for jihad.

Toir Abdusamatov, along with his two brothers, Tokhir and Khasan, was indeed a Nazarov follower. He studied at the same institute with Erkin but was a grade higher. Toir had been captured during the police sweeps following the February 1999 blasts, his sister Mukhlisa told me in a conversation.

The Abdusamatovs' home was raided by security officers a few days after the blasts. Tokhir and Toir, who were at home, tried to escape through the window of their third-floor flat. They used a long mattress for a rope, but Toir failed to get a good hold of it and fell, breaking his leg and pelvis. They still managed to get away and hid in a relative's home, in a room with the door to it barricaded with a wardrobe.

The police raided the relative's place a month later, and the two brothers were arrested. Toir was tortured despite being in a cast for his fractured bones. Erkin believes he made "all those false confessions against himself and others" because of his condition.

When the interrogator returned, he asked Erkin: "Do you know Toir?"

"Yes," Erkin said.

He gave Erkin a pen and paper and said: "Write down what you know."

Erkin wrote about his becoming a Muslim, religious lessons he had taken, and religious books he had read and helped distribute.

"I didn't want to be tortured, didn't want them to bring my parents and sister there, as they had threatened."

When Erkin began to confess to his ties with Nazarov, they started treating him more gently. His spine seemed to have been damaged during the beatings—he had difficulty standing up and kept falling down.

Erkin did his best not to give away any names. Once interrogators brought him an album with two thousand mug shots; each was numbered. Many were apparently photographed after beatings and torture. The names were in a second book—opposite their mug shot numbers. Erkin was told to look through the mug shots and tell them everyone he knew. He put down twelve numbers.

"Good boy," they said.

But their mood changed soon because apart from Nazarov, Erkin picked Osama Bin Laden, the two IMU leaders Tohir Yuldosh and Juma

Namangani, the Chechen warlord Shamil Basayev, other commonly known militants, and the guy who had testified against Erkin.

"How do you know them?" they asked.

"From TV. I really don't know the others."

* * *

Erkin was let out after he had written a statement that effectively meant confessing to terrorism and agreeing to cooperate with the authorities as an informer. "I was against the Constitution of the Republic of Uzbekistan, was plotting to kill Karimov, and then understood that it was a mistake. I ask the state and the president to forgive me, and from now on I will cooperate with the authorities and help them catch terrorists," it said.

He was released under a written undertaking not to leave Tashkent and to regularly report to the prosecutor's office until his trial on charges of drug use, religious extremism, attempting to overthrow the government, and terrorism. Erkin suspected that his parents had paid a bribe to the anti-terrorism chief, Botir Tursunov, to secure his release as they'd had a private talk with him on the day he was set free—maybe that was what was behind Tursunov's show of compassion in his room that day.

For the next two weeks Erkin stayed at home, recovering from the beatings and psychological trauma. Then he returned to the institute and sat tests. To fellow students' questions about his detention, Erkin said it had been a mistake and the authorities released him as soon as they realized it.

His case was now being handled by the general prosecutor's office. Senior Investigator Qolqon Jurayev, who was put in charge of his case, summoned Erkin to his office every two days. He would never talk to Erkin, instead making him hang around for hours in the corridor. The case was probably already prepared, and Erkin was called in to make sure he had not gone on the run and as a way of keeping up the pressure on him.

As he hung around in the corridor, Erkin witnessed various scenes. One morning an elderly man went into a prosecutor's room together with a female lawyer. Sometime later they came out and talked in the corridor within earshot of Erkin. "If I bring my son, will he keep his word?" the man asked the lawyer. "Yes, yes, he will. He said he would talk to him for an hour as a witness and let him go," the lawyer replied. After midday, the man came back with his son. They went into the prosecutor's office. The father and the lawyer came out soon. A few minutes later the son was led out handcuffed.

He heard a story that one of the senior investigators at the chief prosecutor's office, Karshiyev, had once promised to let someone out, saying: "If I don't, you can call me a dog." Karshiyev did not keep his word, and when he was reminded of his promise, he said: "Don't you know that I *am* a dog?"

This standing in the corridor of the general prosecutor's office went on for a few months. Erkin was questioned once during that time, only to be charged with more crimes—robbery, murder, and membership in a religious organization. The charges multiplied as investigators lumped together cases of an endless flow of captured Islamist suspects to speed up their convictions. Erkin knew things were looking like prison.

His trial opened in April 2000 at the Tashkent Regional Court. He was one of eleven defendants, including Toir Abdusamatov, who was being held at the Tashkent prison and was brought to hearings handcuffed. They all, except for Erkin, denied the charges of religious extremism and anticonstitutional activity and said they had all been beaten and abused while in custody. Erkin still believed that if he pleaded guilty to religious extremism charges—like he had done while under investigation—he would get off lightly. However, he told the judge about the beatings and denied drug possession, saying that the heroin found in his pocket had been planted on him by police. He even tried to argue that probably the stuff found in his pockets was not even heroin. But that only irritated the judge, and he told Erkin "not to give him lectures."

At the last hearing the state-appointed defense lawyer asked the judge to give Erkin a three-year suspended sentence. The state prosecutor demanded that he spend eighteen years in a strict security prison. The judge was to deliver a verdict in three days.

Erkin's family found some acquaintance "who had a channel to the judge." The judge was approached on the subject of being lenient toward Erkin. His response was that all he could do, if they paid him three thousand dollars, was to give him a short prison term—six years. The family had no such money, and six years sounded too long to Erkin.

He didn't want to go to jail but was afraid if he ran away, the authorities would go after his father since he had written an undertaking that he would guarantee that his son would cooperate with the authorities. The day before the verdict was "a day of mourning" in their home. A relative visited them that day, and upon hearing about their dilemma, he told Erkin to run. He said he knew some people at the general prosecutor's office, and if there was any trouble with his father, he would help.

"We did not sleep that night. In the morning, I said good-bye to everyone; it was five or six a.m. I did not know where I would go; I just went out and walked; it was dark still. Father gave me a hundred fifty dollars. It was April 13, 2000."

*   *   *

The next day, as Erkin began his new life on the run, the judge delivered his verdict, sentencing him to seventeen years in jail.

He spent his first night as a fugitive at a fellow student's place. The next four months, he lived in a one-room flat rented by his friends for him in a workers' neighborhood around the Tashkent Tractor Factory east of the city. Erkin never turned the light on and used candles for reading, keeping the windows tightly covered with thick blankets.

Through a hole in a blanket, he sometimes stared at a rose in a garden below. At night, at three or four a.m. he would open a window a crack to let some fresh air in, and bringing his nose up to the crack, he would breathe in that air, trying to fill his lungs to the limit.

The old parquet floor in the flat would creak loudly when Erkin performed his prayers. One morning, when he was saying his predawn prayer, a neighbor from one floor down knocked on his door. Erkin quietly watched her through the peephole until she left. She complained to the flat owner about the early-morning noise.

Erkin began to experiment. He wanted to find a soundless way of moving around the house. He came up with a technique of crawling on all fours and slowly moving by sliding his knees, one by one, without lifting them from the floor. From then on that became the way he would move around the flat at all times.

Erkin went even further in his quest not to produce any sound that could give away his presence in the flat. He took showers only when he heard that a neighbor was taking a shower and flushed the toilet only when his neighbors were flushing theirs.

There were mice living in the broken parquet floor of the flat. Erkin asked friends to get him a mouse trap, with which he killed eleven mice over the time he lived there. One day when Erkin was sitting on the sofa and reading by candlelight, he saw a baby mouse coming out of a hole by the radiator. The mouse crept to the middle of the room and began to eat some crumbs from the carpet.

"Probably it was the last surviving mouse. I watched it and watched it and debated whether to kill it or not and decided not to. I felt sorry for it; it was probably the last one and so small."

Meanwhile, more of Erkin's friends linked to Nazarov were getting arrested, and there were fewer and fewer people who could help him hide. He decided to go to Kazakhstan, where, he was told, things were better.

While hiding in the flat, Erkin shaved his head because he was not able to go to a hairdresser. By the time he decided to flee to Kazakhstan, his hair had grown quite a bit, making him look "like a hedgehog." Friends brought him sunglasses, as a kind of disguise.

"I didn't want to wear them, but they insisted, so I looked extremely suspicious when I was crossing the border," he said. He crossed into Kazakhstan without any documents, alone, going around the checkpoint on foot.

Nazarov also managed to secretly move to Kazakhstan in 2000, seeking somewhere safer to hide after nearly getting captured in his hiding place in Tashkent. That day police simultaneously raided several dozen flats in the apartment block where Nazarov was living, including the flat opposite Nazarov's and the one above it.

"While they were searching those flats, there was a soldier with an automatic gun standing in front of our door. But they didn't even knock on our door," Nazarov said. "If they had, I would not have been able to escape, so I began to burn our papers: lists of imprisoned friends, photographs, letters to the prosecutor's office, human rights organizations. The flat was full of smoke, but I could not open the windows, because it would attract attention."

He left the flat the next day.

Notes

The chapter is based on author interviews with Imam Nazarov, his family, and students, Kazakhstan and Sweden, 2006–9.

1. Mir Kaligulayev, *Doroga k Smerti* (Wolverhampton, UK: Black Quadrat, 2005), 76–77.

2. Abdulaziz Mahmudov, "Istoriya zhizni uzbekskogo imama Abdullazhona Utayeva" [A story of the life of Uzbek imam Abdullajon Otayev], Human Rights Society of Uzbekistan, March 8, 2013. http://ru.hrsu.org/archives/4331.

3. Monica Whitlock, *Beyond the Oxus: The Central Asians* (London: John Murray, 2002), 218–21.

4. Whitlock, *Beyond the Oxus*, 202–5.

5. Human Rights Watch, "Creating Enemies of the State: Religious Persecution in Uzbekistan," March, 2004, https://www.hrw.org/reports/2004/uzbekistan0304/

6. Tohir Yuldosh interview with BBC Uzbek Service, February 1992, in Kaligulayev, *Doroga k Smerti*, 46–49.

7. Kaligulayev, *Doroga k Smerti*, 107.

4

A PLACE OF NO RETURN

ONE DAY, TWO MONTHS INTO ABDUMALIK'S STAY AT Zhaslyk prison, the food hole of the cell he shared with a dozen other inmates opened. The inmate on report duty was squatting by the door, as was required; as soon as the hole opened, he was supposed to report that it was cell number such-and-such and that all members were present. If the guard wasn't happy with something, the inmate on duty would put his hands on the tray, and the guard would hit them with a club.

But this time the guard on the other side of the door didn't let him report.

"Don't," he said. Then there was a pause. And then the guard said: "Guys."

The inmates so badly missed hearing normal words because from day one at Zhaslyk, they had only heard swear words and sarcasm addressed to them. Reduced to "worse than animals," Abdumalik said, they were called all sorts of humiliating names.

So after hearing this word—"guys"—they all lifted their heads in astonishment, though it wasn't permitted.

"All this will pass. Be patient," the guard said and closed the hole.

They continued to sit in their squatting positions as tears came gushing out and streamed down their cheeks. All sixteen of them were sitting there, quietly crying. Those few words, that expression of compassion, gave them so much hope. Their minds were racing; they were making all kinds of presumptions; everyone was interpreting those words in his own way. They laid the ground for so many dreams, illusions, hopes: Maybe things are getting better out there? Maybe there has been a government change? Or at least a policy change? Maybe they're replacing the wardens here with less brutal ones? Maybe beatings will stop? Maybe we won't die here? Maybe . . . Maybe . . .

But things continued as normal at Zhaslyk, and their thoughts returned to waiting for death, "because people kept dying around us," Abdumalik said.

* * *

Abdumalik, a younger brother of the dissident imam Obidkhon qori Nazarov, was arrested in their home in Namangan at the end of 1997 on the wave of the official clampdown following the murders of several police officers—a few months before Imam Nazarov, under mounting pressure, would go into hiding in Tashkent. Abdumalik was charged with drug possession and sentenced to nine years in jail. Until August 1998, Abdumalik was held at Fergana prison and then transferred to the Pap colony (a correction facility built like a camp, with its own workshops, and where inmates have a little more freedom of internal movement than in prison). In November of that year he was moved to the Tavaqsoi colony, not far from Tashkent—a light-security facility that convicts would try to get sent to by paying considerable bribes to justice officials.

In early May 1999 wardens at Tavaqsoi assembled the "159s"—the name given to religious prisoners after Article 159 of the Criminal Code, under which they were convicted of religious extremism—in the isolation ward and told them that they would be going to "a very hard place that has been specially designated for you." It confirmed the rumor going around for some time that the authorities were opening a special prison for "religious extremists."

About fifteen to twenty prisoners who made up the 159s from Tavaqsoi were boarded onto a *voronok* (the Russian name for a van for transporting prisoners). They were taken to prison number 64, in Zangi Ota. Waiting for them there was "a special group, very big guys" who at once set about beating up the new arrivals.

"They began to beat us even before our feet touched the ground, so we never managed to stand on our feet," Abdumalik said.

Then they were put in metal cages, their heads were shaven, and, one by one, they started to be moved into a building. From inside they could hear shouts and screams. Suddenly all went quiet—some officers came out in a hurry and reported to their boss that one of the new arrivals was dead. He was fresh out of surgery and died in the corridor from his beating.

The boss said, "Continue."

The new arrivals were given pieces of paper with the national anthem—dubbed "Serquyosh" because of its opening word, which means "sunny," followed by the word "Uzbekistan"—handwritten on them. They were told to learn it by heart. The next morning they were made to sing it at the tops of their voices.

"That was hitting our nervous system, taking a lot of energy, and breaking us physically and morally," said Abdumalik.

The prison building was new, and the water from the taps was white from chlorine. Abdumalik once asked for drinking water, for which he was taken to one of the "beating" cells. He was beaten up, insulted, and humiliated by three guards.

"So are you thirsty? Want some water?" they asked, while hitting and kicking him.

They made Abdumalik scream: "I won't ask for water anymore!"

Abdumalik and the other 159s were kept in Zangi Ota for about ten days, getting regular beatings and being made to clean and wash toilets and cells every night, after the bell for sleep. And the guards constantly frightened them with Zhaslyk.

"This is not your home yet. You haven't gotten home yet," they said.

* * *

In about ten days brand-new handcuffs were put on a hundred religious convicts, and they were loaded into voronoks. They were taken to Tuzel military airfield near Tashkent, where five military cargo planes were waiting on the tarmac with open cargo doors. The planes were surrounded by soldiers holding guns across their chests. Several armored personnel carriers stood nearby. The convicts were ordered out of the vans and to double up and look down while getting into the planes.

"We began to panic, thinking that the new prison must be in Afghanistan, that we were being sold to some country where there was war. I remembered 1941 [World War II]. All those thoughts were spinning in my head. We were totally demoralized," Abdumalik said. "Later, I saw on TV how they [US military] were transferring prisoners to Guantanamo, and that was exactly how we had been treated—all those soldiers on standby around the planes. It's terrible when you're treated like that."

In the plane the convicts were made to sit on the floor with their backs to the board, legs outstretched, arms crossed over their chests, with their right arms tied with a rope to the left arm of the person on their left and their left arms tied to the right arm of the person to the right. Their legs were tied with a rope. They were ordered to keep their heads down all the time.

Their necks would begin to ache soon, and breathing was difficult; for lifting their heads they would get a heavy blow with the butt of a gun. One of them was seriously injured by a blow like this, and he would later die at Zhaslyk, where the planes were taking them.

What they saw when they arrived was an unfinished, unpainted building and many soldiers with dogs. They were eighteen- to twenty-year-old conscripts with expressions of shock on their faces—probably they had been told that they would be guarding very dangerous criminals.

Then the new Zhaslyk inmates had to "run the gauntlet."

"They took us one by one. Those of us still in the voronok could hear the screams of the one who'd just gone. It was agony. Those screams [that we heard there] were special screams, from a special kind of pain and torture. They cannot be described; they cannot be imitated.

"You'd come in; they'd knock you down onto the floor; they'd kick you all over, beat you with iron rods. You'd faint; then more blows and kicks would bring you round. They'd swear at you nonstop and shout, 'Run!' . . . One guy got hit across the face with an iron rod. At least three died right there in that corridor. At the end of the corridor there was someone with a camera filming it all.

"When my turn came, there were blows coming from all sides. Their rubber clubs burst apart; their metal rods were all bloodied. . . . There was nowhere to run; even if you were flat on the floor and unconscious, they kept hitting you, and you'd come round again; you'd get up in horror and try to run, but you wouldn't know where to go. Your clothes would have disintegrated on you by the time you reached the end of the corridor.

"As you entered your cell they'd give you a gown. You'd go in and see others lying on the floor, undressed, with eyes wide open. Some, who still had some strength, helped others to get dressed. Some were just lying there motionless. . . .

"There was one guy from [the western region of] Khorezm, who'd served in Afghanistan [during the Soviet intervention]. They broke his left kneecap. His left knee wouldn't work; he'd get up but couldn't take a single step, yet still they kept hitting his knee. He couldn't walk, so he crawled, but they continued to beat him. It was like going through a mincing machine. When he got to his cell, he was conscious but sat in shock. He could neither cry nor laugh; he had a frozen smile on his face. They only gave him a wooden plank to fix his broken leg a month later.

"There were ten acceptable postures. One was squatting with your hands locked behind your head. That guy couldn't sit like this, so he would sit stretching his legs out in front, but even that was very painful for him, and he'd be crying. The next morning there were about eighty-nine of us left. More died later, from injuries received on that first day."

They were all covered in black and blue marks and had various fractures. Soon the wounds—the marks left by the metal rods on the soles of their feet and on their spines—began to fester and filled with pus. They hurt; they began to smell. The treatment given to them involved squeezing the pus out and cleaning the wound with a piece of gauze, without antiseptics or anything—not everyone could bear such medical aid.

One sixty-five-year-old man suffered badly from his wounds. He cried in pain. His cellmates would call a doctor, but he didn't want to go. He resisted, putting his legs apart at the door and pressing his palms against the door aperture, crying, "No, don't."

They tried to help each other, cleaning each other's wounds as they could, though it was of little use. Some died from inflammations and infections.

* * *

The cells were on either side of a twenty- to twenty-five-meter corridor: five on each side, sixteen people in every cell. The inmates were overseen by about sixty wardens.

They were fed mainly boiled cereal husks, without butter or oil. It took time to get used to it. They had to because refusal to eat was taken as disobedience and led to beating. With time they would begin to wait for their meals eagerly.

"A window would open in the metal door; a ladle would appear and knock on a tray; you'd hold out your bowl, and a hundred grams of food would drop into it. Sometimes no food would come at the set time."

Some of them could not eat at all because their internal organs were damaged from the beatings. "All their internal organs were dead, not functioning. They were dying before our eyes."

From 6:00 a.m. to 10:00 a.m. they had to squat. Abdumalik once put his shoes under his buttocks to make it more bearable. A guard saw his bare toes through a hole in the door.

"Abdumalik Nazarov!" he shouted.

"Yes, *Grazhdanin Nachalnik* [Russian: 'citizen chief']," Abdumalik replied.

"Where are your shoes?"

"It's hot; I've taken them off."

The guard wrote down his name.

The next morning Abdumalik was taken out into the corridor. He was given ten minutes to sweep and wash it.

"I tried. Hurried like mad. They were laughing all the time and teasing, swearing and hitting and kicking me at the same time."

When he finished, the guard asked their boss if they could send him back to his cell. He asked them if he was quick enough; they said yes, and the boss said: "Fine, make him do it again tomorrow."

Abdumalik collapsed from exhaustion and the thought of having to go through that again.

In Abdumalik's cell there was a man from Khorezm in his fifties. He was a nice man, with gray hair and light radiating from his face. Once he was taken out for a beating. He came back in, took a couple of steps as if asleep, fell flat on his back with a loud blunt sound, and lay there motionless, showing no signs of life. The door opened, the guards dragged him out by his arms, and his cellmates never saw him again.

In Abdumalik's first year at Zhaslyk the inmates were made to sing the national anthem, "Serquyosh," "all the time." In the second year they were made to sing the Karakalpak [autonomous region, where Zhaslyk is located] anthem as well, "because among the guards and officers, there were Karakalpaks, too."

The inmates were questioned over and over again about all their relatives and friends. And every interrogation was a prelude to more beating.

"They especially liked beating the soles of our feet. They beat our genitalia, and they would make us stand facing a wall and would beat us from behind with a club."

Sometimes they would see two or three dead bodies, bloodied and mutilated, dumped in the corridor after interrogations. Those who were near to dying would be sent off to the hospital prison in Tashkent and would never

Figure 4.1. Zhaslyk prison inmates marching in the courtyard, 2003. © Author's archive.

be seen again, like Khikmat, a man in his early forties who would shake so violently with fever that all the beds in the cell would shake as well—he died on the way to hospital.

They tried to help each other out as best they could. There was a seventy-year-old man from Namangan who received beatings just like everyone else. But sometimes wardens would allow his cellmates to do the routine thousand sit-ups or hundred push-ups, "after which you could drop dead," for him.

In rare quiet moments, Abdumalik and his cellmates would begin to talk about the outside world, their families and past lives, until suddenly they would hear a scream coming from somewhere in the building. And they would go quiet again. They were always on the alert for sound coming from the corridor, each man waiting his turn to be taken out.

Once the prison was visited by Sayora Rashidova, the official human rights ombudsman, together with the prison administration chief, Radjab Kadyrov. The Zhaslyk administration had made the appropriate preparations: the cells were tidy and sparkling clean; the inmates were instructed on what to say to her. In Abdumalik's cell they did as they had been told, but in the next cell someone told her "the truth," and she broke down in tears, though her tears could hardly lead to any action on her part.

It was a long journey for Abdumalik's wife, Roziya, to visit him in Zhaslyk—about seven hundred kilometers from the eastern edge of the country to the western. When she, her two children, and her father-in-law came for the first time on a December evening in 1999, they were told to wait till the next morning. There are no guesthouses or hotels in Zhaslyk. A watchman put up Roziya and the children in his room for the night. The father-in-law was left outside in the cold and wind.

Roziya would economize on everything at home, saving up so she could take some good food to Abdumalik. Half the food they would bring would be taken away by prison officers, so they tried to mix everything up in their bags, so the guards would not get all the best food.

In October 2000 Abdumalik was transferred to Nukus prison, and three years later he was freed under an amnesty. He went to live in the Kyrgyz city of Osh. One day he and several friends went to a teahouse for the meal of *osh* (a rice, carrot, and meat dish). When the steaming osh appeared, Abdumalik had a sudden flashback to his life in Zhaslyk. A lump came to his throat, and he broke down in tears. Everyone went quiet. Abdumalik kept staring at the plate of osh. He could not speak, could not tell them why he was crying.

"I didn't know how to explain to them what I was feeling, how to convey it so they could understand. Finally I said: 'Do you know what is going on next door in Uzbekistan? Do you care about it?'"

Some of the men at the table began to cry too.

* * *

In the early 2000s, journalists like me reporting on Uzbekistan for Western media received regular phone calls from rights activists with tip-offs that a dead body had arrived from some detention facility and a funeral would be held at such-and-such an address and at such-and-such a time—the local media could never report anything like this. Journalists would rush there to find the neighborhood full of uniformed and plain-clothed police or security officers. The women of the deceased man's family would wail; the men—wearing traditional scullcaps—would sit with their heads down, and an air of pain and hopelessness would hang over them.

There were also letters and calls from mothers and fathers who had for months and sometimes years been trying to find justice after their sons' sudden deaths in detention. One such father was Sotyvaldy Abdullayev. He claimed that in 1999 his son, a hardened criminal, had been tortured to death along with two other inmates while serving a prison term at the Karaulbazar colony near Bukhara. Prison officials said the son had died of heart disease; later the official explanation was changed, and they said that he had been killed as police were putting down a revolt at the facility.

"I managed to find out where my son and the two others were buried, at Said Amir Kulol cemetery. There were metal plates on their graves with the numbers 25, 26, and 27 and a date, November 1, 1999. I spoke to the cemetery mosque imam who had read a *zhanoza* [funeral prayer] for the dead and two gravediggers who had washed the bodies. They told me what the bodies had looked like: mutilated, with blood stains, bruises, and abrasions all over," said one of Abdullayev's letters, sent to rights groups in 2003. After a year and a half of relentless efforts, Abdullayev forced the authorities to exhume his son's body, and an official autopsy concluded that his son had died of torture.

Musurmon Kulmuradov, the son of seventy-year-old Jangil Khudaykulova, was, she said, tortured before her very eyes. Kulmuradov, from the southern Surkhondaryo region, was detained by security officers on November 10, 2002, along with his mother, wife, and two daughters, and accused of trafficking drugs in his stomach. He died the same evening.

"They hit my son several times in the head and body with a wire rope and an iron rod. Musurmon still would not confess, and they brought a pair of pliers and a screwdriver. They pierced his legs with the screwdriver and pinched his body with the pliers in several places. Then they started pulling his fingernails and made him put his hands on the table and beat the fingers with a hammer. . . . They hit him in the head with a metal stick; he started bleeding and fell on the floor unconscious," Khudaykulova wrote in an unaddressed letter, probably just an attempt to document what had happened.

An examination of her son's dead body showed that he had several broken ribs, and there were signs that after his death someone had tried to force several grams of heroin in a plastic wrap down his throat using high water pressure, maybe a hose, Khudaykulova's letter said.

Atrocities going on at Zhaslyk came to light in August 2002. The bodies of two of its inmates were returned to their families for burial with indications that they might have been boiled to death. Both Muzaffar Avazov and Khusnutdin Olimov had been jailed for alleged religious extremism. Avazov's body, in a photograph shown to me by his mother, Fatima Mukhadirova, looked like a red-blue piece of meat. Other inmates wrote to Mukhadirova in a letter, saying that they could hear screams coming from the basement cell where her son and Olimov had been taken for angering guards by openly praying and carrying out other Islamic rites.

"They killed him like a dog. They poured twenty liters of boiling water on him," she said, wiping tears from her face with the palm of her hand, as we sat on *kurpachas* (traditional narrow cotton-stuffed mattresses) on the floor in her house in Tashkent. She said she was proud of her son because his abusers had failed to break his spirit. He had died because of his strong will, because he stood by his religious beliefs, refusing to renounce them.

* * *

These events were happening at a time when relations between Karimov's regime and the United States were at their highest level ever, because after the 9/11 attacks Karimov allowed the US military to set up an air base in the country's south for their campaign in Afghanistan. For Karimov, his alliance with the United States in fighting Islamist militancy was a convenient cover for continuing his crackdown on alleged extremists at home with complete disregard of any kind of human rights.

But the Uzbek government was forced to tolerate journalists representing Western media, and that allowed crimes in the Uzbek prison system to become known outside the country. Avazov's and Olimov's deaths featured in a report by the then UN rapporteur on torture, Theo Van Boven, which he released after visiting Uzbekistan in November 2002. He was invited by the Uzbek authorities under US pressure, as part of apparent efforts to engage Karimov on human rights. The report concluded that torture was routine in Uzbek prisons. Cited and re-cited in almost every foreign media story on Uzbekistan and in every human rights report on the country, Avazov's and Olimov's deaths became for some time the Karimov regime's international label: "a government that boils opponents to death."

That political context made it possible in May 2003 for me, my sister Galima (who at the time was the country director for the London-based Institute for War and Peace Reporting), an AP photo stringer, and a stringer for the BBC's Kazakh-language service named Usen to get permission from the authorities to visit Zhaslyk.

* * *

Our official guide and companion during the trip was Colonel Mikhail Gurevich, the deputy head of GUIN—the main administration for the implementation of punishment. Gurevich was a thin man of average height, balding with gray, fluffy hair, in his early sixties. He wore a grayish suit with a knitted vest under it and a tie.

Throughout the two days that we spent with Gurevich, it seemed he was trying to create an appearance of some secret shared between us, dropping hints here and there that he did not entirely approve of what was going on in the country and within the justice system. Gurevich said repeatedly that he made no distinction between prisoners convicted on religious grounds and those jailed for other reasons, as if trying to draw a line between his administrative job of running prisons and the government's ideological and political campaigns, and absolve himself of the abuses those campaigns involved.

"My job is to feed inmates and clothe them until they have served out their sentences," he said. At the same time, Gurevich never forgot his official mission, and his underlying message to us was that things at Uzbek prisons were not as bad as portrayed by critics.

Our journey started with a flight from Tashkent to Nukus, the capital of the western autonomous region of Karakalpakstan, a desert area blighted by the disaster of a dying sea. The Aral Sea has been shrinking since the 1960s, drying up, it is believed, because of the heavy overuse of its only two feeders, the Amu Darya and Syr Darya rivers, for irrigation. The climate—unbearably hot summers and similarly unbearable cold winters—along with the lack of resources and economic mismanagement, had made the region's 1.2 million people the poorest and sickliest in Uzbekistan.

From Nukus we had to drive a hundred kilometers northwest to the town of Qongrad and then take a train another two hundred kilometers or so farther north, in the direction of Kazakhstan and Russia, to reach the Zhaslyk settlement whose name, which in Karakalpak means "youth," has by default become the name of Uzbekistan's most feared jail. On every leg of the trip we were met and accompanied by plain-clothes men in old Soviet-made cars. We were in the hands of a system that was facing accusations of brutal rights violations, and it was disturbing to see it in action, even if it was only about getting three journalists and a photographer from one place to another. Without uniforms and in their cars devoid of markings, they were scarily invisible.

The railway station at Qongrad could be one of the most desolate places on earth, with a colorless and bare landscape around it and a crumbling station building so small that it could not accommodate any of the waiting passengers to give them protection from the cold and biting wind that blew a mix of salt and dust in their faces. As the people on the platform rushed to get onto an approaching train, picking up their bundles from the ground, it seemed that the dusty, dark-green thundering train, made from tons of heavy metal at some Soviet factory decades ago, was the only thing representing humankind's economic progress here.

On the train we were given compartment number 1, with cotton-padded narrow mattresses thrown on the seats. The compartment was always kept booked for police or other officials going to visit Zhaslyk, so we were treated accordingly, and the conductor kept bringing us milky tea in big tea bowls.

Over the tea, Gurevich calmly dismissed the main allegations and concerns about Zhaslyk raised by rights activists and inmates' families, either prompted by our questions or preempting them because he had obviously done his homework. "These are not schoolchildren; these are criminals," he said about the inmates. Deaths at Zhaslyk, he said, were the result of either fights between inmates or outbreaks of disease. He said treatment at Zhaslyk had been "quite harsh" at the beginning, but now it was "normal." The religious rites were not allowed: "Why should we create special conditions for Muslims?"

According to Gurevich, at that moment about three thousand men were serving terms in various Uzbek jails for alleged religious extremism. The US State Department at the time put the figure at more than six thousand.

Then, to our surprise, Col. Gurevich showed his dissident side, expressing sympathy with religious prisoners, criticizing the cruelty of the justice system, and saying that only democracy could bring change. "We have a tough criminal code. It doesn't allow one article to prevail over another; they're added together, and long sentences are handed down. Courts are controlled by prosecutors' offices. They should give, say, three-year sentences, which would be fairer than, say, nineteen years. The criminal code is not effective; that's why we have too many people in prison," he said.

Most of the religious prisoners, he said, were ignorant. "They just keep referring to the Koran. I tell them: we need to have a real democracy as soon as possible; then you won't be in jail but will be free to propagate your ideas.

"Then they ask: 'Comrade Colonel, when are we going to have real democracy?'"

* * *

After a three- or four-hour slow train ride, we reached the station at Barsa Kelmes, which in Karakalpak means "place of no return." The railway track ended there as if it had reached a point beyond which there was some forbidden land. And indeed we were in a place beyond the world as I, up to that point, imagined and knew it.

Zhaslyk prison was opened in 1999. It was built around what had been designed as a backup landing strip for the failed Soviet piloted spacecraft *Buran*, which was supposed to rival the US space shuttles. The Soviet Defense Ministry had kept a military unit here to guard the strip. It was a modest base, and the facilities were just a building for the command and a laboratory. With the Soviet collapse the *Buran* project was abandoned. The landing strip was never used, becoming a useless massive concrete slab with grass and weeds growing through it, only to be pressed down against its gray surface by the incessant wind. Eventually, in the late 1990s, with the crackdown on potential Islamist-inspired opponents of the Uzbek regime in full swing, the place was handed over to GUIN to convert into a new prison.

From the Barsa Kelmes train station we were taken to a small, typically Soviet flat in one of several concrete blocks around the prison, which had originally been built to house military officers manning the strategic space facility. Our visit to the prison was to take place the next morning. In the flat's living room there was a table waiting for us with a mountain of food on it. The treats included meat pies, chicken, *beshbarmak* (a traditional Kazakh and Karakalpak meat dish), *baursaks* (traditional fried bread rolls), even *saiga* (steppe antelope) meat, and so on—obviously we were being treated like official inspectors of some kind, to be pleased and entertained so that we would pretend not to see any problems. The table was moved alongside a sofa—as people tended to do in Soviet flats given the limited space—and my sister and I sat there, across the table from Alikhaydar Kulumbetov, the Zhaslyk prison boss.

Dressed in a khaki camouflage uniform, Kulumbetov exuded tension. He was a big, heavy man with a thunderous voice and a thick moustache on his broad face. The Zhaslyk prison's wardens, the 240 conscripts guarding the colony, and some inmates called him *khozyain*, which in Russian means "master." Kulumbetov, fifty-three years old at the time, was tense throughout our visit, annoyed at having to host us and answer our questions.

"I am Bagila Bukharbayeva," I introduced myself at the table, maybe too quietly, still finding it hard to believe that I was there and sharing a meal with someone who was believed to be responsible for death by torture.

My words were not audible enough for Kulumbetov, and he roared back: "What Bukharbayev case?" He had misheard and thought I was enquiring about an inmate—he was used to visitors who would plead with him about something on behalf of some inmate or other.

It was hard to enjoy the food and keep conversation going at that welcome dinner thrown by Kulumbetov. Taking note of our host's huge appetite, my sister Galima mentioned that the Afghan general Rashid Dostum was said to be able to eat twenty chickens in one go.

"So what? I could eat that many too and swallow you on top of them," Kulumbetov remarked bluntly, without any hint of humor. This was followed by a heavy silence.

Then it seemed that he had had second thoughts about his remark, and, to mitigate possible damage to his image, Kulumbetov encouraged us to eat more. A woman, probably his housekeeper, kept bringing more food.

He also opened up to us, telling us that he kept himself fit by jogging every morning and going on regular saiga hunting expeditions. Kulumbetov also pointed out his long service record with the Uzbek prison system and noted that he had headed a colony in Bukhara before coming to Zhaslyk.

"I know this system well," he boasted.

When we began asking questions about Avazov's and Olimov's deaths, Kulumbetov went into denial.

"At about ten or eleven a.m. we gave them boiling water for tea. A fight broke out [that day] in the cell between Wahhabis," he began to explain.

But how much boiled water was there? If it was for making tea, how could that be enough to kill two men?

"Each cell gets five liters of hot water. He [Avazov] was ill; they were both ill. They did not die from the boiling water but from their diseases. They did not die here; they died on the way to Nukus," he said in exasperation.

According to Kulumbetov, as punishment for Olimov's and Avazov's deaths, he himself was reprimanded and one guard got thirteen years, another three and a half, in jail, and some others were fired. Kulumbetov denied any abuse of religious prisoners under his watch. "They are making it all up, painting things black. They say that cells are small here, that people hang on bars. We have no [torture] basement. . . . We do not make them sing the anthem. Do you think we have nothing better to do? . . . We are doing everything here to make sure that inmates' rights are not violated. Yes, not everything goes smoothly. And yes, there are those who are not happy," he said, just managing to control his temper.

* * *

The next morning we began our tour of Zhaslyk, which we were told at the time had a total of 538 inmates, of whom 296 were convicted Islamists, mostly Hizb ut-Tahrir members. Through a metal gate we entered a small courtyard with a fountain painted light blue and walked to a checkpoint to the left fortified with a metal door that opened into a short narrow passage, through which only one person could go at a time; then, through a rotating metal barrier, we entered the prison compound.

In front of us there was a rectangular asphalt site without any greenery; the compound was fenced off with whitewashed walls topped with barbed wire. There were a few watchtowers, each manned by an armed soldier. The three-story prison building was some sixty meters from the checkpoint straight in front of us.

We were first led into a one-story building to the left that had ten rooms for three-day visits by inmates' relatives, allowed once every three months. In the waiting hall for visitors there were several sofas, a TV set, a fan, a Karimov portrait on one wall, and his omnipresent slogan "Uzbekistan is a state with a great future" on another.

Then, as we went from one visiting room to another, we began to meet Zhaslyk inmates. Their faces have long since receded from my mind. All I remember is a dehumanized mass of thin, pale men in dark robes and black hats with earflaps on shaven heads, with fear or resentment in their eyes. And all I have now are my hurriedly written notes: names, ages, lengths of prison sentences, and some quotes—messages to a world outside the walls of Zhaslyk.

With some of them I would just manage to write a name and not get a chance to ask further questions, because others were more talkative or because guards would tell us to finish. But often it was because they were not willing to talk. In some cases I could see it was the fear of their jailers, in other cases it was distrust of us, and in others still it was surrender, physical and moral exhaustion, as if they no longer cared about themselves, about their fate, about justice or injustice. The stories of those inmates in my notebook are only two words long: first name and family name.

But others spoke out. Some would speak quietly so that the guards would not be able to hear, and a few answered my questions openly and loudly, looking me in the eye and ignoring the guards.

The first inmate I met in rooms for long visits was Ismoil Nosibov. Born in 1978, he was sentenced to sixteen and a half years for religious extremism and had spent three years at Zhaslyk. "I am not guilty of anything; that's why I'm not going to write a pardon plea," he said. "*Inshallah* [God willing], Uzbekistan will in the future be a caliphate." He was being visited by his sister, who complained that the place was too far from their home, and there was no hotel or guesthouse to stay in, and they had to spend a night on the street.

Abdurakhmon Abdusattorov, fifty-seven years old, was sentenced to fifteen years for religious extremism. "They linked me to the 1999 incursions [by the Islamic Movement of Uzbekistan]," he said. "I had studied at the Transport Institute and was soon to become an engineer, but it was hard to survive financially, so I quit and became a farmer. But they found nitrate fertilizer and also planted nine bullets and a hand grenade in my house.

"It drives me mad that I have to be here. They make us write pardon pleas. We have written several times. So they have cut down my sentence by three years but want to continue to correct me here. Why don't they understand? What if I want to take revenge? They must think about that."

He was the first Zhaslyk inmate who spoke to us about Avazov's and Olimov's deaths. "There are two theories: either they overdid it [the torture], or there was an order from the SNB [to kill them]," Abdusattorov said. He said that the outcry about their deaths triggered some changes at Zhaslyk. "There were inspections from the prosecutor's office, and now treatment is a bit better. We haven't been singing the anthem for a while. There were all sorts of horrible things here before. But I'm afraid we will go back to that. . . . Today it's quiet, but tomorrow there will be a storm," he said.

We walked to the main building and entered it through more metal doors. The air in the building was permeated with an acrid smell. The prison had some forty cells, with about a dozen inmates in each called a "brigade."

We were accompanied by Kulumbetov, Gurevich, and several prison wardens. They said this was for our security. "These are criminals; they might try to take you hostage."

On one of the walls on the ground floor corridor were written the lyrics of the national anthem. In the small library with half-empty wooden bookshelves and several desks, a shelf displaying Karimov's works was right above a shelf of religious books.

Finally we entered the first cell. It was a relatively spacious square room—bunk beds were neatly made up; pillows on every bed were in clean white pillowcases. There was a toilet and a sink in the left-hand corner. There was a table on the right, and some tin mugs were lined up on a shelf in the wall.

I was surprised to see big windows there as I expected them to be always small in prisons. But this building had not been designed as a prison. The windows were barred and had metal shutters on the outside that blocked out the light, and, on windy days, one of the inmates told me, they would bang loudly against the bars.

The inmates were sitting on their beds with their heads down.

"Three inmates died here last year. There is violence and suppression taking place here," Ikboljon Temirov, who was serving a seven-year sentence, said quietly.

"I've been jailed unfairly. Why are we here?" asked Odil Saidamirov, from Andijan, who was in for fourteen years.

Soon we were led out of the cell and taken to a bakery, where we learned that it produced five hundred loaves a day. We were shown the kitchen, where they opened a refrigerator to demonstrate that it was filled with meat, which was supposed to be evidence that the inmates got enough calories and protein. We were told that the prisoners' diet included soups, mashed potatoes, salad, and black bread.

In view of how little time we had been given in the first cell, we tried to be more active and more assertive with our questions in the next one.

Asked if he experienced any ill treatment or torture here, twenty-six-year-old Bakhodir Sobitov nodded. He had been sentenced to sixteen years for religious extremism, and by that time had spent two and a half years at Zhaslyk.

"Since 2000 they introduced this cell system. In 1999 they did whatever they wanted with us. They killed so many people here, but everyone is keeping quiet. No one has answered for that. All our complaints and pleas are ignored," said a prisoner called Saliyev, who was serving a seventeen-year sentence.

"It's got a little better since Avazov and Olimov. Now they're using isolation cells more [for punishment], and they've stepped up psychological

Figure 4.2. Zhaslyk prison inmates having a meal, 2003. © Author's archive.

control over every one of us. They won't let us talk to one another. They put us into isolation cells to pray. They set us against one another.

"There are criminals with previous convictions, so they are used to make us fight each other. They [the criminals] themselves tell us that. They want to introduce criminal laws here."

Next in my notebook I have three names: Shukhrat Abdurakhimov, from Tashkent; Abduvakhab Abdullayev, from Andijan; Ulugbek Gomirov, from Tashkent. They spoke to me all together, hurriedly and in a half whisper, as we sat around the table in their cell.

"They mutilate us here. . . . Something changes before an inspection, and then it's back to 'normal.' . . . Those who killed [Avazov and Olimov] are still here among us. . . . Who can guarantee to us that the same won't happen to our other brothers? . . . . They have shut down the basement for now, but they keep threatening us with it and saying, 'Inspections will come and go, but you will stay.' . . . They're breaking their own laws; they're criminals, not us. But it is we who are in jail."

*   *   *

Akram Ikramov, from Fergana, is the only Zhaslyk inmate whom I can still, albeit vaguely, visualize: thin, of average height, looking younger than his twenty-eight years, dark-complexioned, with staring eyes and sharp features.

A Hizb ut-Tahrir member, he had been so outraged with the authorities' hunt for those like him that, as a way of protesting, he had turned himself in to the SNB in 1999 to show them he had done nothing wrong and had no reason to hide. It failed to impress the SNB. They forced him to admit to planning antigovernment attacks and sentenced him to eighteen years in a high-security prison.

Before beginning his lengthy speech, Ikramov asked if we had come to find out the truth and if our reports would be truthful. He spoke about everything, from the climate to his own Zhaslyk death statistics.

"This prison's in the desert, the worst possible environment. . . . There is salt even in the air. If you drink three mugs of tap water here, you get diarrhea. In the summer of 2000 eighty people got dysentery. . . .

"It's impossible to describe how we were received here, how they have tried to crush us. What you hear is only fairy tales. . . . There used to be real lawlessness here before—they did terrible things to their own brothers. I know what might happen to me after you go. I've buried myself here already. . . .

"When I first got here, they beat me up even before I got to my cell; they beat me unconscious. I still have marks from their clubs on my body. Many of the first ones to arrive here have such marks. . . . They've built this prison to break Muslims. They kill here. . . .

"There are ten postures that we are allowed to be in—hands locked behind the back, hands locked behind the head, and others. To go to the toilet, you have to ask permission. . . . It's beatings, beatings, and beatings. We even used to think sometimes that maybe these guards were not human but robots. . . . In my cell there were sixteen people; four of them died in 1999–2000. . . . They used to kill Muslims just like that.

"Then we heard that the Red Cross was expected to come. Within six months they completely refurbished the place and painted the building for the first time—we did the refurbishment ourselves, day and night. The boss [the prison chief before Kulumbetov] warned us before the Red Cross visit that if anything happened, 'I'll cut off oxygen to you all.' We were only allowed to talk to him on our knees. The Red Cross came in 2001. It was horrible after the first visit. . . . But because everyone [in the outside world] began to criticize conditions here, commissions became frequent, every two months, so they began to change their tactics. Now they're using criminals for beatings and murders. . . . More than twenty inmates have died here since 2000. . . .

"Khusnutdin Khikmatov died three months ago. He always spoke the truth. Nothing worked with him. Then they put him in the punishment cell and beat him with clubs; he then had bleeding from his anus. Then they sent him to Sangorod [abbreviation of the Russian Sanitarnyy Gorod, "Sanitary Town," prison hospital in Tashkent]."

As we listened to Ikramov, Gurevich and the accompanying guards were getting more and more agitated. The wardens stood very close to us, still but tense. Finally someone gave some signal, and we were rushed away to Kulumbetov's office where he and Gurevich tried to repair the damage, saying that the religious inmates are "finished people" who want "chaos" in Uzbekistan.

"If we release them, there will be explosions everywhere," Kulumbetov said.

In his office, in addition to the required portrait of Karimov and his books, Kulumbetov had a sign with a saying attributed to Tamerlane: "Power is in justice."

Still working on his image, or maybe to shorten our time for interviews with inmates, Kulumbetov played us videotapes of shows he had organized in the Bukhara colony, which he had run before Zhaslyk. We watched marching formations of inmates in gray and black striped prison gowns and inmates performing songs and dancing onstage for visiting relatives. Kulumbetov watched the recordings with a look of satisfaction on his face and boasted of the "perfect order" and "rapport" with inmates that he had established there. That was, obviously, not the case with Zhaslyk inmates.

"It's easier with hardened criminals than with religious ones. If you say to a criminal, 'I'll skin you,' he will obey you. But the religious one is not afraid of anything—he always refers to his Allah. . . . This is the most dangerous colony in the country."

But he would not admit any failure at Zhaslyk either. "I am both feared and respected [by inmates]," he said. Perhaps fear was the only language Kulumbetov knew.

We were shown a spacious punishment cell with bare metal bunk beds, where we met Bakhrom Pulatov, from the Fergana Valley, four years into a sixteen-year sentence, who clearly and loudly told us he was in jail "for speaking the truth."

When we were on our way from one cell to another, we heard shouts in the corridor—"Commission! Commission!"—probably an inmate who had heard that some visitors were coming and wanted to speak to us. But we were quickly led away in another direction.

Our guides also refused to allow us to speak to the inmate Shoaziz Ilyosov, who, we were told by some other inmates, had been in the basement with Avazov and Olimov before they were tortured to death.

When we returned to Kulumbetov's office he took a call from some high-ranking official, judging by the change in Kulumbetov's voice from bossy to faltering, and reported to him: "Yes, they're happy; we've shown them everything."

The last thing they did to make us, journalists, "happy" was order about twenty inmates to go outside and play football in the cold wind. Maybe the inmates did not mind and were happy for the chance to get some exercise, but I felt bad for them.

That was the last image from that Zhaslyk visit that stays with me. I kept turning back and looking at them as we walked to the exit: men in dark prison gowns playing football on a concrete site in front of their prison, shut off from the rest of the world by walls and barbed wire, with almost no hope of return.

* * *

On the way back, instead of taking the train, we drove to Qongrad on a dirt track across the steppe. We shared two UAZ off-road vehicles (Russian jeeps).

Preparing for our four- or five-hour drive, Kulumbetov made the woman who cooked for him fill glass jars with soup, pieces of meat, chicken, tongue, pickles, and horse sausage and also pack bread and lots of bottles of vodka. It was all carefully loaded into the vehicles. We made frequent stops during our bumpy ride across the steppe "for a bite and a sip."

Kulumbetov was soon in good spirits from the food and vodka and, sitting in the front seat, shared his dreams with us. "Sometimes I dream of turning into a big eagle," he began. "I would take off and fly to Britain, reach London, and then dive down right into the British queen's palace, snatch and bring her here, and lock her up at Zhaslyk," he said, laughing like thunder, amused by his own fantasy. "That would, of course, provoke a

Figure 4.3. Zhaslyk prison boss Alikhaydar Kulumbetov on a stop for vodka and a bite to eat, as author and two other journalists traveled across the desert to the city of Nukus to catch a flight back to Tashkent after visiting the prison, 2003. © Author's archive.

war! An international scandal! I can see tanks all over the steppe closing in on Zhaslyk, and I'm sitting there holed up with the British queen! Ha-ha!"

Kulumbetov continued to behave like a good host. He made the drivers stop on the Ustyurt Plateau because he thought we should definitely see it—a huge flat platform rising out of the earth. We got out of our cars. The wind was so strong that it seemed it could knock us down any moment or rip off and snatch away our clothes. Our hair was all over the place.

Kulumbetov was enjoying it. First he filled himself up with some more vodka and meat; then he went to the edge of the plateau, spread his arms like the eagle he dreamed of becoming, and, as he stood there defying the wind and laughing, let out a powerful roar: "Aaaarrrrrrrr!"

Maybe this was a way for him to deal with the stress of his job.

Gurevich was drinking all the way, too. By the time we got to the Nukus airport, he was in such a state that he could not talk and walked like a sleepwalker. His face was red; his eyes were blank. They drank more in the airport's VIP room. Then they joined us in the main hall. Gurevich sat next to us. His eyes were closed, and he seemed to be napping. Suddenly, he slumped forward like a mannequin and fell facedown, hitting the marble floor with his forehead. One of his people accompanying us rushed to help him and sat him back down. Gurevich slowly opened his eyes—clearly, he did not understand what had just happened.

We landed in Tashkent and disembarked, and Kulumbetov forgot about us the second he saw his five- or six-year-old granddaughter who was meeting him with his wife at the airport. The little girl ran to him, and he hurried toward her, lifted her up, and kissed her on both cheeks. His face relaxed and brightened with a smile. He was a different man, a loving grandfather.

The horror of Zhaslyk was over for us—for Kulumbetov too, if only for a few days.

Soon after our visit he was fired as Zhaslyk boss and moved to southern Kazakhstan. In February 2007, news came that he had been murdered. The Uzbek rights group that broke the news cited as a source an anonymous former law-enforcement official. The report said that Kulumbetov was "executed" by criminal circles to avenge his despotic treatment of inmates at the Karshi colony, which he had run at some point before Zhaslyk.

5

DISAPPEARANCES

IN LATE MARCH 2004 FOUR MEN ARRIVED IN a dark-blue car at the house of Nyemat Razzoqov in Kakhramon village, about five hundred kilometers southwest of Tashkent, bringing a sack and a half of some stuff.

Nyemat aka's twenty-five-year-old son, Normat, told him that the men were his friends and the sacks contained some fertilizer that belonged to somebody else, and it would soon be taken away. The sacks were put in a shed.

Normat was jobless. After completing his service in the army at twenty, he had gotten a job at the local state farming cooperative but was laid off eight months later. He soon got married and built a greenhouse to grow vegetables. About two-thirds of the residents of their village were jobless. Those who worked for the state cooperative, the only employer in the village, had not been paid for two years.

Nyemat aka was worried that, without anything to do—"he had no proper job and didn't know what to do with himself"—Normat could "become loose," take up smoking and drugs. To prevent that, he decided to introduce a practice of prayers five times a day in the house. Nyemat aka had learned how to pray as a child from his father but had never done it in his adult life. Now it seemed that it could be a way to help his son to not fall into despair about his future.

At about seven p.m. on March 28, Nyemat aka was outside in the courtyard, and his wife was watering flowers when he heard a deafening bang. The next moment a powerful force lifted and threw him into a gap between the house wall and the summer kitchen.

Several minutes later Nyemat aka regained consciousness and started to dig himself out of the rubble, as pieces of debris kept falling on him. He crawled out to find his house, the shed, and the wall around the courtyard in ruins.

On the ground some twenty meters away, Nyemat aka saw the body of his two-month-old granddaughter. His wife, who was in shock but unhurt, saw the baby too and began to wail. Nyemat aka walked up to the baby. She was lifeless. He wrapped the body in a blanket.

The explosion killed Normat, along with several friends who were in the shed at the time making bombs out of the stuff in the sacks they had brought a few days earlier—it was aluminum powder and ammonium nitrate. Normat's wife and twenty-month-old son were injured.

Soon the police came. Nyemat aka was questioned for almost four hours. "It was questioning and more questioning," he said. "My son had not been anywhere. How could he know how to make a bomb out of nitrogen and God knows what else? He would never do it unless he was forced to," Nyemat aka told me a week after the blast and just hours after burying his son. "I myself got a communist education, served in the army in Ukraine, and took an oath. Had I known [about the bombs] I would have chopped off his head with an axe myself," Nyemat aka said.

Nyemat aka recalled that Normat had had a friend called Gayrat who he was at school with. And it was rumored that Gayrat had spent some time with Juma Namangani, one of the leaders of the Islamic Movement of Uzbekistan. "Maybe Gayrat taught my son something," Nyemat aka said.

The site of the explosion was leveled by a bulldozer a day before my visit. All that was left was a wall and two piles of rubble. A torn and dirty carpet was draped on a fence.

The Kakhramon village explosion was followed the same night, March 28, by a shootout in Tashkent between unknown gunmen and police. It started when police attempted to stop a Tico car (a locally assembled Korean model) for a check—the men inside turned out to be armed and opened fire, killing three policemen.

The next day the city's biggest bazaar, the Chorsu, was hit by two suicide bombings carried out by female attackers. In the following two days, there were more shootouts in Tashkent between police and unknown gunmen. The most serious clash took place in an eastern working-class neighborhood, close to the president's Durmon residence just outside the city limits. A group of militants holed up in a flat there and put up resistance against police forces deployed there to eliminate them. Twenty gunmen died in the standoff, according to officials. The authorities said that the explosion in Kakhramon had disrupted plans by a terrorist group to carry out a series of bomb attacks in Bukhara and Tashkent and forced them to begin their assaults prematurely and in a less organized way.

On April 1 there was one more accidental explosion in Romiton, a small town between Kakhramon and Bukhara. It killed a ten-year-old girl who, according to officials, had triggered the blast while playing and injured her elder sister, Farogat Akramova, the wife of one of the alleged bomb makers who had died in the Kakhramon bomb-factory explosion.

The death toll from the four days of attacks and accidental explosions was put by the authorities at forty-seven, including ten policemen, four civilians, and thirty-three militants. Prosecutor General Rashid Kadyrov personally kept media and the public informed, giving regular press conferences in Tashkent. The attackers were said to be Hizb ut-Tahrir members and Wahhabis acting on orders from international terrorists abroad with links to al-Qaeda. Ilya Pyagay, the Interior Ministry's deputy antiterrorism chief, went further than the prosecutor general, telling me that the attackers were from "one of the al-Qaeda branches." He said many of them were using fake documents, but the authorities intended to track down and arrest "every single one."

According to another police official, the first shootout featured a beige-colored Tico car with gunmen inside who started shooting at police after being ordered to stop for a check. They killed three policemen, he said. The official said that the gunmen were headed to the Hotel Intercontinental, the first five-star hotel in Tashkent.

We journalists did not have much faith in the official accounts. Attempts to gather our own information produced only scattered details, mostly minor and confusing.

At the scene of the officially reported standoff between a group of militants and police in a bleak neighborhood of densely packed three- and four-story apartment blocks around the Tashkent Tractor Factory (commonly known as TTZ), there were baffled, tight-lipped police investigators wandering around a destroyed one-story private house. An officer said that in a TTZ flat, block 1A number 20, police had tracked down a group of militants. When surrounded, they came out one by one and "by their own hand" blew themselves up using their self-made explosive devices. Journalists were not allowed inside the flat, which the alleged militants had rented.

No resident of the neighborhood could confirm the alleged collective suicide. The windows in the flat were blown out. But the asphalt driveway and entrance to the block, as well as the facade of the building, did not look like a place where twenty men had blown themselves up just a few days ago. Residents of the neighborhood described the alleged gunmen as being

Figure 5.1. A man walks inside a courtyard of Mir Arab Madrasah in Bukhara, 2008.
© Author's photo.

of dark complexion and speaking some foreign language—something that was hard to make sense of. There were spots of blood here and there. One resident pointed at a bloodstain on an apartment block wall and said that one of the militants had been gunned down there.

At a funeral for one of the policemen killed in the series of alleged attacks, twenty-seven-year-old Aziz Tursunov, his grieving mother said to me that "he sacrificed himself for the president, for the country."

On April 2 the Moscow-based AP photographer Misha Metzel and I arrived in Bukhara to look for clues there. Bukhara's magnificent ancient mosques, minarets, and madrasahs decorated with intricate turquoise mosaic stood, as always, as if above the small and momentary troubles of the present day, breathing peace and commanding reverence.

But the city's residents seemed subdued and worried that the violence could ruin the entire tourist season. The police headquarters was cordoned off with concrete slabs. Police were put on guard outside the mosques and madrasahs.

A policeman standing on watch outside the Kalon Mosque said the police had been on twenty-four-hour shifts for five days. The plotters, he said, intended to ram the regional police headquarters building with a KamAZ truck laden with explosives. "Many have been arrested; they are testifying," he said.

Abdugafur Rozzaq, the chief cleric of Bukhara Region—Bukhara is its administrative center—likened the "Wahhabis" who he said were behind the attacks to communists who "want to dictate their own ideas" and "spread around the world." Rozzaq said, "This is why they are called fundamentalists, fanatics. Like the Taliban in Afghanistan, they got financial aid from Saudi Arabia and then began to establish their medieval laws and rules."

In Romiton I tried to visit the injured Akramova in the hospital, but outside the small whitewashed single-story ward where she was kept stood a special-forces police officer in full gear—with a bulletproof vest and a helmet—who took a warning step toward me and put his hands on the gun across his chest when I attempted to approach the building.

The Romiton District police chief, Talgat Sattorov, refused to be interviewed and only had a disapproving remark for me, for my attempts to find out what happened on behalf of an American news organization. "You go wherever they send you, don't you?" he said scornfully.

All the way from Bukhara to Kakhramon there were police checkpoints. Our car was repeatedly stopped, and our IDs and press accreditation cards were checked by tight-lipped and grim policemen. At one checkpoint a special-forces officer, Alisher, told me that twenty-seven or twenty-eight suicide bombers' belts had been found during the ongoing investigations. "They also wanted to blow up the governor's office, the regional UVD [police department], and the prosecutor's office," Alisher said, as he stood watching passing cars, a Kalashnikov across his chest. He said suspects arrested for the attacks were not cooperating with the authorities and were "behaving defiantly and calling police enemies of the state." But he said the causes were "90 percent social," asking, "How do you live if you haven't been paid for a year?" Alisher said of the suspects, "They are desperate, impoverished people. They say that they are not afraid of death because they have nothing to eat anyway. They didn't even have bread on the table."

When we turned off the main road toward Kakhramon, we were stopped by police again and asked to turn back. They said we could not go to Kakhramon. We turned back and got to the village by a roundabout route.

In Kakhramon, which means "hero," no one appeared shocked or terrified by the explosion in their village just a few days ago. All their frustration and anger was with the authorities for reducing them to a life in poverty. Villagers said they were living hand to mouth on what they could grow in their gardens. Many of them had not held cash in their hands for two or three years, they said. "Nothing like that could have happened if we lived well," a forty-six-year-old villager said of the explosion. He was a thin, unshaven man in shabby clothes with holes in his shoes, leaning against the cracked whitewash on the wall of his house.

* * *

Soon after the violence in Tashkent and around Bukhara, my neighbor Rukhitdin's first wife, Rakhima, and their teenage daughter Odina were subjected to several interrogations by the police. "They mostly asked me about my husband's whereabouts and demanded that I tell them where he was," Rakhima wrote in an open letter to the media and human rights groups on April 16, 2004.

When they questioned Odina they threatened her, saying that they would go after her younger ten-year-old sister, Safiya. "We will not leave either you or your sister alone until you help us find your father," the police told her.

"They set us two conditions: either we helped them find my husband, or they would put one of us in jail. At Tashkent GUVD [city police] there was a special investigation group charged with searching for my husband, and it was led by an investigator named Juma. He was the one who was especially rude to us and used insulting words," Rakhima's letter said.

Odina was interrogated until midnight. Rakhima was kept in custody for two days.

Around the same time, Farrukh, the husband of Rukhitdin's sister Zukhra, was also summoned by police, for the very first time. He went with his elder brother Ravshan. He said afterward that the talk at a district police department that lasted about one hour was just "a formality." The police did not make any allegations against him, but they wanted to know what time he left home for work and what time he returned. And they asked Farrukh not to leave Tashkent for a while.

One day in May, Farrukh's close friend Oqil Yunusov disappeared. Oqil and Farrukh had studied in Saudi Arabia together. Oqil, who had been there on a scholarship from the official Spiritual Board of Muslims, studied Islamic jurisprudence (*fiqh*). After returning from Saudi Arabia, Oqil started a small business and was not doing any teaching or preaching. He and Farrukh remained close and regularly saw each other.

Farrukh was distraught about Oqil's disappearance. He would wake up at night, thinking about him, where he might be, "in whose hands," according to Zukhra. Farrukh looked for Oqil everywhere he could think of, including car parks, because he had vanished with his car. He also called all the hospitals in town. Farrukh visited Oqil's family every other day after his disappearance, hoping to get some news and trying to support them. He thought it was his duty to take care of Oqil's four children. He encouraged Oqil's family to continue searching for him and demand action from the police.

At first, Farrukh did not think that the authorities could be behind Oqil's disappearance. But after several days of futile efforts to trace him, he told Zukhra he believed it was a kidnapping by the government. But it appeared that Oqil's disappearance did not make Farrukh worry about the probability of something similar happening to him. "I'm not doing anything against the law. I have nothing to be afraid of," he told Zukhra, when she asked if he was afraid for himself. But he also said: "If I begin to suspect anything, we'll leave."

Later in May, Imam Nazarov's son Khusnutdin left home in Tashkent and never came back. "On May 16, 2004, after praying in a mosque, Khusnutdin received a cell phone call—someone invited him for evening prayers at Kukeldash Mosque. He didn't go," his mother, Munira, told me. He was taking a shower when someone called again and asked if he could lend him some money. It was spring; there were some neighbors sitting on a bench downstairs, so they saw that one of the cars that were parked outside followed him when he came out. The car had no number plate, according to a neighbor. "Khusnutdin disappeared just like that," his mother said. She and Imam Nazarov had urged him to leave Uzbekistan, but Khusnutdin would say: "Why should they be after me? I do not give any [Islamic] lessons."

Nazarov was at the time hiding in Kazakhstan and was into his sixth year on the run. His home in Tashkent was still under surveillance. His family regularly saw strange cars parked outside their apartment block in the old part of Tashkent. Khusnutdin, who was twenty-eight, regularly prayed and attended Koran reading sessions with his friends. To make a living, he was involved in a small cell-phone-selling business. "If he saw a suspicious car downstairs, he would call and warn us to lock the door. But on that day he did not call or give us a warning," his mother said.

Munira reported his disappearance to the prosecutor's office and all the other official establishments you were supposed to tell in such cases. One day a man appeared at their door saying he was from the Interior Ministry and worked with Minister Zokirjon Almatov himself. He also mentioned that he was from the Fergana Valley, like the Nazarovs, probably so that he would appear more trustworthy. He had a message from the authorities saying that they were not holding Nazarov's son and did not know his whereabouts. When the man was leaving, a neighbor shouted at him: "It's you who did it!" After the man's visit, Munira lost all hope of seeing her son ever again.

Farrukh went missing forty days later. The day before, the family noticed a car with an official number plate and two men inside cruising around their house.

On June 25 Farrukh left home at 10:00 a.m. He was going to drop his and Zukhra's seven-year-old son, Abdullo, and his own father at a park and then shop for some food at the bazaar. Before leaving, Farrukh told Zukhra he would go to the mosque after the bazaar but wouldn't be long.

Zukhra tried calling him an hour and a half later, but his phone seemed turned off. Nobody was able to reach him all day, and he did not come back in the evening. The next day Farrukh's family reported his disappearance to the police. There was some apparent effort on the part of the authorities to investigate his disappearance. Eleven police officers arrived at their house on June 27, searched Farrukh's rooms, and questioned family members. It was established at the very beginning of their investigation that all of Farrukh's mobile phone conversations for the three days prior to his disappearance had been erased from the electronic records of the operator, MTS. They could not explain why.

On the morning of the day Farrukh disappeared, Zukhra said she heard him talking to someone on his cell phone. Farrukh was a little annoyed and said: "I did tell you I'd be there." It seemed that someone was being overinsistent on meeting him. It was probable that more calls had come from that person in those three days leading up to the disappearance, but with all the records gone it was not possible to check. The authorities also said they were unable to trace Farrukh's white Tico car, which he had left in.

Zukhra thought they would find him quickly, "within three days," because the family had connections and friends in various places. She suspected from the outset that Farrukh had been taken by the authorities. Her theory was that one of Farrukh's friends was an SNB agent, and he might have helped them organize the kidnapping. But she was sure that the authorities had no case against Farrukh. By law, they had to bring official charges within three days upon detention or let him go. Their connections would help make sure he was released, she thought. After a month of no news and no progress, Zukhra still believed that Farrukh would be found but decided to resign herself to the truth that his return would take a long time.

Meanwhile, the authorities renewed pressure on Zukhra's family over Rukhitdin, who was still in hiding. Probably they expected that the family would be more likely to give in after the shock of Farrukh's disappearance. Police would come and try for hours to talk Fazlitdin aka into making Rukhitdin come back under guarantees that "nobody would touch him." They also interrogated Zukhra's brother Mukhitdin, trying to get him to "confess" to taking lessons from Farrukh.

Zukhra, nonetheless, began her personal campaign to find Farrukh. She decided to keep pressing the authorities, including through human rights organizations and independent media. "I was like a lioness. I went everywhere, talked to everyone, made demands," she said. "Everywhere" meant mainly various police and prosecutors' offices. Zukhra got in touch with local rights groups—the handful that there were—as well as the BBC

World Service and the US-funded Radio Liberty, radio stations that had Uzbek-language services.

* * *

On August 11, roughly six weeks after Farrukh's disappearance, his family received a letter from a stranger named Dilmurod Turopov. The letter was addressed to the SNB, its chief Rustam Inoyatov, the prosecutor general, and "members of Farrukh Khaydarov's family." It read:

> *Respected Chairman* [Inoyatov]*! I wish to inform you that since childhood I have been going to the mosque in our mahallya, I have been praying and I have been interested in reading the Koran.*
>
> *When independence came* [bringing greater religious freedom]*, I taught myself to read the Koran, and listened to religious audio tapes with sermons by imams of official mosques.*
>
> *On January 13, 2004, I was detained and arrested with CDs of such sermons on me. Later, I was released under presidential amnesty, for which I'm thankful to* [President] *I. Karimov.*
>
> *Before releasing me, SNB officers had several conversations with me. They forced me to write testimony against Farrukh Akmalovich Khaydarov.*
>
> *That young man was a teacher of Arabic at the Egyptian cultural center attached to the Egyptian Embassy. Once or twice I asked him questions about the Arab alphabet book* Muallimus Soniy [*"second teacher," a thin forty-eight-page booklet in green paperback that explains to non-Arab speakers the Arabic alphabet and helps them read the Koran without speaking Arabic; it is still sold everywhere in Uzbekistan*].
>
> *But the SNB officers forced me to write a slanderous testimony against him. They forced me to write that Khaydarov has created an illegal group* [jamoat] *and taught its members.*
>
> *They threatened me with various things. I wrote what they asked me to, but that was not enough for them.*
>
> *They called me again on July 14, 2004. They questioned me from 5:30 to 7:30 p.m.*
>
> *One of the SNB officers who talked to me introduced himself as Farkhod. I found out later that his real name was U. S. Saidkaharov and he was a lieutenant. Another one said his name was Umar.*
>
> *Farkhod, i.e., U. S. Saidkaharov, forced me to sign a "Protocol of official warning"* [against doing something illegal] *that he wrote himself and it also had the name of some investigator called Sh. A. Ergashev on it. But the latter was not present.*
>
> *The protocol written by U. S. Saidkaharov read: "I, Dilmurod Turopov, at the end of 2002 joined a jamoat of the Jikhodchilar* [Jihadists] *religious movement that was set up by Farrukh Akmalovich Khaydarov. Farrukh Akmalovich Khaydarov (nom de guerre—Askar) preached to us ideas of religious*

extremism, fundamentalism and separatism. These actions are punishable under Articles 159, 216, 244 of the Criminal Code."

At the end the protocol read: "It was explained to me that these actions were illegal and that if I repeated them I would face severe punishment."

I told them that I had taken no extremism, fundamentalism or separatism lessons, and that there were no anti-government talks, and all that was slander.

But "Farkhod"—U. S. Saidkaharov—said: "Your Askar is an extremist. If you have attended even two or three of his lessons that's enough. Even if you studied Muallimus Soniy, *that's extremism too."*

For two hours I argued with them and tried to prove them wrong. But they threatened that if I did not sign it I would not leave and would go to jail. They told their people there to prepare handcuffs.

I asked "Farkhod" to change the word extremism because there was nothing like that. "Farkhod" would not agree.

He said: "You did not write this yourself, I wrote it and I will answer for it. You are only signing it to show that you are leaving that path and you are repentant and will not do anything like that again."

He wanted to deceive me with these words. He threatened me for two hours. "You don't know the SNB basement yet. Davron from GUVD [city police] does not know how to beat people. We do, we will teach him."

After he said for the last time that I would not leave if I did not sign it, I was compelled to sign.

But I have been feeling bad since. I've slandered an innocent man. That young man has not done anything bad to me, he never taught me anything wrong and he did not put me on a wrong path.

That's why in this official statement, I withdraw my earlier testimony against Farrukh Khaydarov that I gave at the SNB office. Farrukh Khaydarov never talked to me about jihad, never said anything against the state or about politics. He did not propagate anything.

I only asked him once or twice about things from the Muallimus Soniy *book. I did not take regular lessons from him. The* Muallimus Soniy *book is sold everywhere. It's a book on the Arabic alphabet and is allowed by the authorities. It's not an extremist book as "Farkhod" says.*

I ask you to void the testimony given in my name against Farrukh Khaydarov. It was made up by SNB officers who took advantage of my young age and ignorance of the law, as well as by threat of arrest.

Please help to restore justice and truth.

[Signature] July 21, 2004

After getting the letter, Zukhra went to Turopov's house to thank him, but he was not there. His parents told her that he had gone to Russia with his wife and would not be coming back.

In reality, after writing his letter to the SNB and Farrukh's family, Dilmurod went into hiding. Two years later, in 2006, in Almaty, Kazakhstan, he applied to the UN High Commissioner for Refugees (UNHCR) for refugee status. In February 2009 I met Dilmurod in Sweden, the country that had given him political asylum, and he told me his story. Not everything that he wrote in 2004 in his letter to the SNB and Farrukh's family was true. He had wanted to help Farrukh but without arming the authorities with any information that they could use against him in the event that they detained him again. So Dilmurod omitted in the letter that since the late 1990s, he had been taking Islamic lessons from Imam Nazarov's deputy, Abduvakhid Yoldoshev, and in 2002 took Koran lessons from Farrukh.

Yoldoshev was taken in by the authorities in 1999 amid sweeping arrests among dissident Muslims. He was released several months later but arrested again in 2000 and sentenced to nineteen years in prison. Following Yoldoshev's second arrest, the authorities went after his students. Some of those who had been detained and questioned warned Dilmurod that the authorities had his name too.

In 2002 Dilmurod started attending Farrukh's classes, hearing about them from a friend who was already attending. There were five or six students who gathered once a week to get tutoring from Farrukh on how to read the Koran and the Prophet Muhammad's sayings in Arabic. Their small study group came to the authorities' attention when a friend of one of the students was detained by the security service and was made—through psychological pressure, beatings, or torture—to give away the names of all his friends keen on Islam. Then they got another student, Khasan, who in his turn was made to give away all his contacts studying or practicing Islam independently.

Soon after Khasan's arrest, Farrukh and his students began to notice surveillance on them. Khasan was eventually released and fled to Kazakhstan, but he passed on a message to Dilmurod through his family that he should stop attending Farrukh's classes and that Farrukh was going to be arrested soon. Dilmurod warned Farrukh before going into hiding.

Dilmurod returned home only two years later in January 2004, thinking that the danger had passed. But just a few days later he was arrested along with several friends when they were visiting Imam Nazarov's deputy, Yoldoshev. They were taken to the Shaykhontour District court, made to sign confessions that they had beaten someone up, and sentenced to ten days in prison each. They were placed in cells in the city police detention center and questioned for ten days about their contacts and alleged terror activities.

Dilmurod was questioned by two SNB officers. "Do you know Farrukh Khaydarov? Did you get lessons from him?" they asked.

Dilmurod lied and said that he did not.

"Think well, or else you are not going to get out of here. Do you want to go to jail for twenty years?" So it continued for about one hour, and then they left.

City police investigators warned Dilmurod: "Those guys are from the SNB; you'd better not mess with them. They know everything."

The SNB investigators returned the next day. Dilmurod did as they demanded and wrote a confession about taking lessons from Farrukh. On the tenth day, Dilmurod and his friends were taken to Panelnyy, the grim detention center in Tashkent for drunkards and the homeless.

Dilmurod's parents were making the customary moves in such cases in Uzbekistan to get their son out of trouble. Using their connections, they tried to get the name of someone important enough in the police who could be approached and bribed to get their son freed. A bribe was paid, and the police said they would let Dilmurod out. He was released, only to be detained again before he could reach home. As he headed to a bus stop after leaving the police office, a woman he had never seen before appeared. She ran at him, pushing him and shouting: "Bastard!" Dilmurod tried to pay no attention and walked on, but the same police officer who had just seen him off from the police station caught up with him and took him back in "for attacking that woman."

Questioning resumed. It soon transpired that the purpose of that police maneuver to get him back in detention was to make Dilmurod write a statement that he would cooperate with the police as an informer. Dilmurod wrote it and was finally allowed to go home.

After about a month the authorities began to regularly summon Dilmurod to the SNB, accusing him of ties with Imam Nazarov and of taking terror lessons. He was shown Farrukh's photo and told: "If you deny knowing him we will make you rot in jail."

"Yes, I know him," Dilmurod replied.

"Did you take extremist lessons from him?"

"It's wrong. He did not teach us that."

"We will take you to him right now," the interrogator said. "You are going to die there."

Dilmurod's mother, who accompanied him to interrogations, begged that he sign the confession: "Sign it, Son."

Dilmurod did. Then he wrote that letter to the security chief and Farrukh's family and went into hiding.

* * *

Another letter arrived on August 12, 2004, that appeared to have been written by Farrukh himself. It carried a Kabul postmark dated August 9, 2004. The letter, addressed to Farrukh's brother Rashid said:

> *Hello, dear Ravshan aka.*
>
> *How is your health? Are mother, father, sister-in-law, the nephews, my son Abdullo, Zukhra, brother Bakhtiyor and the others well?*
>
> *Allah is a witness, I know and feel that you all are very worried about me. I beg you to forgive me, but I'm convinced that everything that I am doing is right and in the name of Allah.*
>
> *We, Muslims, have gone on the path of* hijra [the Prophet's flight from Mecca to Medina to avoid assassination] *to carry out our big plans against the regime of infidels which is suppressing Muslims.*
>
> *We had no other choice. In any case, sooner or later we would have been caught by our enemies and then we would not have been able to carry out our planned actions in the name of Allah.*
>
> *Here, together with me are my friends Okil and Khusnutdin, a son of Obid qori [Nazarov]. We could not send you any word until now because we had no opportunities on the road and circumstances would not allow us.*
>
> *After a long journey we reached our planned destination. We found many brothers from Uzbekistan here.*
>
> *Today we met our Teacher. We discussed actions that we are planning in the name of Allah.*
>
> *We agreed that Okil and I will go to another place. As soon as we reach the place where our brothers are we will let you know.*
>
> *Where we are now, there are many students of Qori. They want to leave Khusnutdin here. If you can, please pass this news on to his family.*
>
> *It's very hard here to send letters, it's banned. Okil sent a letter through his friends. We heard it was intercepted on the* [Uzbek-Afghan] *border.*
>
> *Ravshan aka, please do not misunderstand my actions. I hope you will do everything to make sure that my dear ones do not feel my absence.*
>
> *Your brother Farrukh, with prayers to Allah that you have an honest and righteous life and patience.*

The handwriting was Farrukh's, but the letter only reinforced Zukhra's conviction that he was in the hands of the Uzbek authorities. Zukhra wrote an open appeal to the president, law-enforcement agencies, embassies, and human rights groups.

"With complete confidence and without any hesitation, I can say that the letter was written against his will," the appeal said. "It was dictated to him and he wrote it under duress. I have no doubt that this is the work of Uzbekistan's SNB and that they have kidnapped him. It is clear from the letter's style and content. It is clear from the handwriting that the first few lines were written with a shaking hand. This confirms that the person who wrote the letter was under duress and in a state of shock."

Farrukh's parents—his father, Akmal, and his mother, Zhamilya—also publicly protested, writing their own open letter:

"The letter was allegedly sent from Kabul on August 9 and reached us in three days. This does not make any sense. . . . We asked the Main Post Office to clarify this and they told us that letters from Kabul take at least fifteen days to get here."

According to Farrukh and Rukhitdin's friends and family, at least twelve young religious men disappeared in the spring and summer of 2004 in Tashkent. All were linked to Imam Nazarov, Farrukh, or Rukhitdin.

Nazarov's driver, Sagdullaev; Nazarov's son Khusnutdin; and Oqil Yunusov (Farrukh's close friend) all went missing in May. Then it was Farrukh, in June. Then came the disappearances of Abdurasul, Ravshan Imankhojayev, Amanullo (a son of Abdullo Otayev, an imam who himself had vanished in 1992), and Makhmud, who had studied in Saudi Arabia and had been giving Islamic lessons since his return. The friends suggested that possibly there were more disappearances, but many families were too afraid to publicize it or even inform friends, many of whom were by then underground or out of the country anyway.

Dilmurod heard about another apparent state kidnapping in 2005 of one of Farrukh's closest students, Khikmat, in Tashkent. One day he left home in his Nexia car but never got to his place of work at a Turkish firm. He called his office and said he would not be in for a day or two and was never seen again. His parents used all their connections to try to find him but to no avail. One day their servant at home picked up the phone when it rang, and it was Khikmat. He said: "Is mother home?" Someone in the background shouted: "Put it down!" And that was it.

In March 2006 Zukhra went to a district police department—she was finally sent there after spending three days at other law-enforcement and justice offices—to get a response to her inquiry about the official probe into Farrukh's disappearance. The official she met there said they were conducting "a very serious search" and wished her patience. But the clerk there gave her by mistake a letter saying that the official probe was treating Farrukh not as a missing person but a suspected extremist on the run.

*　*　*

Farrukh gave his lessons once a week and every day during the holy month of Ramadan. There were some improvised lessons too, where he would be invited to a friend's for lunch or dinner, and there would be some seventy people waiting for him and wanting him to talk to them about Islam.

Farrukh used to say to Zukhra that her brother Rukhitdin was "like a cloud that pours down with rain on everyone." He described himself as "a well—you have to pull water out of me." It was about their different ways of teaching.

"Rukhitdin did not wait until someone asked a question [about religion]. Everything he said was about religion. But with Farrukh you had to ask first, and then he would begin to talk," Zukhra said.

In 2008 I met two of Farrukh's former students in Tashkent. To give them some extra sense of security and reassurance that by meeting me they would not endanger themselves, I did not ask their names. Both were in their mid-thirties. I will call them Student 1 and Student 2.

The soft-spoken Student 1, the taller of the two, said he had started attending Farrukh's lessons because he had heard that Farrukh was "a knowledgeable man." At the lessons, the students would read the Koran, and Farrukh would correct their mistakes. Then they would discuss some of the Prophet's sayings, with Farrukh explaining the moral messages behind them. Farrukh was a strict teacher, and if one of the students came without doing his homework—learning parts of the Koran by heart—next time he would be asked to recite that unlearned part in front of everyone.

"He knew how to motivate us to learn better," Student 1 said. "So soon we all began to do our homework.

"He explained everything beautifully. He would think before saying anything. Even during a meal, he would try to teach us something. He might tell us some of Muhammad's sayings about food, like 'Eat a little at a time, so everyone gets some.' Or he could ask everyone to say something about food or quote traditional proverbs like the one that says that everyone has to respect food and bread." But Farrukh, Student 1 said, was also a friend and a brother—"everything was open between us."

Student 1 was arrested on July 31, 2004. It was two months after Farrukh's disappearance and a day after the US and Israeli embassies and the general prosecutor's office in Tashkent were almost simultaneously hit by suicide bomb attacks. The attacks killed two of the Israeli embassy's locally hired security guards. The authorities said the alleged attackers intended to blow themselves up inside the targeted buildings, but none were able to get in, and all the blasts, late on Friday afternoon (a strange time, as if chosen to minimize casualties) occurred at the entrances. The attacks came days after the authorities opened a trial of fifteen men facing terrorism charges in connection with the March–April violence in Tashkent and Bukhara Region.

Six security and police officers came to arrest Student 1, kicking open the door of his family's house and beating up his little brother, whom they mistook for Student 1, who was not home at the time. Their shocked father rushed to fetch Student 1 from their other house. "What have you done?" he asked. Student 1 said he hadn't done anything wrong and would go and meet the police and sort it out by himself.

The waiting officers grabbed him as soon as they saw him and pushed him into a police car. The family's two houses were searched from top to bottom. Student 1 was systematically beaten during the first ten days of detention—hitting the soles of his feet with clubs—until he stopped denying that he knew Farrukh. When he said the lessons he took from Farrukh were purely religious, the officer who was questioning him said: "Don't tell us about legal stuff. Tell us about illegal stuff, about weapons, terrorism, jihad. Where do you keep weapons? Where is your explosive suicide belt? What have you been plotting? Where do you get fatwas from?" To Student 1's protestations that he was not involved in anything like that, the interrogator said: "Do you want me to find all that in your house?"

The investigators had one of the books that Farrukh used in his classes—a collection of Muhammad's thirty hadiths. Student 1 suggested they read it. One of them read it in fifteen minutes and said, "It's not what you were studying; you could not have been learning this for six months."

"Islam is not something that you can learn in fifteen minutes. Every hadith has to be explained," Student 1 said.

Questioning in this fashion went on for three months, after which he and a group of other men were charged with organizing a secret religious group, a criminal offense that carried a punishment of between five and ten years in jail.

Their investigator was suddenly replaced before the trial. At his meetings with Student 1 he started off as a tough guy, accusing him of being Farrukh's "right-hand man." But one day he told Student 1 quietly and in a secretive tone: "To be honest, you guys are here for no reason."

"Then let us go," Student 1 said.

The investigator said that since "things are in motion"—meaning confessions had already been squeezed out—he could not call the charges off, but he would add to the case "some mitigating circumstances."

Student 1 and several other defendants were tried on January 7, 2005, as members of an alleged terror cell created by Farrukh. Student 1 would not admit to that, but Zukhra said their families paid bribes to appease the judge. The bribery gave them the hope that the trial would right all wrongs and reveal the truth about their innocence. They told the court that Farrukh taught them "only good things."

"Farrukh aka had such a beautiful nature. I've never met anyone like him in my life. His kindness has had a great influence on me. He told me one hadith: 'Once Oisha opa [the Prophet's wife] was rude to a camel, and the Prophet said to her to be gentle to it.' What I mean is that Farrukh used to tell us such hadiths and taught us to be nice to all human beings. I've learned only good things from Farrukh aka. Allah can be pleased with Farrukh," one of them said in his closing statement.

The trial ended with four of them being released in the courtroom. When the verdict was announced, the four freed men started crying and hugging each other in the metal cage where defendants await their fate. They were crying tears of grief at the same time because their close friend Jalol was ordered to remain in custody for further investigation. One of the freed men hugged Jalol and began to wail.

"It was so hard to see men with tears in their eyes, crying. I never used to cry in front of other people. But here I could not stop myself. Tears rolled down my face," Zukhra, who was in the courtroom, wrote in her diary that evening. "The boys' tears, the way Jalol looked when they were reading the verdict, their parents, friends, wives—they are still in front of my eyes."

Jalol was a devout Muslim, and he would not eat any prison food, considering it ungodly. So he was quite emaciated by the time of the trial. "Further investigation meant another round of torture and psychological pressure for him," she wrote. Jalol was convicted and jailed after a new investigation. He came out of prison in spring 2008.

Student 1 last saw Farrukh a week before his disappearance. It was a Friday, when they and other friends met for prayer at a mosque. Farrukh said he felt that he was being shadowed.

Months after Farrukh's disappearance, Student 1 went to a traffic police office to get his driver's license. On the wall he saw a poster with photos of men wanted by police. Among them was Farrukh. Student 1 froze when he saw the photo. "I forgot why I was there and just walked out, as if someone had knocked me out," he said.

*　*　*

Student 2 was eloquent, sounded well educated, and kept freely switching from Russian to Uzbek and back. He spoke passionately, always looking me straight in the eye, preempting questions, as if seizing the opportunity to get the pain off his chest and share his deeply felt truths.

"There are different kinds of people. You cannot accept just anybody as your teacher. You have to know that your teacher does not just talk the talk; he walks the walk as well. Farrukh was a role model for us. We believed his words," he started.

"Farrukh explained to us what was good and what was wrong, how Islam looks at specific things and why. He would say that this was not good because the Prophet Muhammad explained it like this or that. This is what he taught us: Every man has to reform, improve himself, instead of trying to teach others how to live. When everyone reforms themselves, then society will be different. Show to others that you are on the right path, and others will follow you. Start with yourself. Farrukh was a real teacher; we fully trusted that he had exactly the knowledge that we sought, and we were not worried about him teaching us something bad or wrong," Student 2 continued.

He explained why he and other students of Farrukh's had sought Islamic lessons and why had they had chosen unofficial tutoring.

"We are Muslims—why can't we study our religion?" he began. "What's wrong with studying suras?"

He said that until the late 1980s it had been possible to get Koran lessons at mosques. Now "at official mosques they can and should teach, but they are strictly prohibited from doing that. They are afraid; everyone is afraid. Imams won't teach, even though they have the authority."

This, he said, forced people to study at home. But studying on your own could not get you very far—the Koran is in Arabic, non-Arabic-speaking Muslims need guidance when they begin to learn to read it.

"When I read at home on my own, I would make mistakes," Student 2 said. "But when I was with Farrukh, he would tell me: 'Little brother, that is not correct.'"

They knew that in the atmosphere of the time they were playing with fire, but their desire to learn Islam, their trust in Farrukh, and their conviction that they were not doing anything wrong were stronger than fear of government punishment.

"People like Farrukh were sources of reliable, truthful information. People believed them, trusted them. I would not trust official imams or go to ask any of them to teach me Islam. And they would not trust me either, thinking I might be an SNB agent who was just checking them out," Student 2 said.

Farrukh's advice to his students in case they got detained by authorities was: "Always tell only the truth; do not add anything, but do not hide anything either. Tell them only what we really do," according to Student 2.

"We miss Farrukh. When you lose someone who is close to you, you miss him," he added.

I asked Student 2 what Islam meant to him.

"If I returned to the life I had before accepting Islam, I was someone you could throw into a fire right away. We did all sorts of things before; we were not good people. Now Islam is our life; we weigh everything up: Is it a good thing to do or say, or is it bad? We did not swear to anyone to keep to Islam for the rest of our lives, but when we had learned about it, we asked ourselves, Why was I so blind before? A Muslim begins to see when someone is lying and when he is telling the truth. It's like some kind of detector begins to work in your heart. Everything that a Muslim intends to do, he first puts on the scales: Is it good or bad? There are angels sitting on our two shoulders all the time: the angel on the right side writes down all our good deeds, and the one on the left side writes down all our misdeeds. And on Judgment Day everything will be counted. Allah can see everything," he said.

Student 2 said authorities were suppressing religious freedom because they are "not interested in people getting enlightened."

"It's better for them if people just watch various TV shows, so they are distracted from reality. It is easier to control an ignorant crowd. Islam's main message is there is no God but Allah. That's what we carry in our hearts. The others [rulers] want to be gods themselves. Today rulers want to say that they are gods, so they can do whatever they want. But a Muslim is someone who can say to a ruler like that, 'You are wrong; you are doing evil things; you are unfair to people,'" he added.

He said Uzbeks like him wanted "to study Islam more deeply for ourselves and for our families, because we are responsible for them, but not in order to take to the streets and shout some slogans there."

Neither were they, Student 2 said, practicing Islam to become terrorists.

"Statistically, every fourth person on the planet is Muslim. So if those who say that Islam is a religion of terrorists and extremists are right, there should be no spot in the world left without terrorists, where there would not be bombs going off every day," he said.

* * *

When I talked to Zukhra in 2008, four years after Farrukh's disappearance, she had no more hope left of seeing him again. She seemed to have succumbed to Karimov's regime and was prepared to look at her husband's and her brother Rukhitdin's tragedies from the official point of view.

"My brother and husband did do a wrong thing. Unauthorized teaching [of Islam] was banned," she said. "One should not play games with the state." But, she said, "their only mistake was that they thought that all people were as good as they are."

It was naive to think that the authorities would never find out about their classes, she said. "They only taught people how to read the Koran and answered their questions about religion. The authorities thought they were preparing jihad," Zukhra said. "They were afraid of an uprising because they [the students] wanted to know the truth."

When Zukhra warned Farrukh that his teaching practice would land him in trouble, he would say, "How can I not share what I know? Young people want to know; we are Muslims. I am afraid, but then should I keep all my knowledge to myself?" He also used to say, "They cannot stop religion from spreading. They jail one, and in his place there will come ten new [Muslims.]"

Several months after Farrukh's disappearance Zukhra had a dream about him. In the dream, Farrukh was back at home; he was bearded, looked well, and "talked intelligently." Zukhra asked him how he had been kidnapped, and he replied, "Simply. They said to us, 'Come with us,' and led us away. Very simply. They led us off the street, quietly."

He also said, in the dream, that where he was he met "many people who I knew," including his close friend Oqil, who had disappeared a few weeks before Farrukh. "He said to me that before I had been brought there, they tortured him badly, and now they were going to switch to me." Zukhra woke up before she'd "seen enough" of Farrukh.

Zukhra had been open with her son, Abdullo, about what had happened to his father from the very beginning. She explained to Abdullo that his father had been kidnapped and told him that they might try to do harm to the two of them as well. Therefore, Abdullo was never to talk to or follow any strangers and always had to tell his mother where he was going and what he was doing. If anything happened to her, he was not to panic but should call family.

Abdullo accepted everything without complaining. And he would never complain in the future. He talked about his father for the first time four months after his disappearance.

"Mum, Dad is always in front of my eyes, as if he is talking to me. He says nice things," he told Zukhra.

"What does he say?" she asked.

"He talks but without sound," Abdullo said.

Later it would make him cry when in some public place he would notice a man looking in some way—his face, hair, clothes, figure—like Farrukh. "Look, Mum, that man looks like Dad!" he would exclaim. Abdullo would sometimes go to Zukhra's bedroom, open the wardrobe where they kept Farrukh's clothes, take one shirt, and—putting it on his face—take a deep breath, trying to take in as much as possible of his father's scent. "This will last me for a while," he would say.

Zukhra tried to draw strength from her faith, trying to look at her misfortune as "a test that is designed to teach us to separate good from evil." Another source of strength was Farrukh's letters, about a dozen in total, from the time when he was a student in Saudi Arabia in the 1990s. She first took them out from the chest where she had been keeping them five months after Farrukh's disappearance in November 2004. She read them, "now laughing, now crying, now thinking," for more than five hours, reading each three or four times, realizing how much she missed his words, jokes, his emotional support. The next day she read them together with Abdullo. Zukhra chose the funniest bits, and at the beginning Abdullo laughed a lot. Then he began to sob violently.

Figure 5.2. Farrukh with his son, Abdullo, in their home in Tashkent, 2003. © Family archive.

"I miss Dad," he said in between sobs. Zukhra pressed him against her chest; his heart was madly racing.

"God willing, all will be fine again; your dad will come back, and we will be together again," she said. They sat holding one another for a while, until Abdullo calmed down. Then he lay down and fell asleep.

It had been three months since their wedding. Zukhra was living with Farrukh's family in Tashkent as was required by traditions, doing most of the domestic work as was expected of a daughter-in-law. Her relations with her mother-in-law were not good, and she complained to Farrukh about this in her letters. Zukhra was also preparing to join him in Saudi Arabia in several months.

In a letter written in neat, small handwriting on November 11, 1994, Farrukh said:

> *Assalomu Alaykum, my darling, my flower . . . a star that has come down to earth for me . . .*
>
> *How are you? Are you well? Hope you are not too tired of being a daughter-in-law? Do you get some sleep during the day and night? Do you go to Detskiy Mir?*
>
> *I've got your letter and photograph, thank you, dear wife. I'm now writing looking at your picture. . . .*
>
> *It amazes me how much patience you have been showing these two months. Thank you. You don't show anything even in your letter, but I can understand as well as you do how you feel. It's very hard, very hard!*
>
> *But you must know, one grief is followed by two joys. The longer the sadness, the sweeter the reward, Inshallah. Just a little more patience, patience, patience.*
>
> *There will certainly be an end to this suffering, pain and loneliness, because choices are always our own and there is a reason for every step we take. We are seeking knowledge on the path of Allah and for the sake of that we are seeing such hard days now. But our achievements will be great and Allah Ta'olo [Almighty] will certainly give us a happy and peaceful life in this world and paradise in the other, OK, jonim?*
>
> *Jonginam [my little soul], I have a request, I'd be happy if you would pour out to me all the complaints that you have inside because then they'll be off your chest and you'll feel better—let me be your friend in this. But maybe it would be better if you didn't show them to anyone else?*
>
> *Bring your cotton dresses, the white one, and the one for 80 dollars. You will put it on and wait for me to come back from my studies, OK, jonim?*
>
> *That's it,*
>
> *Your husband who is missing you. My eyes are on the road!*

On the day of Farrukh's disappearance, Zukhra started a diary that she intended to show him after they were reunited so that he would know how much she missed him, how strongly she believed in his return, and how hard she tried to save him. But as months and years went by, her hopes faded away, and the diary became a way of maintaining a connection with Farrukh. She often asked him in her diary to "forgive" her for "being unable to help you."

"We have failed to find you. Sorry! We have stopped all our efforts now," she wrote one day. "I'm starting to feel so intimidated. I don't know how I've lost all my courage. Forgive your cowardly wife. I'm good for nothing. Forgive me."

About a year after Farrukh went missing, his parents expelled Zukhra and Abdullo from their home, saying they never wanted to see them again. They seemed to blame the loss of their son on his connection to Zukhra's brother Rukhitdin. They were regularly visited by the precinct policeman who would tell them that if Rukhitdin handed himself in, their son would be back too. The same message repeatedly came from the Interior Ministry and city police investigators.

In Zukhra's dream on the night of her expulsion, she and Farrukh, holding hands, were walking up a mountain. Farrukh looked sad and was holding Zukhra's hand very tight. When they stopped, Farrukh sighed, closed his eyes briefly, and then opened them and hugged Zukhra: "Zukhra, they humiliated you. Forgive me. I never thought you would see something like this. I am going to disappear again, so I have to speak quickly. I have one request for you: keep talking to Abdullo about me. Don't let him forget me. Please, remind my son about me."

Then he vanished.

6

THE ANDIJAN REVOLT

IT WAS AROUND ONE P.M. ON MAY 13, 2005. Abduvosit Egamov was sitting in a rose bed inside the Andijan Region administration compound. The official building behind him was in the hands of armed rebels busily guarding their hostages, tending the wounded, and bracing themselves for more clashes with government forces.

In the square on the other side of the compound's iron fence, there was a crowd of several thousand townspeople listening to the speakers, who were taking turns on the brown marble platform of a monument to Babur, Tamerlane's descendant who founded India's Mughal Empire in the sixteenth century, to express their grievances against the authorities. Smoke was billowing from the Bakir theater behind the monument and the Sharq (East) cinema hall to the right. Several charred upturned vehicles lay about.

Egamov was too exhausted and shocked to take part in what was going on around him. But in his heart he was happy. It was for his freedom that his "brothers" had risen against the authorities. With a smile on his pale face—a mark of the eleven months he had spent behind bars—Egamov was enjoying being outside, in the sun. He could not believe that he was free.

Egamov was one of the twenty-three men who had gone on trial in the Fergana Valley city of Andijan three months earlier on charges of belonging to an Islamist group. The authorities branded the group Akromia after their founder and leader Akrom Yuldoshev, who had been in prison since 1999. The twenty-three men, owners of various businesses, denied the accusations. They and their supporters claimed there was no organization whatsoever, and they were simply religious businessmen. To many people in the Fergana Valley, they were known as a trust of successful entrepreneurs, who paid their workers well and were dedicated to charity.

That was how much I knew about Akromia when, early in the morning of May 13, at home in Tashkent, I received a call from a colleague, who said that a revolt was under way in Andijan. I made a call to one of the twenty-three defendants' supporters, who excitedly told me that the authorities were "no longer in control" of the city.

Several minutes later I, my sister Galima, her fiancé (the German journalist Marcus Bensmann), and Efrem Lukatsky (an AP photographer from Kiev who had flown to Tashkent the day before to work with me on feature stories) were heading to the airport. The flights to Andijan had already been canceled, so we took the 9:50 a.m. flight to Fergana, another large town in the valley, seventy-five kilometers west of Andijan.

The news of unrest in Andijan was spreading across the country in a wave of quiet anxiety in the absence of any official or independent reports. A fellow passenger in the plane was talking about it in a half whisper on his mobile phone. I strained my ears but only managed to make out a few words: "a military unit," "attack."

The people at the Fergana airport looked quiet and tense. The four of us were in a similar emotional state as we drove to Andijan in a taxi. The driver left us on the edge of the city as the authorities were beginning to block the road with military trucks.

There were still gaps in the cordon and no forces manning it, so, as if not noticing any barriers at all, we went ahead. A man in a military uniform shouted from behind, "Where are you going?"

"To the center!" we shouted back, without turning our heads, and walked on as if knowing what we were doing. We were too close to the story and had no time to waste. The last thing we wanted was to be found out to be journalists. Luckily, the man did not pursue us—perhaps he had not been given strict orders yet not to let anybody in.

The streets of Andijan were deserted. We walked on the tarmac under a sun nearly at its zenith. A tank with its menacingly protruding gun stood in front of the empty Andijan airport building that we passed by.

A mile or two farther along, we saw a lone white Damas minivan—a chance to get a lift—and started enthusiastically waving to the driver. He nodded at our request to take us to the center, which he rightly understood as "where the trouble was."

The rebel territory was marked with a security line—a few cars and a cordon stretched between them. We got out of our minivan and walked up to the two rebels manning the line. Casual and unaggressive, except for the rifles hanging over their shoulders, they seemed to be treating their duties like an everyday task. They checked our journalistic accreditation cards before letting us through.

So, out of the tightly controlled reality of Karimov's Uzbekistan, we stepped onto a small patch of land where his order had been defied and overturned. The rebel control extended to one five-story government building and a square, teeming with young and old Andijan residents. Especially eye-catching were the women squatting in compact groups with their motley headscarves and long flowery dresses. Scores of curious, hyperexcited children and teenagers scurried around the square, as if in a playground, constantly looking for more fun things to do. A few young men were kicking an already battered car and jumping on it. By the burned-out cinema hall there stood an abandoned red fire engine.

I noticed a policeman's hat on the ground and asked someone in the crowd what had happened to the policeman. "He shot a man in the forehead. Then he was seized by the crowd," I was told, left to assume that the policeman had been made to pay for his misdeed.

The scene in front of my eyes seemed surreal. Maybe because of the presence of so many excited children, it seemed like the rebellion of a child against a tyrannical parent—desperate and sincere but sadly futile.

For now, before the inevitable punishment, the overriding feeling among the Andijan protesters was that of euphoria. Standing on the platform of the Babur monument—a twelve-meter bronze horseman with the trail of his long cloak whipped up by the wind—a man prompted the crowd: "If you have something you want to talk about, come on, get it off your chest!"

And people came to the platform one after another and complained about their problems, sharing the frustration and despair that had been building up for years.

"My husband left one and a half years ago to look for a living," a woman in a headscarf began and broke down in tears, unable to continue her speech. The crowd clapped in a show of understanding and support.

"Our aim is justice! Democracy!" shouted another woman from the platform.

"We are worried about our children," said another speaker, a man. "We are doing this [protest] for our children!"

"My six children are without jobs," said another woman. "The factories are not working. The government does not provide anything; they only want bribes from us."

I spoke to people in the crowd, mothers, farmers, and others, taking down their words: "There are no jobs. . . . Uzbek people are suffering. . . . We have forgotten the taste of meat because we cannot afford it. . . . Karimov must go. . . . The food prices must be brought down. . . . One life, one death: if I do not fight today, what kind of life are my children going to have? . . . They give us five kilos of macaroni per person every month instead of pay. . . . Women are forced to do odd menial jobs. Bosses [officials] grab everything for themselves. They care only about themselves."

Suddenly there was a commotion in the crowd, and it made way for two men dragging a tall, heavily built man by the shoulders. It was the Andijan city prosecutor, Ganijon Abdurakhimov, one of the rebels' hostages. Just several hours before, one of the city's most powerful officials, he looked shocked and resigned to his new captive status. He was brought onto the tribune to face the crowd to answer for the prosecution of the twenty-three Akromia members.

"The trial of the twenty-three men was fair. It is a judicial process," Abdurakhimov said in a faltering voice.

"Beat him, kill him!" came shouts from the crowd.

The prosecutor was dragged away.

Then someone announced from the platform that President Karimov was heading to Andijan to talk to the protesters. The news brought smiles to their faces; they cheered and clapped.

Nobody seemed to be paying attention to the noise of military helicopters flying overhead.

* * *

The twenty-three Andijan religious businessmen, as they described themselves, were arrested in June 2004.

Among them was Shamsutdin Atamatov, an owner of a sweet factory that employed twenty-three people. The first interrogation—after he had been snatched by four men in civilian clothes, pushed into a car, and brought to the security-service detention center—went on until 11:30 p.m. and continued for the next two days with the same intensity. His interrogators wanted to know about his business partners, Atamatov told me in an interview.

They said that some antigovernment leaflets had been found in his car and that they had also found a significant amount of money in his office that he was allegedly concealing to evade taxes. Atamatov said he had nothing to do with either the leaflets, which they would not show to him, or the money.

When he refused to sign a confession admitting to possessing the leaflets and money, three men gave him a pummeling with clubs. He eventually signed it after one of the interrogators made a threat against his wife. "You have a wife, don't you? If you don't sign, you will see what happens to her."

The interrogators also showed Atamatov Akrom Yuldoshev's pamphlet "Imonga Yol" (A Path to the Faith). They said they knew that all twenty-three of them had studied the book, which according to government religion experts contained "coded" antigovernment and extremist ideas, and were members of Yuldoshev's "Islamist sect." Atamatov was officially charged with religious extremism, anticonstitutional activity, the creation of a criminal group, and the creation and spreading of materials representing a threat to security and public order.

In September, three months after the arrests in Andijan, the authorities took twenty employees of Turon Productions furniture company into custody in the capital, Tashkent, accusing them of being members of the same group as the Andijan suspects. The charges against them were based on the alleged confessions made by the twenty-three Andijan suspects to belonging to Akromia. In January the authorities arrested another thirteen Andijan men on similar charges.

On February 11, 2005, the twenty-three Andijan businessmen went on trial at Andijan's Oltinkul District court. The prosecutors called more than a hundred witnesses to support their charges, but they all refused to describe the defendants as "extremists" despite facing official psychological and physical pressure.

"One of them [witnesses] was so badly beaten that he had to be taken to hospital," Atamatov said. When he complained about the beating to the judge, he was told the investigators "were simply doing their job."

In protest at the judge's rejection of their demand for a new examination of Yuldoshev's pamphlet and that the jailed Yuldoshev himself be allowed to testify in court, the defendants went on a hunger strike but abandoned it when the authorities attempted to force-feed them.

As the trial went on, the twenty-three men's employees and relatives came and stood outside the court building in silent protest. They came for every hearing in ever growing numbers in a show of striking loyalty to the arrested men and unprecedented defiance of the authorities. Their protests appeared carefully choreographed. They came wearing their best clothes. They would stand in neat rows, men and women separately, or sit on wooden benches that they would bring along every day, making sure they were not in the way of the people and vehicles passing by. The women would bring hot lunch and tea, which would be passed around from hand to hand so that their lines would not be broken and their protest would not be interrupted. Their children would join the protest after school, coming in their uniforms and with schoolbags. Every evening, before going home they would sweep the street clean. They did not chant any demands nor hold any signs or placards. By the last hearings in May, their number had reached about a thousand, according to witnesses.

"We stood so nicely before the court building. There was perfect order. We wanted to know why they were jailing us for nothing," Valijon Babajanov, a brother of one of the jailed twenty-three men, told me in a conversation a few months after the unrest.

It appeared the idea was to pressure the authorities but, at the same time, through their peaceful and exemplary good-citizen behavior, to undermine the official allegations of extremism against them. In addition to the orderly public protests, the defendants' supporters tried using private channels to get the twenty-three men out, which meant bribing the judge—a common practice in Uzbekistan's corrupt justice system.

According to Atamatov, the judge communicated to them through the defense lawyers that he was willing to let all of them walk free from the courtroom, but he could not drop the charges altogether as it would make the authorities "look bad" by raising questions as to why they had arrested the men in the first place. But the twenty-three men and their supporters wanted full acquittal, so no deal happened.

Tensions were building up in Andijan with the trial coming to an end. A rumor was going around that the authorities had drawn up a list of five hundred more persons to be arrested after the trial as suspected Akromia members.

At the hearing on May 11 the defense lawyers and prosecutor made their closing statements. The lawyers asked the judge for a not-guilty verdict for all the defendants. The prosecutor, Mirzoulugbek Zokirov, demanded between three and seven years in prison for nineteen of the defendants, a three-year suspended sentence for another, and to allow the remaining three to walk free, considering that they had already spent eleven months in jail. After hearing the prosecutor's statement, the judge adjourned the session, without setting a date and time for delivering his verdict and leaving the defendants and their supporters in a state of suspense.

Adding to their anxiety, after the May 11 hearing the SNB arrested three active participants and organizers of the protests outside the court building. The next day, they arrested one more activist and questioned some others who had been involved in the protests. It looked like the rumor of official plans to go after more people linked to the twenty-three businessmen was beginning to prove true. Any hope of a positive resolution of their trial was shattered. The pressure on the twenty-three men's supporters reached a critical level. The supporters, as I was told by the rights activist Isroil Khaydarov, who had monitored the trial, were "ready to die for their bosses."

On the night of May 12–13, in his Andijan prison cell, Atamatov and his eleven cellmates were woken up by the sound of shots and commotion in the building. Soon someone started to manipulate their door as if trying to break it open. Startled, they waited to see what would happen next. A few moments later the door opened, and they were told they were free now.

"Everyone in our building was freed; the doors to the cells were broken with iron bars. We came out; there were various people outside. One of them said: 'Those who want to can go to the regional administration building.' It was dark; I did not recognize him. He was with seven or eight other men. Many went, me included," Atamatov said.

The Andijan revolt was on.

* * *

The rebels carried no Islamist attributes; they had no beards, and there was no sign of the green Islamic flag or any banners with Arabic inscriptions. They did not look like a large group, probably about one or two hundred, and about thirty to forty of them were armed with what looked like Kalashnikovs and some lighter rifles.

Armed men manned the security line marking their territory and guarded the seized government building. At least two men were filming the protest—they could have been government agents though. Others tried to manage the crowd, from time to time calling on the chaotic and excited protesters to maintain order.

Galima, Marcus, and I approached one of the rebels, asking if we could speak to their leaders. He led us to the guards outside the administration building, behind an iron fence. Before letting us inside, they checked our journalists' IDs.

By the entrance there were armed guards sitting in chairs. Some men were sleeping on the floor in the corridor. Some rebels were making Molotov cocktails, which explained the strong smell of petrol on the premises.

We were led into an office where we were met by Kabuljon Parpiyev, who introduced himself as the "interim leader" appointed by Akrom Yuldoshev. With him there was a younger man, Sharif Shakirov. They greeted us by shaking our hands.

A forty-two-year-old, fit-looking man of average height, Parpiyev had a thick, dark moustache, and his graying hair was brushed back. He was wearing a clean, ironed light-gray shirt and dark trousers.

Shakirov was thirty-three years old. With dark brown hair, slim and taller than Parpiyev, he wore a mustard-colored leather jacket.

Parpiyev, who said he was a mechanical engineer by profession, was unarmed. Shakirov had a gun hanging on his shoulder. For militant leaders they were, perhaps, too civil and unassuming. Parpiyev said the uprising had happened spontaneously, spearheaded by the twenty-three men's relatives angered by the suspense in their trial and the new arrests made by the authorities among their supporters.

"On May 11, after the last hearing, the situation was that they were to deliver a verdict at the next hearing, but they did not give us a time and place. Everything was up in the air. That angered us," he said. "People rose up. It happened spontaneously; we just played it by ear."

First, the rebels headed to the prison. "There is a military unit by the prison; one shot was fired from there, and it triggered the whole thing. The people stormed the military unit, took weapons, and then opened the prison gates, meeting little resistance there."

Then, Parpiyev said, they headed to the SNB headquarters to free thirteen more "brothers" held there. But the SNB building was well protected, and the rebels were met with machine-gun fire. They were forced to retreat, after returning fire and throwing Molotov cocktails. At around one or two a.m., they took over the practically unguarded and empty regional administration building.

Shakirov said that the authorities later made a failed attempt to retake the building, using "many snipers, from all directions."

The rebels' guns, we were told, were "mainly trophies" seized from the military unit and prison. They estimated that about fifty people had died and around thirty more had been wounded in the unrest so far. The rebels were holding about thirty hostages, they said. "These are soldiers who fired on us,"

Shakirov explained. "They committed an inhumane deed—they shot peaceful people. One of them killed a seven-year-old child. We walked straight at him, right at his pointed gun, overpowered him, and put him facedown."

One of their main demands was Akrom Yuldoshev's release from jail. "If they do that, we will leave here; we are not going to take anything," Parpiyev told us.

Though thus unambiguously acknowledging their link to Yuldoshev—also earlier Parpiyev said he had been appointed to lead the rebellion by Yuldoshev—they both denied the existence of any organization of a religious nature created by Yuldoshev and said that Akromia was a fabrication by the authorities.

"We are just practicing devout Muslims. Everyone has the right to believe," Parpiyev said.

Who they really were, he said, was "an association of businessmen," or "economic union," with more than twenty-five thousand members. "We are middle class. We want them [the authorities] to let us do business. It is a legitimate, simple demand."

"All we wanted was a fair verdict for our businessmen who were unfairly accused of crimes," added Shakirov. "We do not demand that Karimov go. Our only aim is to improve the lives of the people. We want economic freedoms. If we cannot work [do business], we'd rather die. The Uzbek people have been turned into dirt," he said.

Parpiyev said that they had supporters in Kokand and Tashkent and were in touch with them, and there was a hope that they would join their uprising. But he also knew that the authorities were in full control of the rest of Andijan, and the rebel patch was already encircled by government troops who, backed by APCs, took positions about one kilometer around the center.

They made an attempt to negotiate with Interior Minister Zokirjon Almatov, calling him on the number given to them by their hostage, the city prosecutor Abdurakhimov. Almatov initially refused to talk to them but then changed his mind and called them back at 11:00 a.m. to hear out their demands. In a call after 2:30 p.m. he turned down all their demands and bluntly notified them that they were going to be crushed.

"He said he did not care if two, three, or four hundred people died as a result," Parpiyev said. "If they kill us, let it be. Why live like this? Why live if you have no rights? I am sick of living in Uzbekistan."

"Better to die on your feet than to live on your knees," Sharif added, using a slogan popular with communist revolutionaries. Attributed to the Mexican revolutionary Emiliano Zapata and also used by Che Guevara and others, it was an odd reminder of Sharif's Soviet background—everyone who grew up in the Soviet Union would know the phrase—and a strange thing to hear from a leader of an alleged Islamist revolt.

We went outside. I saw a string of torn pieces of cloth stretched across some sections of the regional administration compound with a handwritten sign: "Mines." I asked one of the rebels if they had really planted mines there—he only smiled.

I asked one of the rebels in the compound if I could see any of the twenty-three "brothers" they had freed. He pointed at a man sitting on the ground by the fence. It was Egamov.

Egamov, who was thirty-three, spoke in short sentences. He said he had owned a footwear factory and employed twenty-four people. "I provided for them. I helped schools, a hospital. But some did not like to see me doing well." He said after his arrest he had been tortured to confess to charges of religious extremism.

All that was behind him now. That May Day was probably the happiest in Egamov's life. It was also probably the last day of his life—in a few hours government troops would suppress the revolt, and Egamov would be among those who would never be accounted for.

After talking to Parpiyev and Sharif Shakirov we went to a guesthouse to leave our bags, dispatch our first reports, and get lunch. The guesthouse was opposite a market, which was obviously having a very slow day.

* * *

After 4:00 p.m. we were back in Babur Square. A car was burning on one edge of the square. Some rebels mounted a seized fire engine and were having a ride, with some children running and whistling behind.

I mixed with the crowd, trying to get more interviews and note more details while waiting for further developments, though without any idea of what they could be. A boy of about eighteen came up to me. After asking if I was a journalist, he offered to show me a "dead body." He led me to a charred male body lying in the street to the left of the regional administration. His clothes were burned, and it was not possible to tell if he was a policeman, soldier, or civilian.

The boy, whose name was Nuritdin, said he could show me more dead bodies. We crossed Navoi Prospect. A few moments later, an APC appeared in the distance on the road we had just crossed and sped past between us and the protesting crowd.

It was just past five o'clock.

In a few seconds, the APC was followed by a military truck with about two dozen soldiers in its open top, in full combat gear—camouflage uniforms, helmets, and bulletproof vests—poised and holding their machine guns at the ready. Boys in the crowd whistled and hurled rocks at the truck, and the soldiers opened fire.

In no time, the whole square was under a barrage of fire coming from all sides. It seemed that troops were closing in from all directions, though surely they were firing from positions taken well in advance. Like this, without warning, the government began the suppression of the Andijan revolt.

The protesters' euphoria amid burning buildings, upturned vehicles, and dead bodies; the guns in the rebels' hands; the hostages; the storming of the prison, the parading of the city prosecutor—however against the law it all was, it still made some sense. These were actions by people driven to despair by a government that systematically violated the law and their basic rights. The government onslaught—a cold indiscriminate butchery of people—in a split second threw us into insanity.

When the first shots were fired, Nuritdin and I were by the walls of School No. 30, opposite Babur Square. I at once instinctively fell to the ground. Nuritdin shielded me with his body as I, cowering by the wall, dialed the AP Moscow Bureau and, shaking and clutching my mobile phone and pressing it against my ear way too hard, began to describe what was happening. We were living a nightmare, stunned by the punishing and piercing sound of nonstop gunfire, mixed with human screams and the noise of the helicopters flying low over our heads.

Before my eyes, which, if I did not have to do reporting, I would probably not have dared open, there was a defenseless crowd under fire: children, old people, women running in all directions, not understanding that the safest thing was to lie low. A teenage boy fell to the ground a few meters from me with a bullet hole in his temple and blood trickling onto the gray asphalt—one family had just lost a son, grandson, brother. It felt like a black cloud had come and covered this small piece of land, closing it off from any light, any sense, tearing it away from normality, from anything to do with humanity.

After I was done with reporting, Nuritdin said we had to run for some cover. Doubled over, we ran around the corner. There, two young men were carrying an old man with a wound in his thigh. The old man was groaning. The young men were trying to get him to tell them his name and home number, so they could call his family.

Running for a place to hide, I, Nuritdin, and two other young men who had joined us went inside the school, entered the first door that was open, and ran upstairs, finding ourselves in a corridor with windows on one side and the classroom doors on the other. The doors were locked. We ran back downstairs and in the courtyard saw a small one-story building, which could have been a storage room or an electric generator. It looked like there was a loft in it. I don't know who saw it first and who was first to think we could use it as a hiding place, but a few moments later we were helping each other to climb in there.

It was a small loft, in which we could not even sit up, only lie on the dusty floor. There were some bricks and wooden boards inside, which we used to prop up and block the door.

We could not see what was going on in the square. The gunfire, screams, and helicopter noise continued but some distance from us. I felt utterly helpless. Nuritdin, a total stranger to me just a few minutes ago, continued to act as my bodyguard, placing himself between me and the door.

We stayed there crouched and trembling for about one hour, intently and desperately listening to the sounds outside. Suddenly the skies burst into heavy torrential rain. As the rain lashed outside, as if drawing a curtain over the horror that we had just witnessed, the sound of gunfire died down until we could hear only sporadic shots.

I stayed in touch with Galima from the start of the shooting. She and Marcus hid in a gutter when it started. A bullet tore through Galima's backpack and a notepad inside—she found out only when they got back to the guesthouse when everything calmed down.

The photographer, Efrem, had left the square a few minutes before the start of the shooting. He'd gone to the guesthouse to send his pictures—maybe it saved his life. His photographs would later become almost the only independent visual proof of the uprising and how many people it involved.

When the shooting and rain subsided, Nuritdin said we had to try to get to his place. I too thought we had to leave "the crime scene," for government forces could soon come back to mop up the area.

Across the street from the school there was a park. Nuritdin said that once we got there we would be safe and could get to his home through the park. The challenge was to cross the street—to the left was the square, which appeared to be quiet and empty now, and to the right, about one hundred meters away, there stood a police van. Holding our hands up in the air to show we were unarmed, Nuritdin and I ran across the street. Once in the park I kept thinking to myself, "Nobody's shot at us."

We reached Nuritdin's home through the rain-washed park and narrow, unlit alleys of his mahallya. It felt like the town that a couple of hours ago had been in a state of elation, taking a breath of freedom, was now back down on its knees, drenched in blood and petrified.

Nuritdin lived with his aunt's family and grandfather. No questions were asked, either about me or what happened in Babur Square. In silence, we had supper sitting on the narrow cotton-stuffed mattresses laid on the floor around a traditional low table.

The grandfather, Nuritdin's aunt, and I ate together from one small bowl—fried potatoes with two or three small pieces of meat on top. With her fork, the aunt pushed the meat to me—I was entitled to it as a guest.

After supper, half lying on pillows, the grandfather, who had a long white beard, mentioned that in 1898 in Andijan there had been another revolt "like today."

"It was against the Russian general. The rioters seized the Russian military barracks. They were frustrated peasants. They all were shot or hanged afterward," he said. "Who is going to answer for all this?" he asked about today's bloodshed.

I had to write and file a story for the AP. My laptop was at the hotel, and Nuritdin had no computer. He said he would take me to an internet café in their mahallya. We walked to the café through dark alleys to find it closed.

But in an Uzbek mahallya everyone knows everyone, and it is normal to show up at a neighbor's door when you need help. Nuritdin and I headed to the internet café owner's home.

He agreed to come with us and open his café for us. Without any agreement, we were all whispering to each other. The internet café was a tiny room, about two by three meters, with two old desktop computers, which were very slow to start. There was no internet connection. But at least I could type up my story as a WordPad document. We did not turn on the light as a precaution.

As I sat there in darkness, describing the protest and the shooting, someone knocked on the door. Nuritdin and the café owner carefully opened the door. There was a young man there, asking if he could come in and have some water. He was covered with blood and mud and in a state of shock. He said he had been in the square when the shooting began and survived by pretending to be dead as he lay among dead bodies.

I dictated my story on the phone to the news editor in Moscow, Judith Ingram, and we went back to Nuritdin's.

*   *   *

Sounds of sporadic fire could be heard till early morning, as I tried to get some sleep on a mattress thrown onto the floor in one room with Nuritdin's sister-in-law and her children.

As darkness fell away, like from another reality, another world, I heard a call for the morning prayer. The voice of the muezzin ringing over Andijan's mahallyas, over the dead lying on the streets drenched in blood, sounded so poignantly mournful and so utterly timely and relevant. For breakfast we had bread and tea, sitting on a *chor poya*—a large low, usually wooden, outdoor bed—in the courtyard.

As I was finishing my bowl of tea, Nuritdin polished his black shoes. He was dressed up, wearing a clean white shirt and dark trousers; his hair was oiled and neatly combed. He looked purposeful and serious as if preparing himself for an important day.

Watching him polish his shoes, his aunt gently joked, "Look at yourself! You are like a real hero."

I wanted to go back to the square and see the aftermath. Nuritdin was determined to accompany me. In the mahallya there were people in twos and threes out in the streets, probably sharing what they knew or heard of the previous night's events. They stopped their quiet conversations as we approached.

On Cholpon Prospect, despite the evening rain, there were large pools of blood and pieces of scattered yellow-gray human brain, lost shoes, flip-flops and sandals of various sizes, and many empty missile and bullet shells. As we got closer to the square, I began to notice dead bodies—all men, with gunshot wounds, lying on the edge of the street or in the gutter along it.

Apart from me and Nuritdin, there were several people, mostly young men, wandering around: some looking for their friends or relatives, others, apparently, there in protest and anger. When they found out that I was a journalist, they shouted questions at me, "Why did they do this? Why did they kill children and women? Why did they shoot their own people?"

A man said he was looking for his friend named Akhmed, who had left home yesterday to go to the maternity hospital to see his wife and never returned. Another said his neighbor had lost his eldest son, a seventeen-year-old. A woman, whose name was Khalida, said that the soldiers had shot people even when they had raised their hands in a gesture of surrender. She said the rebels "had stood up for the people." Another man said that about seventy people had died on the spot where we were standing, and later the bodies were taken away in a ZIL bus.

They took me to a courtyard off the street to show me about five corpses covered with white cotton fabric. All were men. The heads on some corpses were smashed as if having taken a hit from a big missile. They said that I was late, that soldiers had been there before dawn collecting dead bodies, loading them onto trucks and taking them away; that the soldiers took care to first remove children's and women's bodies; that the women's bodies were stripped of jewelry.

We reached Babur Square. All the way there and in the square itself there was no sign of police or military. The regional government building stood abandoned.

On the marble platform of the Babur monument that the day before had served as a free tribune, there now lay about a dozen dead bodies wrapped in white fabric. I kept a body count on the way to the square. Altogether, including the bodies in the square, I counted twenty-three dead.

A young man was weeping aloud over the dead. "There is no justice for common people. The terrorists are our government. Why did they kill their own people? Our women, children! They were unarmed!" he said, beating his chest with a fist. His name was Daniyar Akbarov, an Andijan jail inmate who had been doing time for murder until the storming of the prison by Akromia rebels.

Amid my interviews in the square I received a call from Galima, who said that they had been held by security officers and told to leave the city within thirty minutes, or else the authorities could not guarantee our security. It sounded like a veiled threat—they could do anything they wanted to us and then blame it on the rioters. I consulted AP editors in Moscow, and they advised that Efrem and I should leave Andijan.

On the way to the guesthouse, Nuritdin and I stumbled onto two or three government security positions that they had set up in the shaded

Figure 6.1. Bodies of protesters killed by government troops laid in Andijan's central Babur Square, May 14, 2005. © Denis Sinyakov.

neighborhoods around Babur Square. There would be a tank or an APC with two or three soldiers crouching or standing by the walls of the traditional whitewashed Uzbek houses with their hands on the guns across their chests. We would instinctively slow down and raise our hands in the air while passing under their cold gaze.

At the guesthouse, we packed up and headed to Fergana. The policemen at the security point on the edge of Andijan carefully studied our IDs and copied the information, our names and the media organizations we worked for, into their logbook.

On the other side, a few dozen meters from the Andijan town border, we saw a car with a Reuters news agency crew, who had just attempted to enter the town but been turned back. The city was already sealed off—the regime was back in control and at liberty to do to its residents anything it wanted, away from the prying eyes of the world outside.

In the next few months the Uzbek government would move to force foreign reporters out of the country and close down foreign aid groups' offices. Furious at US officials' criticism of the regime's response to the Andijan revolt, President Karimov would also close down at very short notice the US air base in the south, near the country's border with Afghanistan.

* * *

The Andijan unrest was the first ever popular revolt against President Karimov's government—and the only one during his twenty-six-year rule. As it has emerged from witness accounts and reports by human rights groups, the regime prepared its suppression plan well. Whoever mastermined it obviously treated all those gathered in Babur Square—the armed rebels, their hostages and unarmed supporters, rights defenders, journalists, and simple onlookers, including elderly people, women, and children—as one legitimate target, "terrorists," as they would say later.

As if warming up for the main onslaught planned for later, during the day troops periodically drove by Babur Square in APCs or military trucks, firing randomly into the crowd, every time leaving some dead and wounded. The first drive-by shooting was at around six or seven in the morning. At the time the three- or four-hundred-strong crowd was mainly made up of the rebels, who were involved in the prison attack and other overnight skirmishes, and released prisoners.

At around ten in the morning another APC drove by and fired on the crowd of protesters, which by then had grown by a few hundred more people and included women and children. This attack killed ten to twelve people, including a young boy and a woman, according to various witnesses.

"One five-year-old boy was running in the street. A soldier shot him from a truck. His mother ran to him; she was shot too," a witness said.

At around noon government forces fired on them again from an APC and killed ten to fifteen people. In about two hours there was another similar shooting. The wounded had initially been taken to hospitals, but later, when the square was encircled by government troops, they were taken inside the regional government building and given first aid by medics from among the protesters.

Meanwhile, government snipers were taking positions above the square, and troops were being pulled up to the town center. A journalist saw "a column of military vehicles," consisting of four heavy military trucks and ten jeeps, going up central Navoi Prospect. "Inside were men armed with automatic guns pointed at people," the journalist told Human Rights Watch. By the regional police headquarters there was "a huge number of policemen, fully armed and in bullet-proof vests."

The bulk of the forces were used to block off approaches to Babur Square. By around four in the afternoon the square was effectively sealed off. The protesters were left one corridor to leave by, along the town's main Cholpon Prospect.

It would become clear later that the idea was to drive them like a herd of sheep into a trap, a butchery zone. Concealed behind a barricade of three buses and at least two APCs, a squad of soldiers entrenched behind stacks of sandbags and snipers on the roofs of the buildings and trees around were poised to open fire. The people would have no choice but to run right at their guns.

As I witnessed myself, the revolt crackdown plan was set in motion shortly after five p.m., with an APC and a military truck speeding past the square and opening fire on the crowd. At the same time other troops moved in from behind the regional administration building and side streets, pushing the people toward Cholpon Prospect.

There are no accounts of the rebels trying to return fire.

When the first wave of shooting subsided, leaving about twenty dead and an unknown number of wounded, the people in the square led by the rebels divided into two groups and, placing their hostages in front of themselves, moved into Cholpon Prospect. The first group was made up of about three hundred people, mostly men, with a large number of hostages in the first row. They held up pieces of white cloth in a sign of surrender.

The Andijan rights defender Lutfullo Shamsutdinov was following the first group on his bike and watched how they were literally mowed down as they ran into the ambush awaiting them on Cholpon Prospect by the Technical Construction College and School No. 15. He said the troops opened fire as soon as the crowd got closer to them. "The fire was coming from two APCs. The soldiers lying on the ground fired from machine guns."

The people fell to the ground, and "the bullets were swooshing over their heads, coming down like rain. . . . Some three hundred people died before my eyes."

One survivor said that as he lay on the ground, he could feel how everyone's bodies were shaking with fear under the piercing metallic noise of gunfire. "The military fired at us for about fifteen minutes nonstop, then shot at those who stirred or showed any sign of life," he said. "Some tried to scream; mostly they were requests to stop firing, and others cried for help. I heard a child's voice which cried, 'Mummy!'" the man said.

Another man from the first group who survived by hiding behind a tree said he saw how a man's head "split in two, the way a watermelon splits in half," after being hit by two bullets.

The second, a considerably larger crowd of people fleeing Babur Square, included many women, children, and old men, whom the men put in the middle to shield from bullets. They too had a few hostages in front of them. The gap between the two groups was about five hundred meters, or ten to fifteen minutes' walking time. They came under persistent fire in the ambush zone but suffered fewer losses.

"They would fire on us; we would fall to the ground. When the shooting stopped, we would get up and walk on, leaving the dead behind like lost shoes. They would fire again; we would fall to the ground again and wait until the firing stopped and then get up and walk again, leaving more dead behind," one survivor said, describing to me their passage through the ambush zone.

The human rights activist Shamsutdinov said that the hostages, including Prosecutor Abdurakhimov, were "the first to be killed by the soldiers" because they were in the first rows. The Human Rights Watch report said all but four of the hostages were killed in the government crackdown. Obviously the authorities never even considered saving the hostages.

About six hundred people, including about one hundred fifty women and twenty children, survived the Cholpon Prospect ambush and walked throughout the night toward the border with Kyrgyzstan. In the border village of Teshiktosh, which they reached by about six in the morning, they ran into another military ambush, which left another seven dead. The others managed to cross the border.

* * *

With the revolt put down, the authorities had a lot to cover up and many people to punish for their involvement. The authorities' immediate job was to deal with the injured and dead in Babur Square and Cholpon Prospect.

No ambulances came for the wounded. Some were collected by relatives, but many were finished off by soldiers, according to many witnesses. A survivor of the Cholpon slaughter who hid in the technical college that night saw two APCs "driving right over the corpses lying in the road," lighting the road with their headlights.

Another survivor, Rustam, who hid in the same college, saw five heavy KamAZ trucks and a bus with soldiers arrive at the scene at around five a.m.

"The soldiers would ask the wounded, 'Where are the rest of you?' When they responded, they would shoot them dead and load them into the trucks. There were no ambulances there. . . . The soldiers were clearing the [area of] bodies for two hours, but they left about fifteen bodies where they lay."

The authorities' postrevolt reprisal operation was codenamed "Filtering." Its purpose was to identify and capture the rebels and their supporters and silence the witnesses.

Isolated shooting could be heard in Andijan till the evening of May 16 as part of official "mopping up" raids, the human rights activist Shamsutdinov said. The exit roads were blocked to stop any more people from fleeing to Kyrgyzstan. Sweeping arrests were immediately made in the Bogi Shamol neighborhood, indicating that many of the rebels and their families lived close together.

The security service took over control of the town hospitals. All those wounded in the unrest were treated as "terrorists" or their accomplices and moved to the Regional Emergency Hospital, which was turned into a detention facility. In the next few days, in this heavily guarded hospital the wounded were interrogated and tortured, and some of them were executed without trial, according to witness accounts. A worker from one of the hospitals told Human Rights Watch that when he came to work on May 14, he was told to "go home and rest." When he returned two days later, all those wounded in the unrest were gone.

Valijon Babajanov went outside on the morning of May 14 looking for his missing mother, two sisters, and a sister-in-law, who were among the crowd of protesters in Babur Square when the shooting began. Having not found them dead or alive, either in the square or on Cholpon Prospect, he went to the city morgue.

"I saw very horrible dead bodies; one had half of his head missing; nobody could identify them. They were all without clothes. There were rows and rows of dead bodies. There was a terrible stench."

Those arrested faced inevitable abuse and torture, which some would not survive. "Someone was arrested in Cholpon Bazar, and three days later they returned his dead body," the human rights activist Isroil Khaydarov told me in a conversation in Kyrgyzstan a few months later.

One of the men detained in the postcrackdown sweeps said he and several others had been made to strip naked and were beaten with rubber truncheons by stocky men in military uniforms. "They ordered us not to look

Код формы по ОКУД 5103835 2

Министерство здравоохранения СССР

Наименование учреждения Обл. отд. суд. мед. Андижанской об.

Медицинская документация
Форма № 106/у-84
Утверждена Минздравом СССР 19.11.84 №1130

ВРАЧЕБНОЕ СВИДЕТЕЛЬСТВО О СМЕРТИ № 208

(окончательное, предварительное, в замен предварительного № ___)

Дата выдачи « 15 » мая 2005

Место для

1. Фамилия, имя, отчество умершего Умаров Бобирджон Тахирджанович

2 — 2. Пол: муж—1 жен—2 (подчеркнуть)

3 — 3. Дата рождения: год 1974 месяц июнь число 16

4 — 4. Дата смерти: год 2005 месяц мая число 13

5 — 5. Для детей умерших в возрасте от 6 дн. до 1 мес.: доношенный—1; недоношенный 2 (подчерк.)

6 — 6. Для детей, умерших в возрасте от 6 дн. до 1 года: масса (вес) при рождении ___ граммов

7 — 7. Место постоянного жительства умершего: область (край) республика Узб. Рес.
Анд. район
город—1, село—2 (подчеркнуть) Андижан (вписать)
ул. Сайхоб дом 62

8 — 8. Место смерти: а) область (край), республика Узб. Рес. Андиж.
район ___ город (село) Андижан

8б — б) смерть последовала: в стационаре—1, дома—2, в др. месте—3 (подчеркнуть)
на улице
(вписать где)

9 — 9. Смерть произошла от: заболевания—1, несчастного случая вне производства—2, несчастного случая в связи с производством—3; убийства—4; самоубийства—5; род смерти не установлен—6;

10 — 10. Причина смерти установлена: врачом; только установившим смерть—1; врачом, лечившим умершего—2 патологоанатомом—3; судебно медицинским экспертом—4 (подчеркнуть)

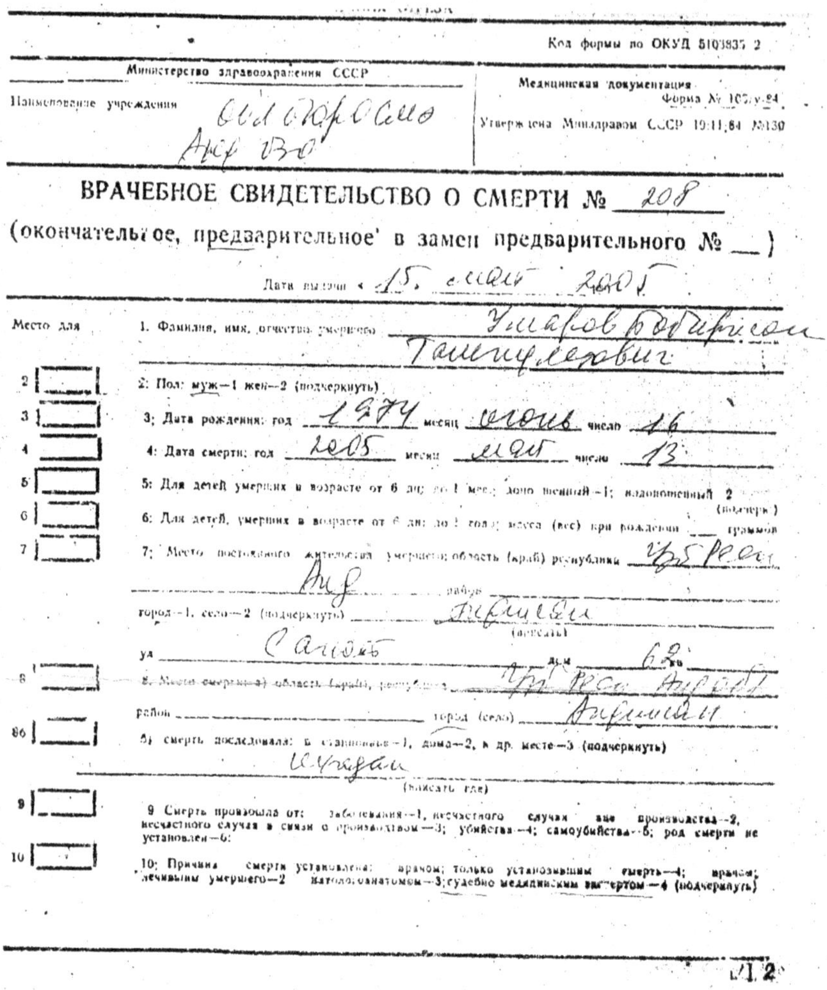

Figures 6.2 and 6.3. A scanned copy of death certificate no. 208, issued by the Andijan Regional Forensic Medical Examination Office on May 15, 2005, for Bobirjon Umarov, born June 16, 1974. According to the document, he died on May 13, 2005, from a gunshot wound in the pelvis area. Copies of a total of seven similar death certificates were given to me by Andijan human rights activists after the uprising.

11. Я, -врач _____ *Темерове ии* должность *Суд*

Ф. И. О.

удостоверяю, что на основании: осмотра трупа — 1, записей леч его врача в медицинской документации — 2, предшествующего наблюдения — 3, вскрытия — 4 (подчеркнуть нужное) и делена последовательность патологических процессов (состояний), приведших к смерти, и установлена следующая причина смерти:

I. Непосредственная причина смерти a) _____
(заболевание или осложнение основного заболевания)

заболевание, вызвавшее или обусловившее непосредственную причину смерти (основное (первоначальное) заболевание указывается последним) б) _____

в) _____

II. Другие важные заболевания способствовавшие смертельному исходу, но не связанные с заболеванием или его осложнением, послужившим непосредственной причиной смерти

_____

_____

_____

12. В случае смерти от несчастного случая; отравления или травмы; а) дата травмы (отравления)

год _____ месяц _____ число _____

д) при несчастных случаях, не связанных с производством указать вид травмы: бытовая — 1, уличная (кроме транспортной) — 2, дорожно-транспортная—3, школьная—4, спортивная—5, прочие—6 (подчеркнуть)

в) место и обстоятельства, при которых произошла травма (отравление)

_____

_____

13 Врачебное свидетельство выдано: наименование медицинского учреждения *ОЗ*
бюро Суд Экс Во

_____ врач выд _____ свидетельство о смерти _____

14. Врачебное свидетельство провер органах загс врачом, ответственным за правильность заполнения врачебных свидетельств о смерти.

_____ 199 г. Подпись _____

Figures 6.2 and 6.3. (*Continued*)

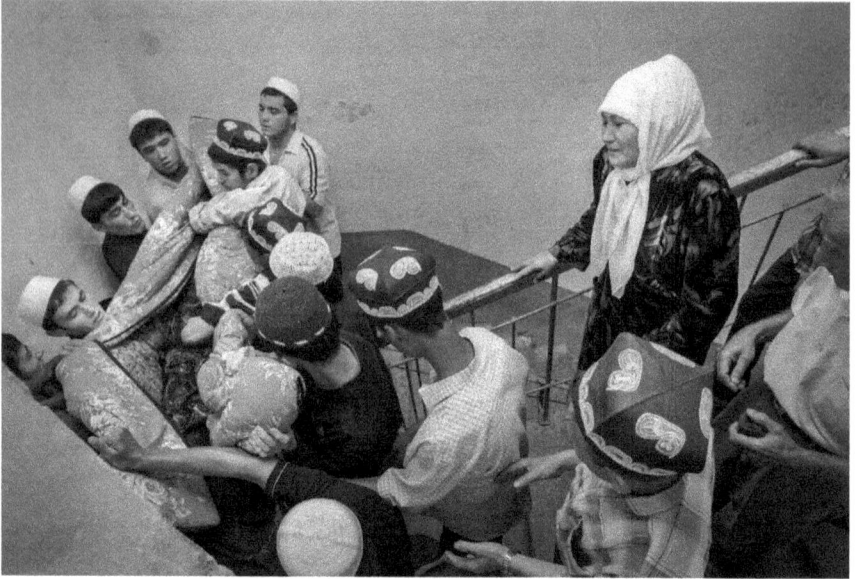

Figure 6.4. Family members carry for burial the body of an Andijan resident killed by government troops in suppressing the May 13, 2005, uprising. © Denis Sinyakov.

up, but just to look down at the floor. We stood there naked, and they took turns to kick us and beat us with truncheons. They would put guns to our heads and threaten to shoot."

Witnesses said busloads of suspects would be regularly brought to the Andijan police and security-service headquarters for several days after the suppression of the revolt, and their basements and warehouses would be overfilled with them. Some detainees were kept in prison trucks, twenty people in each, because there weren't enough cells to put them in. There were not enough handcuffs for all the detainees, and they would instead use the shoelaces from the detainees' own shoes.

At least twenty-five people did not survive the interrogations. Their bodies were returned to their families with bruises, cuts, and stab or bullet wounds and missing nails or sexual organs. One such victim was a woman who had been wounded on May 14 and, while in hospital, pressured to testify that her son was one of the terrorists behind the revolt. She told her family that all the wounded had been given two choices: to die a painful death or testify against their relatives. Her body was returned to the family on July 22 showing signs of violent death, including bleeding around her mouth.

Figure 6.5. A woman grieves by fresh graves of those killed in the Andijan violence, May 2005. © Denis Sinyakov.

Khaydarov and other activists went around to the homes where there had been deaths to express condolences and make a list of the dead, but the people would not talk to them fearing official reprisals. The grave digger Juraboy Abdullayev, who was involved in burying the crackdown victims, was a nephew of Khaydarov's friend. He told Khaydarov that the grave diggers were ordered to put two bodies in each grave in a burial site in Bogi Shamol. The graves were marked only with numbers.

"He was afraid to say how many [they had buried] because they [the grave diggers] had been given instructions by the SNB [not to speak to anyone]. But he did speak to us, and the next day he was stabbed to death by unknown people," Khaydarov said.

Khaydarov himself had been summoned to the SNB every day and warned that if he spoke to anybody about the May 13 events, he would go to jail. He eventually fled to Kyrgyzstan, where in October 2005 I met him in the city of Osh.

"You cannot imagine how scared I am," he told me. He disappeared soon after our meeting, and his fate remains unknown.

The authorities said 189 people died in the May 12–13 violence, and most of them were armed "terrorists."

According to the report "Andijan Refugees Speak Out" published in 2010 by survivors who are now living in various Western countries as refugees, about four hundred were killed in the Cholpon Prospect ambush alone. It said around a hundred more died in Babur Square or other skirmishes or were tortured to death in the postrevolt mop-up.

According to Human Rights Watch, as many as 245 people were given prison terms ranging from five to twenty-one years between September 2005 and January 2006 for their alleged roles in the Andijan uprising. Among them was the rebel leader Parpiyev, who had survived the crackdown and fled to Kazakhstan but was captured several months later and handed over to the Uzbek authorities. His and most of the other trials connected to the Andijan unrest were behind closed doors.

The second leader, Sharif Shakirov, was killed on Cholpon Prospect—heavy artillery fire hit him in the chest and tore off his arm.

Notes

The chapter is based on the author's personal account; author interviews with Andijan refugees in a camp and elsewhere in Kyrgyzstan, May–June and October 2005; International Crisis Group, "Uzbekistan: The Andijon Uprising," Asia Briefing no. 38, May 25, 2005, https://d2071andvipowj.cloudfront.net/b38-uzbekistan-the-andijon-uprising.pdf; Human Rights Watch, "Bullets Were Falling Like Rain: The Andijan Massacre May 13, 2005," 17-5(D), June 2005, https://www.hrw.org/report/2005/06/06/bullets-were-falling-rain/andijan-massacre-may-13-2005; Human Rights Society of Uzbekistan, "Andijan Refugees Speak Out," special report, November 2010, http://en.hrsu.org/archives/836.

7

THE ROAD TO UPRISING

IN AN INTERVIEW IN THE SEIZED GOVERNMENT BUILDING on May 13, 2005, the Andijan revolt leader Kabuljon Parpiyev said that they were "an association of businessmen" with twenty-five thousand members, and one of their main demands was freedom for Akrom Yuldoshev; according to the government, it was the jailed Yuldoshev who commanded the revolt from his prison cell. Our conversation in the tense atmosphere of a violent uprising was brief, and I did not ask Parpiyev for more details about what he described as an "association" and its connection to Yuldoshev.

After the uprising had been put down, the protesters who escaped Uzbekistan all unanimously denied the existence of any kind of group of which they could have been members and which could have organized the revolt. In my many interviews with them in the UN refugee camp in Kyrgyzstan—on a narrow patch of land hidden between two hills just a few hundred meters from the Uzbek border—they all stuck to the line that they had come to Babur Square after hearing about a popular demonstration going on there and that President Karimov was expected to come and speak to them. They kept saying that they were ordinary businessmen, craftsmen. "Look, I've made these shoes myself," one of them said, pointing at the shoes on his feet. "They are excellent quality. Can you see? I am a shoemaker; I am not a terrorist."

Among the refugees was Yuldoshev's wife, Yodgoroy, as well as his daughter and a sister. Yodgoroy too said to me that she had joined the protest by accident and denied that her husband had created any organization or had any involvement in the revolt.

Their defensive narrative was understandable. They were shocked and subdued by the government's cold-blooded execution of their family members, friends, and neighbors. The government was accusing them of being

ГОВОРЯТ ПОСТРАДАВШИЕ И СВИДЕТЕЛИ

В Ташкенте продолжается судебный процесс над 15 особо активными участниками андижанских событий, обвиняемых в совершении террористических актов и других особо тяжких преступлений. Суд продолжает заслушивать показания потерпевших и свидетелей.

Ранее мы сообщали о том, что суд уже заслушал показания пострадавших, и слово предоставлено свидетелям. Но оказалось, что приглашенных в Верховный суд и желающих дать свои показания много больше. И поэтому на процессе наряду со свидетелями продолжают выступать пострадавшие. В их числе люди, исполнявшие свой долг по охране правопорядка и просто обычные граждане, волею случая оказавшиеся в водовороте трагических событий.

Еще 10 мая сотрудник милиции Хуснитдин Мирзаев в ходе проверки паспортного режима обнаружил в Андижане непрошеных гостей. Его жестоко избили, но ему удалось бежать. В числе заложников были сантехник, работавший в хокимияте Ш.Раимжонов, и военнослужащий К. Хакимов.

16-летняя Зиеда Муминова 12 мая вечером поздно возвращалась с базара на "Дамасе" через центр города. Но машину остановили, людей высадили. Дальше пришлось идти пешком. Она увидела пылающее здание театра. Затем толпа вынесла ее на площадь. Вооруженные люди стреляли в воздух. Не понимая, что происходит, она в испуге шла с людьми. Зиеда попыталась уйти, но в этот момент шальная пуля ранила в руку.

Какая-то сердобольная женщина сказала: "Не пытайся сейчас отсюда уходить, тебя могут застрелить. Видишь, что делается".

На следующий день к вечеру девушка вместе с толпой наконец покинула площадь. С этими людьми она прошла почти 40 километров до границы с Киргизией.

Муминова подтверждает, что их не преследовали военные, в них не стреляла милиция. У самой границы некоторые из женщин решили повернуть назад, вот тогда и раздались выстрелы. Стреляли те, кто сопровождал их с оружием в руках. Ей удалось бежать, но она вновь была ранена.

Военнослужащие из Ферганы Дильмурад Абдужабаров и Икбол Мадрахимов рассказывают, что по тревоге их перебросили в Андижан.

— До последнего момента мы думали, что это учебная тревога, — говорит И.Мадрахимов. - И только увидев возле ворот воинской части несколько погибших людей, поняли, что произошло чрезвычайное происшествие.

Военных, прибывших из Ферганы, направили сформировать блокпост на одной из улиц Андижана, который впоследствии оказался на пути тех, кто уходил с площади.

— Когда колонна людей приблизилась к нашему посту, к ним навстречу без оружия вышел капитан Джураев и объявил, что есть приказ открыть коридор и все могут уйти, только нужно оставить оружие, - вспоминает Д. Абдужабаров. - В ответ раздался выстрел, Джураев упал. Затем почти двадцать минут нас непрерывно обстреливали.

По словам Д.Абдужабарова, военных пытались окружить, бросили в них гранату, осколками которой были ранены несколько солдат. Тогда же против них них был применен слезоточивый газ.

— На какое-то время нас буквально парализовало. Я запросил по рации помощь, - говорит офицер.

Подоспевший бронетранспортер подобрал раненых, но капитана Джураева до медицинской части живым не довезли.

Ситуацию возле блокпоста дополняет И.Мадрахимов: "Нам поставили задачу обеспечить защиту населения, не допустить захвата заложников, без команды не стрелять".

По его словам, в бинокль было видно, что впереди колонны шли связанные сотрудники милиции, за ними женщины и дети. В этой толпе скрывались вооруженные люди.

Судьи задают ему уточняющие вопросы.

— Вы стреляли в людей?

— Первые 20 минут мы не могли поднять голову. Затем начали прицельно стрелять по вооруженным людям.

— С вами был бронетранспортер, затем подошел еще один БТР. Велась ли стрельба из этой техники?

— Нет, из БТРов огонь не велся. Одна машина пришла только за тем, чтобы забрать раненых...

Процесс в Верховном суде продолжается.

Б.Мадаминов.

ПРАВДА ВОСТОКА

7 октября 2005 года

Figure 7.1. A scanned article from the official Uzbek Russian-language newspaper *Pravda Vostoka* (Truth of the East) published on October 7, 2005. The article entitled "Testimonies of victims and witnesses" covers the trail of those accused of staging the May 13, 2005, Andijan revolt. According to the article, all the shooting was done by the rebels.

terrorists and pressuring Kyrgyzstan to hand them over. (The Kyrgyz authorities would give in and hand several of them back in breach of international conventions.)

In 2006, in my quest to get to the bottom of the story of the Andijan revolt, I had another meeting with Yodgoroy, who by then had ended up in Boise, in the US state of Idaho, with a group of other Andijan refugees. I stayed for two nights with her and about a dozen other women, all of whom were living in a single flat. They had never left Uzbekistan before and probably had never even imagined traveling abroad. Now they were my hosts in this northwestern US state famous for its potatoes, thousands of miles away from home.

The reception they gave me exceeded even the lavish conventions of Central Asian hospitality. It seemed every woman in the house had made some dish or dessert to treat me to, and the table was bursting with food. They staged a concert for me, taking turns to dance or sing. They even included a patriotic song about Uzbekistan and a belly dance (with their bodies fully covered). I watched it all sitting on the sofa with Yodgoroy, smiling and clapping to show appreciation but feeling terribly embarrassed by this private entertainment as if I was some kind of royalty or slave owner.

They told me that they had given a similar performance for a US diplomat visiting them in their temporary refugee camp in Timisoara, in western Romania, where more than five hundred of them had been taken by the UN from Kyrgyzstan before permanent asylum was found for them in various countries. They had also given the US diplomat a surprise welcome by lining up in a corridor and bursting into a storm of applause the moment he opened the door and entered. It gave him a fright. "He probably thought that he had entered a house full of terrorists!" the women told me, laughing.

They took me to the local zoo. Our group, with my Andijan hosts in their long dresses and headscarves, attracted curious looks from other zoo visitors, to which they responded by smiling and loudly saying, "Ha-a-allo!"

The VIP reception they gave me, the concert and other hospitality, was an attempt to show me that they were normal people, not religious zombies. They were a sad, lost group of women, like fish out of water, abruptly taken out of their homes, away from their families and everyday chores and worries, and placed in a completely alien environment. They all badly wanted to go back.

"We have left our hearts there," one of them, Nailya, said to me. Her children, aged two and four, were back in Uzbekistan, and she wanted nothing but to be reunited with them. By then she had been separated from them for a year and a half. "For a mother, it is terrible to be parted from her children. It is a punishment." She said she knew "the real situation" back home, meaning the possibility of being prosecuted for rebelling, but, "despite everything, we want to go back."

"Why didn't I live with my mouth shut? Why did I go out [to protest]? Who has ever given Uzbek women the right to go out and speak out?" she said. Nailya said she joined the protest because her husband had. He was now in jail.

It was obvious that Yodgoroy was the boss—nothing in this all-female household could be done without her nod of approval. I shared a small bedroom with her, and as we prepared to go to bed, she told me about her husband, how exceptionally bright, good-hearted, and religious he was. She explained how he had courted her before they got married—she was teaching at a school, and Yuldoshev, a jealous suitor, would disrupt her classes by knocking on the door and demanding she come out for a word. But again, Yodgoroy denied that her husband ever created any kind of organization.

However, while in the United States I also met another Andijan refugee who had broken away from Yodgoroy and the rest of them. She said she had done so because there was too much control over her private life. She wanted to get her son, whom she had left behind in Uzbekistan, to the States, but Yodgoroy would not let her.

She was the second Andijan protester, after the revolt leader Parpiyev, to say to me that they were members of some kind of organization. The word she used to describe it was "sect." She said the members could only marry among themselves, but she stopped short of giving me any more details, even anonymously. Some of her family members were still with the group, and she did not want to cause them trouble.

A few years later I got in touch with her again, and she agreed to tell me all she knew about the group. She offered to write down for me her own story as a member of the sect, starting with how she had joined it. Several months later I called her to ask if she was making any progress. She said she had been busy but still wanted to write. More months went by, but there was still no word from her. We spoke again once or twice more. She seemed to have real health- and family-related reasons for the lack of progress with writing and asked for more time. But more and more months went by, and nothing ever came from her, and she stopped answering my calls and emails.

One person who has helped me to take a look inside the closed world of Yuldoshev's organization was Hotam Hojimatov. An ethnic Uzbek from the city of Osh in the Kyrgyz part of the Fergana Valley, he used to do business with the sect's members and had personal contacts with their leaders. He later left for Russia and was given Russian citizenship.

He was running a human rights group in the Russian city of Ivanovo helping Uzbeks fleeing persecution at home when, a month after the Andijan revolt, he was arrested at the request of the Uzbek authorities for alleged involvement in the unrest—which he denies. He was released under pressure from rights groups and left Russia for Europe, where he now lives as a refugee.[1]

From there he has shared with me what he knows about the Birodarlar, or "brothers." That information has been confirmed and expanded by another Uzbek dissident, who for some time was close to the group, though never a member. He spoke to me on the condition that I not use his name.

*   *   *

As a young man, Akrom Yuldoshev rode along Andijan's tree-lined streets on his bike and dreamed about a just world. Intellectually a cut above his peers, he was good at mathematics, but his most passionate interests were history and philosophy as he pursued a formula for human happiness. When studying at the Andijan Cotton Growing Institute, he regularly challenged lecturers on philosophical issues, won victories in philosophical contests, and waged a personal campaign against bribe taking among lecturers. Those were Soviet times still, and the main philosophy taught and propagated was Marx's communism, with its promise of a fair and frictionless economic and social order without rich and poor. Yuldoshev was a keen believer in this, leading his school's communist youth league Komsomol and planning to join the Communist Party.

At the start of perestroika in 1986, Yuldoshev was twenty-three years old. With a young man's enthusiasm, he started to study the mushrooming new ideologies that were offering their own solutions to humankind's miseries. The first teaching that Yuldoshev got interested in was that of the Hizb ut-Tahrir party. Its recruiters had approached him themselves, singling him out for his leadership qualities and charisma, and he became a member. Yuldoshev, however, soon became disillusioned with Hizb ut-Tahrir and left around 1992 with a group of associates. At the same time, he studied and discarded Wahhabism—another popular teaching at the time—and concluded that none of the new ideologies on offer were any good.

He thought he had his own vision of how to build a new, fair society. With that in mind he and several associates bought plots in Andijan's Bogi Shamol area, starting what later would become a large community tightly bound by Yuldoshev's ideas, as well as economic and family ties. They would call themselves Birodarlar, the plural for "brother" in Uzbek.

Many in Andijan had laughed at Yuldoshev's idea of creating his own teaching. But public skepticism did not dampen his determination, and he got on with his independent study of the Koran so that he could understand Islam without any middlemen. He did not speak Arabic and read the Koran in its Uzbek translation by Alouddin Mansur, a theologian from the Kyrgyz town of Kara Suu, on the border with Uzbekistan.

Mansur did the translation in 1992, calling it *Quroni Karim Izohli Tarjimalari* (Translation and interpretations of the Koran). He was known for his anti–Hizb ut-Tahrir stance and was distrusted by many believers in the valley for his alleged cooperation with the Kyrgyz and Uzbek authorities in their hunt for religious dissidents.[2]

The reading of Mansur's interpretation of the Koran "fundamentally changed Akrom Yuldoshev's life," according to Hojimatov. It inspired Yuldoshev to work out his own utopia, whose ideological foundation he laid down in his pamphlet "A Path to the Faith." The pamphlet was about "how to live so there are no divorces, courts, crime, or joblessness," Yuldoshev's sister told me in a conversation a few weeks after the Andijan revolt. He concluded from his study of the Koran that Muslims were unhappy despite having "such a good religion" because they did not understand it "correctly," his sister said.

"The Koran can be understood only by intelligent people," Yuldoshev concluded, and he "decided to devote himself to helping people" understand it.

Any trained Islamic cleric would have looked down on Yuldoshev's attempt to teach Islam to others without knowing Arabic and having no formal training himself. But Yuldoshev believed his understanding of the Koranic messages was right.

His pamphlet, written between 1992 and 1994, according to various sources, and *Quroni Karim* would become his followers' two main textbooks. The fourteen-page pamphlet, which I've read in Russian translation, starts off with the explanation that man has material, social, spiritual, and physical/biological needs. But the spiritual needs are the most important, and only through satisfying them can people solve their material and social problems. The pamphlet is available on the internet, posted by a lawyer who defended the twenty-three Andijan businessmen linked to Yuldoshev. It says that Allah, through the Koran, shows "a path to happiness" and a solution to people's "material and moral sufferings." That path is religion, he says, and "today the religion of truth is Islam," "a perfect religion." He says that some people "stray off the path" and follow "mistaken" beliefs. "One group holds on to the laws of the mosque, another strongly insists on the laws of the state, a third group gives supremacy to the laws of science, and yet others confine themselves solely to prayer lessons. Yes, each group claims it is on the right path. Of course, they are not responsible for each other's mistakes. But there is only one truth!"

The pamphlet also calls for unity among "dear brother Muslims" and says they all should "beg Allah to free us from the anger that we hold against one another." It says, "Let us unite. If we do so, we will restore Islam, and it will reach its perfection." The pamphlet, which is written like an abstract essay, does not say how that unification would or should happen nor how Islam can be "restored" nor what exactly is meant by the "perfection" of Islam, which seems to be the core and goal of his ideology.

The historian Adeeb Khalid in his book *Islam after Communism* describes the pamphlet as "a discourse on religion and spirituality," "a call for individuals to take responsibility for their own actions in light of a faith derived primarily from the Koran and hadith." Khalid concludes that it is "clearly the work of an autodidact innocent of traditional Islamic learning." He finds "not one word" about plans to seize power.[3]

* * *

Having started off as a group of about a dozen people, the Birodarlar expanded slowly but surely, to a great extent thanks to Yuldoshev's charisma, eloquence, and seeming learnedness.

"You would not get bored talking with him for hours. He would support his arguments citing suras from the Koran, as translated in *Quroni Karim*. He would tell you the exact page each sura was on. . . . You would get the impression that he knew the Koran very well. He would also give you examples from math, physics, and other natural sciences," Hojimatov said.

The Birodarlar ranks were boosted by the disappearance in 1995 of the prominent Andijan imam Abduvali qori Mirzayev, according to Hojimatov. Mirzayev was a formidable authority among the Fergana Valley Muslims, and his disappearance left many of his followers feeling lost and disorientated. There was also a sense of chilling fear among his students and sympathizers, as nobody doubted that he had been abducted by the authorities. Yuldoshev's group, which was only just emerging and therefore not yet targeted by the authorities, presented itself as an appealing alternative.

Yuldoshev remained influenced by Marxism in creating his own utopia. Apparently still loyal to the central idea of Marx's philosophy that relations between human beings are defined by the way they produce and redistribute food and other material values, Yuldoshev completed his own ideology with an economic model—something missing in the Hizb ut-Tahir ideology.

Hizb ut-Tahrir positions itself as exclusively a political organization. Its view on economy is quite simple—abolition of the "corrupt" capitalist economic system. It is also not interested in spiritual, educational, and welfare activities as these are nonpolitical and distract from the political goal of reestablishing the caliphate.[4]

Yuldoshev had an industrious and entrepreneurial mind, and business activity would become central to the life of his sect. Marrying communism with Islam, Yuldoshev replaced the communist postulate that the means of production must be nationalized with the Islamic principle of zakat, which requires every Muslim to donate one-fifth of his income to help the needy and poor. The Birodarlar were obliged to contribute 20 percent of their income to one common fund.

Yuldoshev's economic model proved to be extremely efficient. His simple idea of combining religious devotion and hard work was something that had been "stumbled upon" and tried many times before in human history. But the concept of a return to Islam and opportunity for free private entrepreneurship perfectly met the two main aspirations of most ordinary Uzbeks across the country, especially so in the valley, in the chaos and uncertainty of the early days after the Soviet collapse. Yuldoshev's model also made good use of the Uzbeks' strong tradition of living in close communities, with every mahallya existing like a large family with its own leaders, or elders, and helping each other when needed.

* * *

One of the first Birodarlar businesses was the famous Andijan cafe Shinam, run since the Soviet times by the Shakirov family—Bakhrom and his five sons. Bakhrom Shakirov, a friend of Yuldoshev's, and his sons would, as the organization took shape and grew, become part of the Birodarlar leadership.

The Brothers steadily opened more businesses, and by 2004, when the authorities launched their campaign against them, they were running a sizeable consortium of companies with interests in construction, transportation, furniture making, and other industries. They also had followers with their own businesses in the capital, Tashkent, and the Fergana Valley town of Kokand. They carefully managed their finances, using profits and contributions from members to expand old and open new businesses. Their companies became known throughout the valley and beyond for the high quality of the products and services they provided.

The Birodarlar won government contracts to build schools and sports facilities. Their furniture was so famous for its quality that the regional governor placed an order with them to furnish his office. Produce from their bakeries and sweet factories sold out quickly at bazaars across the valley. They paid their workers well and also regularly engaged in charity work, helping hospitals and schools, sponsoring sports events, and helping the poor and sick in their local communities.

"If you have any problem, come and tell me; otherwise, I won't know and won't be able to help," one of the Birodarlar workers said their boss would say to them. And the problem could be anything from a leaking roof to a sick mother needing medical treatment.

All this was attracting more and more people to join Yuldoshev's group. They were offering good regular pay and social security amid the general economic decline gripping the country. People were ready to queue for months to get a job with one of their companies.

But the business success and charity activity were only one, visible, side of Birodarlar life. The invisible, carefully hidden side was their growth into an Islamist organization with a rigid hierarchical structure that allowed totalitarian control over the rank-and-file members.

In addition to Marx's ideas, Yuldoshev borrowed some Hizb ut-Tahrir ideas and methods in designing and developing his organization. Like Hizb ut-Tahrir, which seeks to emulate the Prophet Muhammad's steps in establishing a caliphate, Yuldoshev decided that he and his followers would revive Islam in its original pure form following in the footsteps of the Prophet.

They believed they were currently in the "Mecca period," when the Prophet was only preaching the new faith and not yet waging any wars on its enemies. Many of the rituals, now central to Islamic practice, like yearly pilgrimage and fasting or five-time daily prayers, were yet to be introduced in the later "Medina period."[5] For this reason, within Yuldoshev's organization there was no strict ban on alcohol or smoking, and men were not obliged to have a beard. Their women dressed in the traditional Uzbek way—headscarves and long dresses over ankle-length loose cotton pants.

Similarly, in the initial stages of their quest to build an Islamic state, Hizb ut-Tahrir members are allowed to drink alcohol and behave in other "ungodly" ways in order to blend in so that they can penetrate government and army institutions. The Birodarlar too thought that at this early stage of their ideological-religious pursuit they had to put aside some of their principles and accept the laws and practices of the society outside their sect. To avoid official extortion, they regularly bribed various government inspectors and officials "to keep them quiet by giving them the toys and icons that they worship," Hojimatov said.

They believed that it would be in the Medina period that they would take over power in Uzbekistan. They thought they would do it peacefully, in a similar way to Hizb ut-Tahrir, by spreading their ideology, building up the ranks of their followers and supporters, and penetrating government institutions—establishing sufficient influence, starting with Andijan Region.

Yuldoshev was revered by them as someone who spoke on behalf of the Prophet Muhammad and helped them understand Islam. They apparently likened themselves to the Prophet's first disciples who followed him, initially secretly, despite the hostility of the rest of their community.

To build a strong core of leaders, the Birodarlar were first and foremost interested in recruiting the most active and respected Andijan community members. These core members would then attract trustworthy people from among their friends, family, and neighbors, who in turn would bring their trusted people. Later their expansion would be driven largely by their economic success, attracting to them jobless people and others seeking a better living. The Birodarlar companies hired new workers by recommendation from old members. The new worker would be given a probationary period, during which his supervisors would study his character and behavior. If the new worker proved to be loyal and hardworking, he would get promotions and better pay. Then, after getting a taste of the material benefits of being with the group, he would be slowly initiated into the ideology, which involved studying Yuldoshev's pamphlet.

Yuldoshev built a strict hierarchical system of management of his organization. "Their internal rules resembled those of a military organization and at the same time of a religious sect. They are like a religious version of the socialist system," Hojimatov said.

Every member had a supervisor above him who had his own supervisor above him and so on. Everyone was to obey his or her supervisor's command without question. They also had to regularly report to their supervisors all their personal issues, both concerning family and work relations.

The supervisors had the power to demote a worker or cut his pay for any disobedience, as this meant a sin for which you would burn in hell and Allah would no longer hear your prayers. The longer you stayed with the group and the more loyalty you showed to the group, the more authority you would be given, which meant more people under your supervision.

From the outset the Birodarlar relied on Uzbek society's traditionally strong family ties, with whole large, extended families—parents, sons, daughters, uncles, cousins, in-laws with their own extended families, and so on—gradually coming into the fold. With time, to further consolidate the group, marriages were allowed only within the group, and matches were decided by the leaders. This, along with the economic incentives, would make leaving the group very difficult. Those who left were considered to be turning away from Allah and therefore leaving Islam altogether.

Hizb ut-Tahrir similarly relies on social networks and informal institutions like friendship and neighborhood networks; it has strict criteria for membership, taking in only those who fully accept the party's beliefs and methods; at the primary level members are organized in small, usually five-strong, cells. It attempts to create "a collective identity that engenders a sense of solidarity on the part of group members," according to the researcher Emmanuel Karagiannis.[6] Hizb ut-Tahrir's draft constitution for the future Islamic state also contains elements of socialism, like guaranteed employment and free health care and education for all.

* * *

Because of his past link to Hizb ut-Tahrir, whose members were harshly persecuted by the authorities, Yuldoshev was kept on the security service's radar screens. The authorities couldn't not know about his attempt to create his own Islamist group. He was repeatedly summoned and warned that his preaching of Islam was undesired and anticonstitutional. Yuldoshev continued to create his network, but more secretively.

In 1998 when he was at a local bazaar, someone started a fight with him. He was detained by the police, and they found drugs in his pocket.

Yuldoshev's wife, Yodgoroy, said the fight had been staged and the drugs were planted by the police. Yuldoshev was jailed but amnestied in six months.

Perhaps, at the time, the authorities could indeed not see anything too dangerous in Yuldoshev's activities. Returning to his wife a copy of Yuldoshev's pamphlet seized during the search in his house after the arrest, the investigator told her that nothing illegal was found in it and advised that they should get it officially published, to avoid further trouble over it.

Yuldoshev intended to follow the advice, but before he could do so, he was taken in again amid the sweeping arrests across the country following the February 1999 bombings in Tashkent, which Karimov's government used as pretext to go after every kind of dissident in the country. This time Yuldoshev was given a seventeen-year sentence for alleged antigovernment activity.

Yuldoshev suffered severe beatings following his arrest, as a result of which his ribs were broken, cutting through his lungs. Later in jail, with his lungs damaged, he contracted tuberculosis, according to his follower Abdullah.

"He did not bend under any pressure, and he did not seek any help. He refused to write to human rights organizations," he said. "He was not against the constitution. Karimov has no more loyal citizen than Yuldoshev."

Kabuljon Parpiyev and Bakhrom Shakirov, and Shakirov's sons acted as the group's leaders in the absence of Yuldoshev. Parpiyev, Bakhrom Shakirov, and his son Sharif were also jailed after the 1999 Tashkent bombings. Parpiyev was released in 2001 under an amnesty. Sharif was freed in 2002; his father, a year later.

Two of the Shakirov brothers, Shavkat and Shakir, were among the twenty-three Brothers jailed in 2004. Sharif and Parpiyev led the 2005 revolt, and the two other brothers, the twins Khasan and Khusan, were actively involved in it.

Sharif and Shakir were killed in the suppression of the revolt. Khasan, Khusan, and Shavkat were captured and jailed. Their father, Bakhrom, having in effect lost all his sons, ended up as a refugee in Europe.

After the uprising, the authorities showed Yuldoshev on state TV publicly confessing to instigating his followers to launch jihad. He reportedly died in prison in 2010.

* * *

Figure 7.2. Akrom Yuldoshev, the founder of the group behind the Andijan uprising. YouTube screenshot of his official TV "confession" that he commanded the revolt from his prison cell. https://www.youtube.com/watch?v=mgsUuwGiuLg.

As journalists and researchers tried to make sense of the Andijan uprising, one theory emerged that linked the arrest of the twenty-three Birodarlar leaders to the dismissal a few weeks earlier of the Andijan Region governor Obidov, with whom, it is said, they were on good terms. In the corrupt Uzbek system of government, a business can only survive through the regular bribing of government officials in exchange for protection from various other agencies seeking to live off them—the higher the protector, the safer your business is. The Birodarlar regularly paid substantial bribes to local authorities, and possibly the governor was one of the recipients—the furniture in his office was made by the Birodarlar. According to the theory, the Birodarlar refused to pay "tributes" to the new governor, Begaliyev, who set out to establish his own control over the region's economic assets. In retaliation, the new governor used their religiousness to target them as extremists.[7]

However, the arrests of Birodarlar members in Tashkent, following the Andijan arrests, could indicate the hand of the central government rather than revenge by a local official. At the same time, in an environment where anyone pious could be seen as a suspected extremist or could be easily turned into one for any kind of reason, one "tip-off" from a local official to any law-enforcement official in Tashkent would have been enough to trigger the Tashkent arrests.

Still, Yuldoshev's long-term imprisonment and the earlier arrests of other Birodarlar leaders could suggest that the authorities had long been treating them as Islamists. In need of an excuse for killing scores of unarmed members of the sect, the Karimov government was quick to categorize their revolt as jihad and terrorism, backing up its theory with Yuldoshev's questionable TV confession and testimonies extracted through torture from his followers arrested after the uprising.

Despite their having a utopian idea of creating an Islamic society in a distant future—with hardly any of them, even among the leaders, knowing how exactly it would happen—the Birodarlar May 13 revolt was not an attempt to overthrow Karimov's government and seize power. The uprising was planned but, nevertheless, a desperate and ill-conceived action—a bid to do something, anything, to save their network from destruction, probably, first of all as an economic and social safety net.

The group had its own "security service" and instructors who started preparation for the revolt three months ahead. More than a hundred of the most trusted members had undergone firearms training in the mountains of Kyrgyzstan's Jalal-Abad Region. Only the top leaders knew what was going on. The rank and file were kept in the dark.

Those who were expected to be actively involved in the revolt were told to be ready for "an action that could change their lives." They were also told to be ready to die. As a reward they were promised paradise.

They wanted to show the government that they were a force to be reckoned with. The Birodarlar leaders believed that, since nobody had risen up against the government before, the very element of surprise would guarantee them popular support and force Karimov to hold talks with them. They had even appointed people for such talks.

They thought the whole thing would be over in a few hours or days. They overestimated their own strength and miscalculated the government's potential response. Their sheer numbers, financial resources, organizational efficiency, discipline, and connections within the local government made them overconfident. But they were cornered too. It was obvious that the authorities would not stop until all their members were in jail and the organization was totally wiped out. They were left with no choice but to "die standing."

Notes

1. International Historical and Educational Charity and Human Rights Society, "Ivanovskiye Uzbeki budut osvobozhdeny," Memorial (website), March 2007, https:// memohrc.org/ru/news/ivanovskie-uzbeki-budut-osvobozhdeny-0

2. International Crisis Group, "Central Asia: Islamist Mobilisation and Regional Security," Asia Report no. 14, March 1, 2001, https://d2071andvipowj.cloudfront.net /14-central-asia-islamist-mobilisation-and-regional-security.pdf.

3. Adeeb Khalid, *Islam after Communism: Religion and Politics in Central Asia* (Berkeley: University of California Press, 2007), 194.

4. Emmanuel Karagiannis, "Political Islam in Uzbekistan: Hizb ut-Tahrir al-Islami," *Europe-Asia Studies* 58 (2), 266–267.

5. Zeyno Baran, *Hizb ut-Tahrir: Islam's Political Insurgency* (Washington, DC: Nixon Center, 2004).

6. Karagiannis, "Political Islam," 270.

7. Fergananews.com, "Godovshchina krovavykh sobytiy v Andijane. Kommentarii ekspertov, politikov, zhurnalistov," May 12, 2015, http://www.fergananews.com/articles/8535; EurasiaNet.org, "Andijan massacre linked to local power struggle—source," September 29, 2005, https://eurasianet.org/andijan-massacre-linked-to-local-power-struggle-source.

8

THE SHYMKENT RAID

SHYMKENT—A KAZAKH BORDER CITY WITH AN ETHNICALLY mixed population, including a considerable Uzbek minority, and not much law and order (at the time of the events described below)—was an obvious destination for many Uzbeks fleeing persecution at home. In the late 1990s and early 2000s, it was easy to cross into Kazakhstan bypassing the few official checkpoints—through the gardens and backyards of private houses sitting on the border. Borders between the Soviet republics had existed only on maps. As political differences, economic disputes, and distrust grew between the Central Asian leaders after the Soviet disintegration, they moved to make the borders physical, but it took years to reach demarcation agreements, mark out the frontiers, and begin to control them.

Shymkent, located about a hundred kilometers northeast of Tashkent, was founded in the twelfth century and grew into a center for trade between nomadic and settled Turkic tribes. Now it is Kazakhstan's third largest city with more than nine hundred thousand people—a mix of mainly ethnic Kazakhs, Uzbeks, Russians, Chechens, Tatars, Koreans, and Uighurs.

The Kazakhs have been slow to let go of their old nomadic traditions in favor of Islam. A nineteenth-century Russian historian wrote that, in response to questions about their religious identity, Kazakhs usually said, "I don't know."[1] Also, because under Russian colonial rule huge numbers of Slavs had settled in the Kazakh steppe and many children of the Kazakh elite had been educated in Russia, the Kazakhs emerged out of the period of Russian-Soviet rule more russified than the Uzbeks, which also contributed to the weakening of their "attachment" to Islam.

But after the Soviet collapse, Kazakhstan too saw a surge of interest in Islam and its new interpretations offered by various home-grown and foreign preachers. Historically closer to the more religious Uzbeks, southern

Kazakhstan has always had stronger Islamic traditions than the other parts of the country, and by the late 1990s there were many unofficial mosques throughout the region, which were by and large ignored by the authorities.

Under the Communist boss turned president Nursultan Nazarbayev, Kazakhstan at the time was going through a speedy transition to capitalism—a process that involved massive workers' strikes, privatization of industrial enterprises, and sale of the country's extensive natural resources to foreign companies. "Unofficial" Islam in Kazakhstan was seen at the time as a marginal trend. According to a 2005 report by the Kazakh researcher Sanat Kushkumbayev, since getting independence in 1991, Kazakhstan had seen "practically no attempts to create political movements or parties based on Islamic slogans."[2]

In a few years Salafism would begin to find followers in Kazakhstan's socially deprived western regions, and in 2011 the country would see the first suicide bombings targeting security and law-enforcement forces. In 2012–13 Kazakh fighters would begin to appear in jihadist ranks in the Middle East.

But in the early 2000s Hizb-ut Tahir was the most visible Islamist group in Kazakhstan, and it was most active in the south. To a great extent, its spread was fueled by the crackdown on dissident Muslims in Uzbekistan, and it focused on spreading the word about this and condemning Karimov's policies. Kushkumbayev's report mentioned the detention of several Hizb ut-Tahrir members in southern Kazakhstan in 2000–02 with leaflets calling for the creation of an Islamic state but said that did not indicate the existence of "a mass and active network of Islamist groups in the country."

One of the most outspoken Hizb ut-Tahrir activists in Shymkent at the time was Vadim Barsenev. An ethnic Russian in his early thirties, he had had a rough childhood, leading to a conviction for drug dealing at the age of fourteen. By the time I met him on a reporting trip in May 2004, Barsenev was a zealous Muslim and defender of religious rights. In this new capacity he had gotten two more convictions, though—one for an unauthorized rally in 2003 against Karimov's regime and "his killing of our brothers" and another for breaching public order by arguing in a mosque. He argued against the official imams' position that since he and other Hizb ut-Tahrir members were Kazakh citizens, they had to abide by the country's constitution.

"I told them: I live not in Kazakhstan but in the land of Allah, and on Judgment Day I will be judged not by the Kazakh constitution but by the laws of Allah," Barsenev said. He sported a neat beard, was relaxed, and talked about his run-in with official mullahs and police with a smile, as if he found them entertaining.

He believed Karimov's repression of Muslims was only helping groups like Hizb ut-Tahrir win more followers. "In the entire former Soviet Union, Hizb ut-Tahrir is spreading because of Karimov's repressions. Karimov is like a mad dog that broke loose and went on the rampage," he said. Thus, Karimov was only hastening his own demise because "the only force that can break him is Islam," he said.

After the string of antipolice bombings and shootings in Uzbekistan in 2004, the Uzbek authorities said two of the suicide bombers involved in the attacks were Kazakh citizens. The Kazakh security service confirmed the claim following an investigation, saying the two were members of an Islamist group based in the country's south. They made arrests among the group's members and tightened control over Islamists.

* * *

In summer 2000, along with three followers, Imam Nazarov secretly moved to the Kazakh border village of Abay not far from Shymkent. Several of his other loyal followers continued to visit him there from Tashkent for Islamic lessons and to get him food and other supplies. But in a few months, one of them, Shokhrukh, was arrested.

Fearing that under torture Shokhrukh might give away his whereabouts, Nazarov moved to Shymkent and stayed there for the next five years. With time, more of his followers—including Erkin, a student of Nazarov's, and Farkhod, who had taken lessons from Farrukh—moved there, followed by their families. Nazarov himself was joined in Shymkent by his youngest son, Daudkhon, and his disappeared son Khusnuddin's wife, Mamlakat, and her three children.

There was no visa requirement for them to stay in Kazakhstan, but they had to legalize themselves by getting registered with the migration authorities, which would mean giving themselves away. They were sure that the Uzbek authorities had passed on their details to the Kazakh authorities and a search was on for them. Under security agreements, the two countries' governments exchange information on their fugitives. Official corruption, however, allowed some of Nazarov's followers to get three-month registration papers and keep renewing them without being put on official records.

They all mostly depended on the money sent by their relatives in Tashkent. But some who had migration cards started some small businesses,

Figure 8.1. A poster outside a police station in Kyrgyzstan's southern Batken Region with mug shots of alleged Islamist militants wanted by the Uzbek authorities, 2007. Similar posters could be found in Kazakhstan regions neighboring Uzbekistan. © Author's photo.

like selling construction materials and plumbing equipment. One of them opened a butcher's shop; another worked at an internet café. Those without any papers would go outside as little as possible, relying on their friends and sympathizers from the local Muslim community to get food and do other errands for them. They lived in permanent fear, knowing that they were still within the Uzbek government's reach.

Imam Nazarov would almost never go outside. He continued to give lessons to a core of his students. His other followers in Shymkent would never see him. They worked out a system of secrecy. There were trusted liaison men who would maintain contact between a certain group and the core group around Nazarov. Some of them were in touch only with Nazarov.

Nobody, apart from Nazarov, knew how many of them exactly there were in Shymkent. Mirakhmat, who was an aide to Nazarov and lived with him and his family in Shymkent, said he knew about fifteen other students of Nazarov's hiding at the time in the town, along with their families. They often moved houses and used code words in their telephone conversations. They diligently followed all the news from home for signs of any change for better or worse and also news about Karimov's contacts with the Kazakh president Nazarbayev—every time the two met, there was a chance that Karimov would demand that Nazarbayev step up the hunt for the runaway Uzbeks sheltering in Kazakhstan.

Erkin was joined in Shymkent by his wife, and in their five years there they had two sons.

"We lived in poor conditions, in cold houses," Erkin told me. "The first few months were especially difficult, though actually it never got much easier."

Erkin wanted to buy a Kazakh passport but failed to find a reliable channel. So he and a few others in their group bought fake Kyrgyz passports, which was an easier and cheaper option—two hundred dollars apiece. But the "passports" were of such poor quality that using them was out of the question.

When they had to see a doctor or rent somewhere to live, they used false names and made up stories about themselves and why they did not have identification papers and other documents. It would get seriously problematic when their wives had babies. Medical care is free in Kazakhstan, and their wives would be admitted to maternity hospitals, but doctors would refuse to discharge them until the fathers registered the newborns with the authorities. Eventually, they would have to pay a bribe to the doctors or bring them flowers, chocolate, or other small presents to have their wives discharged. Erkin's neighborhood pediatrician was the wife of a district police chief, and every contact with her was a stressful affair, as he was afraid she would suspect something and tell her husband.

They had to avoid busy public places like bazaars, where there would always be police patrols out in the streets not so much for maintaining order but for opportunities to harass and extort money from someone. One day in 2003, Erkin and his friend were detained by police at a bazaar as they window-shopped for leather jackets. The police figured out from their dialect that they were from Tashkent and assumed they were in Shymkent for shopping and therefore were in the money—the Uzbek authorities at the time had closed many markets inside the country as part of new trade restrictions, and many Tashkent residents would come to Shymkent for shopping. But Erkin and his friend had only three thousand tenge, which was worth about twenty dollars, between them, too little for a shopper. Suspecting they were hiding their money, the police dragged them out of the bazaar and gave them a good body search. Having found nothing, they had to make do with the three thousand tenge and let Erkin and his friend go. They never went to any bazaars again—any encounter with the police could lead to an identity check and deportation to Uzbekistan.

Having lived in Shymkent for some time, Erkin began to see why the city and southern Kazakhstan in general were called "Texas" in the rest of the country. "Shymkent *is* Texas," he said. "The people are rough there." He added, "Though there were kind people too."

He told me a story about his landlord, Temirkhan, who once decided to sell his house and found a buyer who wanted the house to be vacated immediately. But Erkin needed time to find a new place—considering his legal situation, it was going to take some time. The buyer kept insisting "in a mean way" that they leave. Temirkhan then threw at her the thousand-dollar deposit she had paid and said the deal with her was off.

* * *

When a link was established between the attacks in Uzbekistan in March–April 2004 and an Islamist group in southern Kazakhstan, Karimov swiftly, in his usual blunt way, accused Kazakhstan of harboring terrorists. The Kazakh authorities tightened security, and Nazarov's group immediately felt the effect of it.

"It got more difficult. There were frequent identity checks," Erkin said.

Erkin and his friends often discussed their future, wondering if they could ever live as free people again. "We had no idea about the existence of the UNHCR," Erkin said. "We only got as far as agreeing during one of our discussions about 'what to do' that there must be some organizations that help people like us. But we were afraid to turn to such organizations: what if they too said that we were terrorists?"

At the beginning of 2005 Mirakhmat, Nazarov's aide, "took the risk," Erkin said. He went to Almaty and submitted his documents to the UNHCR office. Then so did Abduvosit Sadykov and after him Abdurakhmon Ibragimov.

Upon returning to Shymkent, Ibragimov gave the details to the others—most importantly that he was not treated as a suspect or fugitive, and although it would take time for them to process his case, he was already legally under UN protection as an asylum seeker.

"When he asked who else wanted to apply, I raised both hands," Erkin said. "Tokhir [Abdusamatov] did too."

They invited a UNHCR representative to come to Shymkent, and in March 2005 they met her in the office of a local human rights organization. They told her their stories and gave her their documents. They were told that they would be interviewed further before a decision could be made on giving them refugee status. Two months later came the Andijan uprising.

"The UNHCR got busy with the Andijan refugees. Summer passed; then November came. We were still waiting to be interviewed," Erkin said.

Farkhod, on the other hand, had before the Andijan unrest been thinking about staying in Shymkent for good. "We sent our eldest daughter to school; we thought we would stay in Kazakhstan and get citizenship," he said.

"Then came the Andijan [uprising], and all our hopes were shattered. It was a shock for us. More people were fleeing Uzbekistan; checks and inspections got more rigorous in Shymkent. We heard that we were being searched for more seriously now."

In late June, in an apparent demonstration of solidarity with Karimov over the Andijan revolt, the Kazakh authorities carried out a large-scale operation to uncover illegal migrants and announced the capture of two alleged participants in the uprising. In Almaty in July they detained Lutfullo Shamsuddinov, a rights activist from Andijan who had been sought at home for providing independent information on the massacre. Uzbekistan demanded his extradition. It took the UNHCR weeks of intense negotiations to secure his release.

Nazarov too began to look for a way to leave Kazakhstan for somewhere safer. Mirakhmat approached the UNHCR office in Almaty on behalf of Nazarov, without revealing his whereabouts. "A process of taking him out of Kazakhstan was already under way," Mirakhmat said. "Nazarov was waiting for a good moment to make a move."

* * *

With Nazarov's group feeling more insecure than ever after the Andijan massacre, it was a bad time for Rukhitdin to appear in Shymkent. After going into hiding in 1998, he had stayed in Tashkent until 2004 or 2005, until he got a fake passport with which he left for Ukraine, according to Nazarov. From Ukraine Rukhitdin had continued to visit his family in Tashkent via

Shymkent. He came again in August 2005, traveling with a Kyrgyz passport in the name of Ravshan Aripov.

The reason why Rukhitdin, number one on the Uzbek government's wanted list, had managed to stay in Tashkent so long, go to Ukraine on a fake passport, and travel back and forth without being exposed was his "hard-to-remember" features, an "elegant" way of dressing, and a cultured and confident manner, Mirakhmat told me in a conversation. "Nobody would think he could be a fugitive," he said.

Still, after coming to Shymkent in August, Rukhitdin sought Nazarov's advice concerning his safety if he stayed in Shymkent for a while.

"It's up to you, but if you stay, you will have to be very careful. There are SNB officers here; they are searching for us. It is going to be dangerous, and you will have to stay in most of the time," Nazarov said.

Rukhitdin decided to stay. In November he arranged a meeting in Shymkent with his mother. Rukhitdin said he wanted to see her to say good-bye because he was planning to go soon to some other foreign country. Rukhitdin wanted to get a farewell present for his mother and took her to a bazaar, so she could choose something. But Manzura opa would not let him spend any money on her.

After seeing Rukhitdin, Manzura opa told the rest of the family that he looked "very well" and seemed to feel safe in Shymkent.

"It's not like Uzbekistan here," Rukhitdin assured her.

A week after his mother's visit Rukhitdin was captured.

* * *

On the morning of November 24, 2005, Abdurauf Kholmurodov, one of Imam Nazarov's most trusted people and also a close friend of Rukhitdin's, went to see Rukhitdin and Alizhon Mirganiyev in their rented flat. There was a rule within their group that everyone should regularly check in with the others by making quick calls. Nothing was heard from Kholmuradov that day after he set off for Rukhitdin's flat. He did not answer his mobile phone.

"There had been instances before when some of us got detained by police during identity checks, but they would always let us go for money. But he [Kholmuradov] did not reply for a whole day, and we got worried," Farkhod said.

Later that day Alisher Mirzokholov, who was Imam Nazarov's driver, got a call on his mobile. He said to the caller, "I'll be there soon," and left home, saying he was going to Rukhitdin's. Mirzokholov was supposed to come to the imam's after sunset but did not turn up. They called Mirzokholov, and he answered, shouting, "I did give you the money; leave me alone. Stop calling me!" It sounded like he was trying to protect the true identity of the caller, at the same time signaling to the caller about big trouble.

Nazarov and Abdurakhmon Ibragimov, who had a car, went to Rukhitdin's to find out what had happened. Nazarov stayed in the car while Ibragimov went to the flat. They agreed that he would ring Nazarov as soon as he was in the flat. But time went by, and there was neither a call nor any sign of him returning.

Nazarov was now seriously worried. He also spotted two cars in the street that he thought could be police surveillance cars. He got out of Ibragimov's car, took a taxi, and went to the house rented by Erkin and several others.

The men sat together to discuss the situation. They were missing five people: Rukhitdin, Alizhon Mirganiyev, Abdurauf Kholmuradov, Alisher Mirzokholov, and Abdurakhman Ibragimov. It was clear to Nazarov and the others that the Kazakh authorities had tracked them down. The finger of suspicion was pointing at their recent guest—a student of Rukhitdin's who had visited him in Shymkent a few days earlier.

Azizbek Rakhimov had taken Islamic lessons from Rukhitdin in Tashkent in the 1990s. Following the Andijan violence he was involved in the anti-Karimov protests outside the Uzbek embassy in London, where he was studying under an Uzbek state scholarship program. Around November 17–18, 2005, he arrived in Almaty from London and then traveled to Shymkent and stayed with Rukhitdin for two nights.

"Then, we guess, he illegally crossed the [Uzbek] border and went to his hometown, Kokand, because he wanted to see his family. But the authorities would have been expecting him there. He would have been arrested at home by masked men and taken to Tashkent. He was obviously tortured and gave them information on Rukhitdin's whereabouts in Shymkent," Mirakhmat said.

It appeared that Rukhitdin and Mirganiyev were arrested in a raid on their flat. Abdurauf Kholmuradov was shadowed after his visit to the flat and seized somewhere in town. Mirzakholov was trapped through a phone call—probably one of the already captured men was forced to make a call and invite him to Rukhitdin's place. In the evening they got Ibragimov, when he came to check on Rukhitdin and Mirganiyev.

The five missing men were from among Nazarov's dozen closest followers—the ones who were in daily contact with him and on whom he depended. All were from Tashkent, except for Ibragimov, a former muezzin of Nazarov's Tokhtaboy Mosque, who was from Andijan. Nazarov and his remaining students began to think frantically what to do. They knew that the Kazakh security service, the KNB, would soon know exactly where to look for them.

"It was clear that we had to lie low," Farkhod said. "Always, if there was anything, any risk to our security, we would pack our bags and move to a new place. We mastered it to such a level that we did it automatically."

They immediately evacuated the places known to the captured men. Nazarov, however, stayed in his house for two more days, until November 26, even though one of the five missing men, Mirzokholov, knew the address—so strong was his trust in his driver.

His followers, meanwhile, now had an uphill struggle to urgently find somewhere to live for more than twenty people. First, everyone moved in with Erkin's family because their place was relatively newly rented, and none of the captured men knew the exact address.

"So in our three rooms there were six men, five women, and eleven children," Erkin said. "I got on with looking for a new house to rent. My looks were closer to Kazakh, and I could speak Kazakh a little."

He spent the next two days in search of somewhere, setting off at six in the morning and coming back late in the evening, without any success. Then Erkin suggested that they should at least ensure the safety of the women and children. He went to a local Muslim friend and begged him to let their women stay with him for a little while: "We have no choice. Please, give us one room for the women and children."

The man thought for a long time and finally agreed—he gave them his car to move the women and their stuff. Erkin was the only one among the men who knew where the women were going.

* * *

Then they got on with getting rid of their household stuff, which was all at Erkin's now. No one wanted to take it. Finally one friend agreed but said he would take everything except the religious books. The six men—Erkin, Farkhod, Sharafutdin Latipov, Tohir Abdusamatov, Shoirmat Shorakhmetov, and Nozim Rakhmonov—finished moving the kitchenware, bedding, and similar things by around ten p. m. on November 27.

Everyone was tired, but they still had to repair the metal gate that had broken because they had opened and closed it too many times during the day as they moved their belongings. Three of them went to fix and lock it. Outside they noticed a Lada car with tinted windows and no number plate. On any other day they would immediately suspect it was a police surveillance car, but this time they were too tired to pay attention.

They cooked supper and sat down to eat. Just as Erkin took a spoon, he heard someone banging on the gates.

Erkin and Tohir went out to courtyard and heard the words: "Open! It's UVD YuKO [the South Kazakhstan regional police department]. Open the door!"

Erkin and Tohir shouted, "Coming!" and rushed inside to tell everyone to run. Everyone jumped up from their seats. Erkin was the last to leave the house because he wanted to get his mobile phone and the hard disk from the computer with all his correspondence on it.

In the courtyard there was a summer kitchen and a thick gas pipe extended out to it at chest level. Everyone was jumping onto the pipe and then up onto the roof and into the backyard. Erkin tried to get onto the pipe but kept falling. "I was jumping and jumping," he said.

The police were continuing to bang on the gate, already trying to break it open and shouting, "Open now!"

Erkin thought that this was it for him and prayed, "Allah, it'll take you no effort at all to help your slave. Do you have to leave me at this minute?" He continued, "And suddenly I managed to get onto the pipe, though the police were already three to four meters behind me. I got onto the roof, then ran, then jumped onto some barrels below and fell to the ground in the backyard. Two friends were trying to open the backyard gate there; I rushed toward them, but there was a policeman behind me. He fired his gun; the bullet hit the gate.

"The guys ran away from the gate; I wanted to get to it too but dropped my cell phone—all my contacts were in it. I bent down to pick it up. One special-forces officer caught up with me and grabbed me by my left arm.

"Still bent over, with my right arm picking the phone up from off the ground, I raised my head and looked in his eyes. He looked in mine. I pulled my arm, and he let go of it. I ran.

"Behind me, I could hear that they had caught Shoirmat Shorakhmetov.

"They were shouting, 'KNB, stop! Or I'll shoot!'"

Erkin climbed onto the fence and fell into the gap between their fence and the fence of the neighbor's house. The gap was about fifty centimeters wide, a fire safety requirement designed to stop fire from spreading from one house to another. There were some plants growing there and fallen leaves, in which Erkin buried his head, though the rest of his body was exposed for everyone to see. He also buried his hard disk in the earth.

He heard two officers jumping from one rooftop onto another over his head. The shouts continued for a while but gradually everything calmed down.

Soon the police officers knocked on the gates of the house next door, beside the walls of which Erkin was lying. The owners were an elderly Russian couple. The police asked them if they had a flashlight; the couple said no.

The police lit a match and checked the gap along the fence. Someone spotted Erkin's track suit top and said, "Someone's dropped a track suit top."

Erkin thought, "That's it; I have to come out." But then he decided not to move until they themselves approached him. But instead they left.

Then it went quiet. Lights went out in the house.

Erkin tried to move—he stretched his leg, but it made a rustling sound. He heard steps approaching him from the neighbor's yard. The person came up to the fence and jumped up a couple of times, trying to see what was making the noise. Erkin pulled the track suit top over his head and stayed in that position until he heard the 4:00 a.m. train passing.

He had a chronic cough, and as he lay there he had the palm of one hand always pressed against his mouth. His legs went numb. At night he heard some of the officers involved in the raid drinking vodka in their now abandoned house.

After hearing the train, Erkin slowly got up, making one move at a time and waiting for two minutes before making another. He climbed over the fence into the neighbor's courtyard, got onto the stack of firewood by the shed and then onto the shed roof, and climbed over the wall into someone else's courtyard, ignoring the growling of their two dogs. He climbed over their fence and got out into the street.

"All the neighborhood dogs began to bark. I walked along the street. I was all dirty and dusty," Erkin said. "I kept thinking about our women and the other guys—what happened to them? It was close to morning prayer time, so I decided to go to a mosque, clean myself up there, pray, and think. But then I thought that maybe the special services would expect me to show up there. I changed my mind."

Erkin went to a local friend's house. He knocked on the door three times.

"Who is it?"

"Erkin."

"Are you on your own?"

"Yes."

"Are you sure you weren't followed?"

"Yes."

He let Erkin in, hugged him, and began to cry.

"I was too shocked to cry," Erkin said.

But the friend had no hiding place, like a basement, in his house. The attic was too dangerous because neighbors might notice him there. He took Erkin to another friend's, but that friend did not want to put Erkin up even for one day. He gave him his cell phone though. Erkin called Ziyad, another student of Nazarov's in Shymkent.

"Erkin, Erkin, is that you? You! Are you by yourself?" Ziyad said.

"Let's meet. Name me a place," Erkin said.

"Go where I lived three years ago. Take a bus."

Erkin waited there for a long time. Finally Ziyad came in a taxi and picked him up. He told Erkin that all the women were safe.

Then they called the Almaty-based reporters of Radio Liberty, the BBC World Service, the known Russian rights activist Vitaliy Ponomarev in Moscow, and Human Rights Watch representatives.

"We told them we needed help," Erkin said.

* * *

Farkhod too managed to escape that night. When they were caught by surprise in their house, Farkhod, like everyone else, climbed onto the roof and ran.

"Someone was chasing me; I ran and ran until the roofs ended," he said.

He jumped down into somebody's courtyard. The dog there started to bark. The walls around the courtyard were too high to climb over, so Farkhod started knocking on the door, screaming, "Let me in—help!"

But no one opened. Farkhod rushed into a shed that was crammed with firewood. A few minutes later the security officers knocked on the gates, ordering those inside to open them.

"I was praying to Allah for escape but thought that was it, and I would be arrested," Farkhod said.

The man of the house opened the gate; the officers came in and started searching around the courtyard with their Alsatian dog. The dog was quiet when they approached the shed.

"Where is he?" the officers asked the owner of the house.

"I don't know. I'm looking for him with you," the man said.

His son added, "Maybe he ran away along the roof?"

The officers left. Farkhod could not believe his luck. With a pounding heart he decided to stay put in the shed.

The police came back in an hour, but they only asked the man of the house to go with them to "where those Muslims were" and act as a witness while they did the paperwork after searching the house. The man went and came back soon.

Farkhod stayed in the shed all night. In the morning the owner of the house got onto the roof with a neighbor to check if it was damaged during the night chase. As they inspected the roof, the man told the neighbor that only one of the six Uzbeks raided last night had managed to escape.

"They made punching bags out of those Uzbeks. If I had it my way, I would have shot them all dead," he said. He was ethnic Russian.

Before hearing that, Farkhod was considering coming out and asking him for help, but now he understood that it would be a bad idea.

"I was terrified. I decided to wait," he said.

He spent the day and another night in the shed and ventured to leave it only early the next morning. Behind the shed there was a narrow passage, alongside a pigsty and a henhouse. The disturbed pigs began to snort, and the hens began to cluck as Farkhod squeezed past and got onto the roof of the next-door house.

From the top he saw that it was the last house in the row and jumped down into the street. The noise of the pigs and hens, now joined by a barking dog, got even louder. Farkhod walked on.

He took the SIM card out of his phone and broke it, to avoid getting tracked through it. He walked until he reached a taxi stand. He had some money in his pocket and asked a taxi driver to take him outside the city to a place where he and his friends had once gone for a picnic—he wanted a safe place to think about what to do.

* * *

The other four—Sharafutdin Latipov, Tohir Abdusamatov, Shoirmat Shora-khmetov, and Nozim Rakhmonov—were captured. With the police at their heels, one of them called Nazarov to give him a warning and maybe to hear a word of support or advice.

"We are surrounded; we are on the roof. They [the police] are armed; they have dogs," he told his teacher.

Nazarov was too shocked for words. A moment later, the caller hung up. Nazarov immediately contacted the other men in their group and told them to leave their houses, leaving behind their wives and children.

The wife of one of them was in the hospital with some illness. Their two children were sleeping at home. He asked the imam, "How can I go and leave the children on their own?"

"Go now. Leave your children to Allah," Nazarov told him. The man was crying.

The same night, the Kazakh authorities raided Nazarov's house, which he had left the day before. Mirakhmat was still in the house, as well as all of Nazarov's belongings, including his laptop, his books and papers, and his children's identification documents. When Mirakhmat heard loud banging on the front door, he climbed over the fence into a neighbor's yard and then into the street and "ran for my life," he said. "It was a cold, foggy night. There was a rubbish dump two hundred meters down the street. I hid there. In about thirty minutes the house was stormed by a large group of KNB officers." Mirakhmat stayed hiding in the dump until local friends sent a car to pick him up.

One more house rented by Nazarov's followers was raided that night in Shymkent, but all the men were already gone. The authorities did not touch the women.

Nazarov, believing that all six of the men who were in Erkin's house had been captured, called their families in Tashkent to deliver the news.

"They were all crying," he said.

By the morning around fifteen relatives of Nazarov's captured or missing students had arrived in Shymkent. Among them were Zukhra and Rukhitdin's second wife, Mukhayo. They went to the South Kazakhstan regional police and security-service offices. No official or officer in either place would talk to them. Grief-stricken, they wandered the long corridors until they were yelled at and told to get out.

Some of them visited the house raided on November 27. Later, in a letter to rights organizations, the mother of Tohir Abdusamatov said, "When we visited the place where they were arrested, we saw blood stains on the walls, windows, doors and floor. Neighbors said that that night they heard screams, groans and swearing coming from the house."[3] Still they hoped that their men were being held somewhere in Kazakhstan and it would be possible with the help of rights activists and international organizations to get them freed.

After failing to get anything in Shymkent, Zukhra and Mukhayo came to Almaty with a handwritten note on half a sheet of A4 paper by a rights activist in Tashkent to his colleagues in Kazakhstan. It read:

> *Esteemed Zhenya, Zhemis, Sergei!*
> *The person who brings you this note of mine is someone I trust. She intends to go to the Kazakhstan International Bureau for Human Rights and Promoting the Rule of Law concerning one important matter.*
> *It's my great hope that you will be able to assist them regarding this issue.*
> *All the best.*
> *With sincere respect and greetings,*
> *Tolib Yakubov [signed] November 25, 2005*

But it was too late to do anything. In a few days, news came from lawyers in Tashkent that the nine men were in the hands of the Uzbek authorities. After their capture, they were secretly handed over to the Uzbek authorities in breach of both Kazakhstan's national extradition laws and the international convention on refugees and torture that it is party to.

Farkhod stayed outside Shymkent without contacting anyone for a day, thinking about what to do. Then he remembered about the UN and decided to try to get to their office in Almaty. He returned to town and went to a local friend, who bought Farkhod a jacket and a bus ticket to Almaty and directed the bus driver, who was a friend of his, to help Farkhod if anything happened. On the approaches to Almaty the bus was stopped by police. A policeman got in and began to check everyone's IDs. He stopped two rows before Farkhod's and got off, probably because the documents of everyone he had checked until then were in order.

Farkhod was met in Almaty by another friend and taken straight to the UNHCR office.

"There was a big surprise waiting for me there: my parents were there and also Rukhitdin's sister and wife. We hugged and cried."

Those who escaped arrest in Shymkent moved over the next few months to Almaty.

Imam Nazarov, along with his son Daud and a Kazakh friend from Shymkent, who was supposed to act as their bodyguard, took a bus to Almaty on New Year's Eve 2005, assuming there would be fewer police on the roads because of the New Year's celebrations. After a twelve-hour journey, at around four a.m. on January 1, 2006, they arrived at Almaty's Sayran bus station, where they were met by Mirakhmat. The snow-covered streets were deserted.

Erkin also took advantage of the New Year's lull, leaving Shymkent on January 1 with his wife, two sons, and Mukhlisa, the wife of Tohir Abdusamatov, who was captured, with her two children.

The UNHCR began to deal with their cases—about sixty people altogether.

* * *

It was then, while they were waiting in Almaty for the UN to process their cases, that I first met Imam Nazarov. We met in a flat he was renting in a Soviet-built four- or five-story concrete apartment block. Marcus Bensmann (my journalist brother-in-law) and I were brought there by Mirakhmat, with whom we had been in touch since after the Shymkent raid.

Nazarov met us at the door. Thin, with sunken cheeks, he was wearing a buttoned-up white shirt not tucked into his black trousers. We sat around a coffee table laid with bread, salad, and fruit. Nazarov said that since going into hiding, he had been living "in constant danger."

"Now danger increases; now it decreases," he said. But he said life was about tests and trials. "We will live in a carefree way, without problems, only in paradise. Here there will always be challenges, in the form of Karimov and others. These are tests from Allah, tests of our faith. Despite all the difficulties, you should not give up even for a second. Allah will help; he will give you more, if you do not give up. A man must be an optimist. We pin our hopes on Allah; we lean on Allah. We have faith in Allah, that your fate is written and you cannot escape it," Nazarov said.

Despite these words and his calm demeanor throughout our conversation, his inner tension and emotional exhaustion were obvious. He felt guilty before his captured followers and was bitterly disappointed with himself because of his failure to find words of consolation for the one follower who had called him minutes before being captured.

"I still cannot forgive myself. I did not know what to say to them, how to help," Nazarov said.

Figure 8.2. Imam Nazarov, his daughter-in-law, children, and grandchildren at Almaty airport before departing for Sweden, March 2006. © Ian MacWilliam.

"Why didn't I say, 'Don't be afraid; Allah will take care of you,' to support them? I failed to do that."

He said his students had followed him to Shymkent because they wanted to be near him. For security reasons, while in Shymkent he would not see most of them. "But they were happy just to live in the same town with me," Nazarov said. "We lived like this for five years. They believed in me, and I had to take care of them."

Nazarov's case was treated by the UNHCR as a priority, and as early as March he and his family were flown to Sweden. The others had to stay in Almaty longer. Erkin had to wait until August; Farkhod, a whole year. They received a little aid from the International Red Cross but still would not have been able to survive without the money sent by their families in Uzbekistan. Again they had to live in cramped rooms, often without heating or bathrooms.

And they did not feel much safer than in Shymkent. The UNHCR had to coordinate with the Kazakh authorities the process of handling their asylum requests, and each asylum seeker had to get registered with the Kazakh migration police, giving them their names and addresses. The Kazakh authorities took their chances when they could to detain and extradite Uzbek refugees quietly, without attracting the attention of the media, rights groups, and the UNHCR. Between December 2005 and July 2006, the Kazakh authorities attempted to detain four asylum seekers from among Nazarov's followers in separate cases when they were registering themselves with the migration authorities. Abduvosit Sodikov and Khayrullo Tojiyev, who were detained in February, were threatened with being secretly handed over to Uzbekistan unless they revealed the whereabouts of Imam Nazarov. All were let go following UNHCR intervention.[4]

Notes

Based on author interviews with Imam Obidkhon qori Nazarov and his students in Kazakhstan, 2006, and Sweden, 2009.

1. Alma Sultangaliyeva, "Evolyutsiya Islama v Kazakhstane," *Central Asia and the Caucasus* 4 (1999), http://www.ca-c.org/journal/cac-05-1999/st_06_sultangal.shtml.

2. Sanat Kushkumbayev, "Islam in Kazakhstan and Ethnic Identity," in "Islam, Identity and Politics in Post-Soviet Space," special edition, *Kazanskiy Federalist* 1 (13): 91–100.

3. Vitaliy Ponomarev, "Bezhentsy iz Uzbekistana v stranakh SNG: ugroza ekstraditsii (may 2005 – avgust 2007)," 12 (Moscow: Memorial Human Rights Centre, September, 2007), http://old.memo.ru/uploads/files/283.pdf.

4. Ponomarev, "Bezhentsy iz Uzbekistana," 16.

9

THE YOUNGEST BROTHER

RUKHITDIN WAS A BIG CATCH FOR THE UZBEK authorities—one of their most wanted for seven years. The cliché verdicts used by the authorities in almost every trial of alleged extremists since the 1999 bombings would mention Rukhitdin as the Tashkent *amir* (leader) of the IMU. His mug shot had been on either the wall or the desk, under a glass pane, in every antiterror official's office. Over the years it had become ingrained in the minds of all police and security officers, rank and file and further up, that Rukhitdin was one of the biggest and most dangerous Islamists—whether or not some of them were conscious of the fact that the whole campaign against alleged terrorists was based on fabrications and torture. In the first days after his arrest many curious police staff popped into his SNB cell to see the big catch with their own eyes. Some, especially the hired thugs with their pumped-up muscles, were quite disappointed to see his nonathletic physique.

"Are you Rukhitdin?" they would ask, with a look of surprise, to make sure.

"They expected to see some kind of a Rambo," Rukhitdin told his visiting sister.

Some of them, instead of beating Rukhitdin, would say a prayer together with him.

All nine men captured in Shymkent were put through the standard welcoming and interrogating procedures for terrorists used by the Uzbek justice system, to which the concept of suspects is unknown. As Rukhitdin's family heard from the other men's families, one of them lost his mind as a result of the beatings and torture and ended up in a mental hospital; another had his twelve gold teeth pulled out by hired thugs. He was thrown on the floor, one man held him while another pulled the teeth. One last tooth would not come out, and they asked the MVD detention center's doctor to pull it out with pliers—without any anesthetic. They had new teeth made for him later.

Rukhitdin's lawyer Ira, who was the first to see him in detention, told the family that "his hair has gone completely white and there is no color in his face at all." His hands were blue from "a fall," according to him. Through the lawyer, Rukhitdin passed on a letter to his father and mother:

> *Bismillohir Rahmonir Rahim.*
> *Assalomu Alaykum dear Father and Mother.*
> *Every day I pray to Allah asking for good health for you. I also believe that you pray for me daily.*
> *Please do not worry about me. Everything is good in all respects. So far they have been treating me very well. To my own surprise. That's why you shouldn't worry at all. Please pass on my regards to everyone.*
> *I kiss your hands and put them on my eyes. I will be at your service when I am freed. Please look after my children.*
> *Assalomu Alaykum.*

Family were allowed to see Rukhitdin two months after his capture, after he had been moved in January 2006 from the secret service's detention center to the police's. And they would for some reason only let women—his mother, sisters, and wife—see him. When Zukhra saw him for the first time after his arrest, she did not recognize him.

The meeting was in the MVD courtyard. Zukhra stood there waiting. There was a man standing by the door and looking at her. Only when he called her name did she realize it was her brother. His face was so sunken that "there were only eyes left on his face."

Zukhra had seen him only once since he had gone into hiding eight years ago. He was still in Tashkent and saw her in the street when he was passing in a car. He stopped the car, came out to say a quick hello, gave her a hug, went back into the car, and was gone.

Fazlitdin aka was not allowed to pass even a letter to Rukhitdin. He still wrote one and brought it to the investigators to show that he only wanted to say hello and a few words of support. The investigators decided it would be "too comforting." Fazlitdin aka attempted another letter, or rather a note, to say happy thirty-ninth birthday to his son on August 8, 2006:

> *It's your birthday today, son. It must be written that you'd be marking it in jail. But be strong. It will pass. I believe that your investigators are educated and clever people. Everything will be fair.*

But this note wasn't allowed to be passed on to Rukhitdin either.

Rukhitdin was charged with an attempt to overthrow the constitutional order, terrorism, religious extremism, illegal border crossing, and other offences, thirteen altogether. He had been one of the authorities' most wanted men for seven years, which would suggest that they had strong enough, or at least some kind of, real evidence against him. But when they caught him, they built a case against him based on the written confession that he signed after being shown a video recording of a rape of his six-year-old daughter.

In early April 2006 the child, Rukhitdin's youngest, was lured out of an internet café by a teenager. He took her to a construction site, had his way with her, and then brought her home.[1] The family found her "all bleeding," standing on the steps by the second-floor door in their apartment building. They took her to a doctor.

"What happened, little one? Have you caught a cold?" asked the doctor, after laying her on the bed.

"No, it's something else," the girl replied, her eyes wide open.

Her aunt Mavlyuda asked, "Why didn't you shout for help?"

"It would have put me to such shame," said the girl.

The police showed unusual efficiency in solving the crime. They deployed several dozen officers to search for the rapist, and he was caught straight away.

In her diary, Zukhra described what happened as "unimaginable horror." She and the girl's mother, Mukhayo, were invited to the Shaykhontour prosecutor's office to be informed about the results of the investigation.

"That dog [the rapist], his mother, uncle, two witnesses, and some twenty policemen were waiting for us. We all went to the scene where it all happened. He described everything that happened there," Zukhra wrote in her diary.

Mukhayo begged the police not to tell Rukhitdin about what happened.

"Sure," said a policeman. "How can we tell him something like this?"

But Rukhitdin was not only told but shown the video of what happened. After that he signed everything they wanted. Neither Rukhitdin nor his family asked investigators how they had obtained the video and who had filmed it. (There could not have been security cameras at the construction site where the crime took place.) To them, the fact that authorities had the video and used it to make Rukhitdin sign confession papers could only mean one thing: that the rape had been organized by authorities to that very end.

The opening of Rukhitdin's trial in September 2006 was put off three times. Initially planned to be held in Tashkent, it went ahead only after the authorities had found a new venue—the small town of Chirchik, forty kilometers north of Tashkent—to minimize public attention.

The small court building in Chirchik had been cordoned off by several dozen armed policemen. No family, journalists, human rights activists, or other observers, nor even one of the two lawyers hired by Rukhitdin's family, were allowed to attend the swift three-day trial. The court was ready to rule on the case after listening to just three witnesses, according to Rukhitdin's lawyer Irina Mikulina, who represented him at the trial.

"You are only toys in the hands of the authorities," Rukhitdin told the judges and prosecutors in his closing speech. "You will answer for what you are doing before Allah. You may sentence us to any length of time; you may sentence me to death by a firing squad. A day will come when I will see the light of day, and then you will answer for everything."

Rukhitdin was given seventeen years.

Fazlitdin aka used his connections to get an appointment with one of the Prison Administration bosses to beg him not to send Rukhitdin to Zhaslyk or the other most notorious colonies where all the convicted religious extremists were usually placed. "I have made inquiries and heard that you are a good man; otherwise, I would not have come here," Fazlitdin aka told the official. "I am afraid my son might be taken to Karakalpakstan [Zhaslyk]. We, his parents, are old and ailing; how will we be able to visit him if he is sent there? Leave him in Tashkent Region, please."

"OK, go on your way. We will let you know," said the official.

The official kept his promise, and Rukhitdin was sent to the Zangi Ota colony, in the mountains near Tashkent, which was the best possible choice.

Rukhitdin's mother, Manzura opa, died fourteen months after his sentencing. She had been unwell since the news of his capture in Shymkent. She passed away on November 15, 2008, after three days in a coma.

As her mother lay motionless, Zukhra hugged her and whispered in her ear: "God willing, I will be a happy woman. I will have more children. Just like you helped me nurse Abdullo, you will help me with your new grandchildren. We will live together in a beautiful house. You will live with me. We will get a car for Abdullo, and he will take us around to visit relatives and friends. Only pray for us."

A teardrop appeared in the corner of one of Manzura opa's closed eyes.

* * *

Rukhitdin's confinement conditions allowed a parcel a month and a three-day visit by family every three months. For three-day family meetings there were special rooms in the colony, each with a kitchen.

From December 27 to 30, 2007, Zukhra and Abdullo visited Rukhitdin in the Zangi Ota colony. While Zukhra cooked in the kitchen, Abdullo tried to keep Rukhitdin entertained. He recited poetry, danced, told him all the jokes he could remember, and showed his ability to read the Koran.

Abdullo, who was nearly twelve at the time, also had many questions. He started with the main question in his heart: "Uncle, I will soon be coming of age. Teach me; what do I have to do?"

"I have never seen Abdullo this happy before," Zukhra wrote in her diary after the visit. "No other man has ever spoken to Abdullo so intimately and with so much care and love. I was so happy to see the two of them lying together, hugging. I think Abdullo has found a good soul that he can connect with."

Rukhitdin praised Zukhra for giving "a very beautiful upbringing" to her son. "I have been thinking a lot about your son, wondering what kind of person he is now. His views are deep; his manners and the way he carried himself are just like his father's. Now that I have seen you and your son, my heart is content," he told Zukhra.

Zukhra and Rukhitdin also spent time remembering and crying about Farrukh.

"We had missed each other so much that those three days were not enough for us to see enough of each other. I don't know how those three days just flew by. I said things that I could not say to anyone else before and got answers to my most important questions," Zukhra wrote.

"Every night he kissed us good night and every morning woke us up with a kiss—all three days. His love, his respect, his desire to protect us from everything bad—it all healed my heart. I felt healthier, stronger after being with him."

When it was time to leave, Abdullo, crying, threw himself at Rukhitdin's chest. "Uncle, let me come to visit you every three months."

Seeing that, Rukhitdin and Zukhra cried too.

"Your son misses a man's attention," Rukhitdin said.

Despite her feeling of relief after meeting Rukhitdin, a month later Zukhra was writing in her diary that dark thoughts about her life were back, and she was thinking about taking her life. "I am one step from slipping down, from doing something bad," she wrote in February 2008. At the time she was spending a lot of time by her mother's grave, sitting there crying or just staring at the ground, unaware of time and leaving only when she started getting cramps.

Her dark thoughts couldn't but turn to Rukhitdin as an almost obvious reason for Farrukh's kidnapping as a way to pressure the family to turn in her brother. "I love my aka [Rukhitdin], but it's he who has destroyed my happiness," she wrote in her diary on February 6.

In August 2008 Rukhitdin was transferred from the easygoing Zangi Ota colony to the harsher Kyzyl Tepa (Red Hill) No. 47 in the central desert Navoi Region, as punishment for his refusal to read Karimov's book. One day he had been called into the Zangi Ota colony chief's office, given a book, and told that he was to read it and make a fifteen-minute presentation on it the following day.

"It's a thick book. To understand it properly and make a proper presentation, I need a week," Rukhitdin replied.

"Do you know who this book is written by?" the officer asked.

"By whom?"

"By Karimov."

"Then I am not going to read it at all," said Rukhitdin.

For that Rukhitdin was severely beaten and sent to Kyzyl Tepa.

In September when he was visited in his new colony by his wife Mukhayo and sister Mavlyuda for the first time, they found him broken and "falling apart." Mavlyuda said he looked like "a skeleton" with drooping skin on his face. He could hardly walk as the soles of his feet were ruptured and bleeding. His moral state was similar: "He says one word and then begins to cry."

Fazlitdin aka went to Kyzyl Tepa after hearing about Rukhitdin's condition, but he was not allowed to see him. "You are giving him a hard time. I have heard that he has lost weight, that he is pale. Are you not feeding him well?" Fazlitdin aka asked one of the officials there. "He is knowledgeable; he knows religion. My son speaks many languages; he used to teach people like you. He is my most respected and loved child."

"Your son is stubborn," was the reply.

Two months later Rukhitdin was beaten up again and placed in an isolated cell for four months because his wife Mukhayo tried to sneak out a letter he had written to his second wife, Rakhima.

* * *

Apart from Rukhitdin and Zukhra, one more devout Muslim emerged from among Fazlitdin aka's eight children. Usmon, the youngest child in the family, was born in 1975. According to Fazlitdin aka, "just like Rukhitdin, he was a very clever child" and learned to read and write before starting school. He graduated from it with honors.

As an elder brother and the brightest child in the family, Rukhitdin was a role model for Usmon throughout childhood. But perhaps because of an eight-year age gap between them, they were never very close. By the time Usmon finished secondary school in the early 1990s, Rukhitdin was already living the secret life of an independent preacher, keeping his family, including Usmon, out of it.

"He always forgot about me," Usmon said.

Still, like so many other young Uzbeks at the time, Usmon and some friends embarked on studying the Koran.

"It was something new. When something new comes, it seems to you that it's what you need, and you try it. We used to live under a Communist regime. There was a spiritual vacuum. There was emptiness in our souls," Usmon said.

In 1995, encouraged by his father, who hired biology and chemistry tutors to prepare him for entrance exams, Usmon entered the prestigious Tashkent Medical Institute. Two years later, he decided to go to an Arab country to study Islam properly and "learn languages, new cultures, see the world," Usmon told me when I interviewed him in 2009 in Sweden. Usmon said he resented the society in which he lived—in his words, its slavish mentality and all-pervading moral hypocrisy. He felt an urge to break away from it. He felt, he said, that if he stayed in Uzbekistan, he would never grow as an individual, would never be able to move on.

Usmon had friends from Yemen among his fellow students at the medical institute, and they helped arrange an invitation for him to study at the Al Iman University in the Yemeni capital, Sanaa. Fazlitdin aka gave his consent to Usmon's plan to go to Yemen on condition that Usmon would continue studying medicine there. Usmon did not mind, but fees at medical schools in Sanaa were too high.

Usmon began attending the Al Iman University, whose compound was as large as a village with a mosque that could accommodate more than four thousand worshippers and where tuition, housing, and food were free for students. The university was founded in 1993 by Abdul Majid al-Zindani, a follower of Yemeni Salafism, less radical than Saudi Wahhabism. He was an active supporter of the jihad against the Soviet troops in Afghanistan and a spiritual mentor to Osama bin Laden. The latter is said to have been among the university's donors, but Zindani has denied that.

Western governments have linked Al Iman's students to terror plots, attacks, and weapons smuggling in various parts of the world. Some of them were implicated in the attacks on the USS *Cole* in October 2000 and the French tanker *Limburg* in October 2002 off the Yemeni coast. In 2004 Zindani was declared by the UN and the United States "a specially designated global terrorist," after which for a while he was not able to go to Saudi Arabia, the main US ally in the Islamic world.

But now with Yemen being torn apart by civil war, as I write in 2017, Zindani is a member of the exiled government of President Abdrabbuh Mansour Hadi, residing in the Saudi capital, Riyadh. The war with the Shia minority Houthi rebels backed by Iran broke out in 2015. Saudi Arabia, with US, British, and French intelligence and logistical support, openly backs the ousted government militarily.[2] The war has caused a large-scale humanitarian crisis, with millions of Yemenis facing food insecurity and having no access to safe drinking water.

In 2014 Zindani's Al Iman was taken over by Houthi rebels and closed down. Now, with Saudi money, Zindani has plans to build new universities in parts of Yemen controlled by the exiled government, the independent Yemeni journalist and blogger Nasser Arrabyee told me in an interview from Sanaa in 2017. Arrabyee said the Saudi intervention, which is supported by the United States, has given a boost to militant jihadists, including the Yemeni branch of al-Qaeda.

Back in 2009, at the time of my conversation with Usmon, he spoke with admiration about Zindani, though he was aware that "he is considered very dangerous by the USA, and they want the Yemeni authorities to hand him over to them." He said, "He interprets the Koran in a new, scientific way. He has invented a drug for AIDS. There are some *ayah* [verse from the Koran] that no one can understand, and he's found clues to them. He has written a book jointly with the embryologist Keith Moore called *The Evolution of Humankind*. He has students from many countries."

Usmon embarked on studying ayahs, hadiths, *tafsir* (Koranic verses, sayings of the Prophet, and commentaries and interpretations of the Koran), and religious laws at Al Iman. In 1999, he made a traditional pilgrimage to the holy Islamic sites in Saudi Arabia and decided to stay there for some time, "to see what it's like there," after getting a scholarship from the Islamic University. But he was disappointed with Saudi Arabia because of the strict government control over foreigners, "constant checks," and restrictions on movement. He also thought that people in Yemen were more open and cultured than the Saudis.

Soon Usmon was struck down by osteoporosis, a disease that destroys the bones, causing them to slowly lose their density and become fragile. Because he was in constant pain, Usmon had to quit his studies and return to Yemen. One of Usmon's friends from Al Iman, Ali, who was from Palestine, invited him to Hadhramaut Valley in southern Yemen, where he was learning religion from Sufis and Shafiates. Shafiates are followers of the Shafi'i school of Islamic law, one of the four main schools in Sunni Islam, which is dominant in Yemen.

Usmon set off to the valley in 2000 when he began to feel a little better. In his words, it was while living with his friend Ali in Hadhramaut Valley that Usmon got his religious education and found faith. "Ali helped me understand religion through his own life. He did not teach me anything, only how to read the Koran. I learned things just by watching him, the way he lived."

Ali had an insatiable thirst for religious knowledge and spiritual search and knew by heart thirteen interpretations of the Koran. Usmon called him "one of the biggest teachers in my life." He said, "He studied so much, so hard. He never slept. I saw him sleep only once, on the steps, with a book in his hands. . . . He gave all of himself to faith. He never asked for any money or any help from anyone. He ate only twice a day—a piece of bread and some sour milk. He was the first person to show me true religion, as I understand it now."

Ali was also a compassionate friend, spending all his savings on Usmon's medical treatment. "I have never met anyone like him. He cares so much about other people, always wants to do something for others," Usmon said.

Back in Uzbekistan, the authorities put Usmon on the wanted list, deciding, according to Fazlitdin aka, that he had gone to follow Rukhitdin, who was at the time in hiding in Tashkent. Usmon was declared by the authorities to be a member of Hizb-ut-Tahrir. Fazlitdin aka went to an investigator and argued with him that Usmon did not even know what Hizb-ut-Tahrir was, but to no avail.

Usmon stayed in the Hadhramaut Valley for about one year and then returned to Sanaa. The disease continued to develop. He was in pain all the time; he could not sit, stand, or walk. Sometimes he gave Arabic lessons to foreigners for money.

"Problems started after 9/11," Usmon said. The Yemeni authorities decided to close down Zindani's university, accusing him of supporting terrorism.

"9/11 was blamed on Bin Laden, who had studied in Sanaa. Look how everything comes around and directly hits our family," Fazlitdin aka said, echoing Usmon, during an interview in Tashkent.

The university to which Usmon was still formally attached was closed down, and foreign students were to be deported. He was seriously ill and without means, but going back to Uzbekistan would have meant arrest and prosecution on extremism charges.

Security officers and police were repeatedly calling his family in Tashkent, asking about his whereabouts. Fazlitdin aka did what he could to get Usmon off the wanted list. He wrote many letters to prosecutors and security officials, denying the allegations against Usmon. Finally, some official said he agreed that Usmon was innocent, and he should not be afraid to return. But neither Fazlitdin aka nor Usmon himself believed those words.

Stranded in Yemen, Usmon survived doing odd jobs, working in cafes and once in a hotel as a cleaner, waiter, or cashier. "They paid pitiful money; it was hardly enough for anything," Usmon said. But because of his disease, he could not last in any job for more than two or three months. So often he would sink into even deeper poverty.

* * *

On May 15, 2005, two days after the Andijan uprising in Uzbekistan, Usmon was arrested in Sanaa. This was a time when the Yemeni authorities launched another crackdown on foreigners in order to deport them, as part of antiterrorism measures under US pressure. Usmon was taken by presidential security guards while waiting at a bus stop near the presidential palace. They thought he looked suspicious, he said.

"Who do you work for? When did you arrive? What are you doing in Yemen? Why aren't you leaving?" the security officers asked Usmon.

They kept Usmon in the basement of the presidential palace for one night. The next day Usmon was transferred to the political security prison.

There interrogators' questions changed to, "What do you have against our president? Do you have links with al-Qaeda? What do you think about Shiites?"

There was no beating and no torture. Finally, they said they had nothing against Usmon and would send him out of the country. They said they would transfer Usmon's papers to the immigration service, so they would deport him to any country of his choice. But they must have forgotten about him, and Usmon languished in jail for the next eighteen months.

He was placed in a high-security prison, where "the food was impossible to eat . . . but treatment was good." The hardest thing was not to see the sun—a walk was allowed only once a month. He was allowed to go to the toilet four times a day and "too bad if you wanted to go in between those times." Inmates staged frequent riots, which would be suppressed by special forces using tear gas. Then the inmates would get a beating and would be given a talking to. There were about twenty to twenty-five people in each cell who would lie on the floor "like firewood."

Usmon's illness would not let go. When he got too sick, ten armed soldiers would escort him to a doctor. In the street, people would gather around and stare at him, and the soldiers would try to disperse them. Doctors would say that it was nothing serious. The prison bosses did not seem to believe that Usmon was really ill either. Once an officer whispered in a doctor's ear, "Is he faking it?" The doctor whispered something back. But fellow inmates looked after Usmon, giving him the best food and the best mattress, despite his objections.

Usmon was transferred to the migration service's detention center after the escape in February 2006 of twenty-three al-Qaeda members, who dug a 140-meter tunnel from the toilet to a nearby mosque.

"Some of them were part of the al-Qaeda nerve center in Yemen," Usmon said.

The prison administration was apparently given a dressing down for allowing the escape, and as a result some prisoners were moved. The conditions in Usmon's new cell were "so much better"—with a toilet in it—that he considered himself "free," though sometimes there would be no water for up to a week. Usmon had dreams that gave him hope that he would be freed and leave the prison "with my head held high."

About six months after his transfer to the new prison, the facility was visited by a man who went around asking why each of the inmates were there. "Who else can tell me his story? Who else?" he kept asking.

Usmon was quite ill that day and was lying on the floor—he was not going to talk to anybody. But one inmate pointed at him and told the visitor, "There is one guy from Uzbekistan."

The visitor said to Usmon, "Get up." But Usmon was too unwell.

A man from Saudi Arabia told him Usmon's story. "He is here for no reason. He is ill. Why are they keeping him here?"

The visitor was an opposition MP, Ahmed Saif Hashed, who was on the Parliament's Freedom and Human Rights Committee. Hashed took up Usmon's case and started pressing for his release, raising the issue in Parliament and his own *Al-Mustakilla/Mostakela* newspaper. The story was picked up by other media outlets.

"Newspapers wrote about me every day; I became a big problem for the authorities. Various delegations began to visit me in prison—from the prosecutor's office, Parliament, political security office, and foreign ministry. They all came [to prison] to have a look at me. I didn't expect there would be such a fuss over me," Usmon said.

The authorities were forced to hold a trial for Usmon.

"It was a circus. They tried me for sitting in prison, for having no registration [with the immigration authorities] for the period I was in prison," he remembered.

"You have had no registration since May 2005," the judge said.

"I knew it was a false accusation but did not say a word against it. I simply wanted to see the sun again, to be around people," Usmon said.

He was released in late September 2007.

His family in Uzbekistan had meanwhile traced him in the Yemeni prison through the Red Cross. On May 5, 2006, a Red Cross representative visited him in jail. After his release the organization made sure his case was taken up by the UNHCR.

One day, while Usmon was waiting for the UNHCR to find a country to give him asylum, a man from Washington came to question him, Usmon said. "He took my fingerprints and scanned the iris of my eye. He lied to me that they were considering giving me asylum in the US, but he was from the CIA or something. He questioned me to check if I was linked to al-Qaeda. He spoke perfect Russian," Usmon said.

On November 15, 2007, Usmon cried all day for no reason. That was the day of his mother's death. He only found out about it from his family the day after.

In summer 2008 he arrived in Sweden as a political refugee.

* * *

I went to see Usmon in the Swedish town of Bracke in February 2009 after meetings in Stromsund with Imam Obidkhon qori Nazarov and his followers. One of them, Kamoliddin, who was also living in Bracke, gave me a lift there in his car.

During the hour-long journey in the company of his family—his wife, teenage daughter, and four-year-old son—we listened to religious songs in Arabic. Some tracks, beautiful and soothing, sounded like mantras or songs of an inspired lover. Strapped in his baby chair, the four-year-old Sirojiddin was singing along and swaying as if in a meditative trance.

When we reached Bracke, we first stopped at Kamoliddin's flat to drop off the family. They made me eat supper with them. I had to agree out of respect for Uzbek hospitality rules, even though I was impatient to see and talk to Usmon, especially as I had a train ticket for early afternoon the next day.

All over Kamoliddin's flat, on the walls, the bathroom door, kitchen cupboards, and the refrigerator, there were quotations from the Koran. Little Sirojiddin explained to me over supper that if you do not eat your meal with pleasure and gratitude to Allah, you can be sure that genies will come and join you in eating from your plate. He said I could choose any room in their flat for the night and that next time I came he would teach me more things.

His parents also said they wanted me to stay the night with them. I realized there was some concern among my hosts about my plan to stay with Usmon. It appeared that they—Nazarov himself or someone else or some kind of council—had decided or recommended that I should stay with Kamoliddin's family. Maybe they wanted to find the most discreet and decent solution. Considering the etiquette they followed regarding women and considering that Usmon and his wife had been married only for about one month by then, they thought the presence of another woman in the house would not be appropriate.

The life of Nazarov's community in Sweden was fully dictated by conservative rules. There was strict segregation of men and women. All women wore hijab and would avoid contact with men outside their families—if they bumped into a man on the street or stairs, they would quickly turn their faces away. They would also not show their faces to male visitors in their homes, keeping to the kitchen or other rooms. Their daughters as young as four would wear hijab too. All the men had bushy untrimmed beards and wore short trousers, imitating the Prophet, who wore a robe that did not reach his ankles. They believed trailing garments to be too lavish and a sign of pride.

Or maybe they wanted to limit my time with Usmon because, as it turned out, he was a dissident even inside their small community of refugees.

Before our meeting in Bracke, my last memory of Usmon was from 1997, the year he left for Yemen. I had probably last seen him outside our apartment block in Tashkent, maybe on its entrance steps or on the staircase by the elevator, and we probably greeted each other in passing. In my mind he was still that slender young man with the face of a poet.

I felt a pang in my heart the moment I saw Usmon's stooped figure—like that of an old man from the ravages of his disease—standing in the hall of his flat to greet and invite me inside. He was thirty-three at the time. His face was more mature and rounder than I remembered and also adorned with a moustache and a small beard on the tip of his chin.

We had never been friends and never said much more than hello to each other. Our closest contacts were in a distant past when he, a five- or six-year-old boy, had rung our doorbell to ask if my youngest sister, Balkhiya, who was a year younger than him, would come out to play with him in the courtyard. Their childhood friendship was short-lived because Usmon's elder brothers kept teasing him about his friendship with a girl, which was unmanly in their opinion, and saying that my little sister was his bride and he was going to marry her. They started calling him by my sister's pet name, "Botya." Perhaps to save himself from such taunts, Usmon stopped asking Balkhiya to come out to play. Or maybe their friendship ended like mine and Zukhra's because they went to different schools.

But like all longtime neighbors, we have remained involuntary witnesses of each other's life journeys, hearing scraps of news about each other from our parents and neighbors. Also I know that I will remain forever linked with him, Zukhra, and Rukhitdin by those shared childhood memories—our courtyard with maple trees and sycamores behind a green fence, cherry and apricot trees that blossomed every spring under our windows, those concrete steps that we all walked up and down many a time to enter our apartment block, and our faint memories of one another's child and teenage selves, playing games in the playground or carrying our school bags or bringing home bread or milk. Maybe those bonds are strengthened even more by that sense of community that is so strong in Uzbekistan and by the shared pain for our homeland.

Now in this neat, small flat in a remote snow-covered Swedish town, fifteen hundred miles from our home city, I felt like I was seeing a close relative with whom I had been separated for a long time by twists of fate. Maybe Usmon felt something similar. For him there was no question of me staying somewhere else that night. "She is my friend. She is staying here," he said.

I was keen to hear out his story. Of the three closest men in Zukhra's life, all of whom have become devout believers in Islam, Usmon was the only one whom I could meet in person. His experience was different from those of Rukhitdin and Farrukh, who after studying Islam in Arab countries came back to Uzbekistan and gave unauthorized lessons, staying there or nearby even after the start of the official persecution of people like them.

Usmon, because he had been away for almost eleven years, in Yemen, became in a way an outsider. He did not belong to any group of dissident Muslims in Uzbekistan and watched "the rise and fall" of Islam in his home country from a distance.

* * *

Over a meal and tea served by his wife, Usmon told me about his life in Yemen and shared his thoughts about things going on in Uzbekistan. Usmon was merciless to his troubled homeland, blaming its miseries on the Uzbeks themselves—in his words, their submissiveness and inability to stand up for their rights and truth. He spoke with passion and conviction, sometimes sounding like a revolutionary, sometimes like a preacher.

Usmon described as "useless rubbish" the religious disputes that flared up in Uzbekistan in the early 1990s between the government-supported conservative clerics and new-wave preachers seeking to introduce "a pure Islam." He said that he and Rukhitdin were among those who followed the new trend. "We were all Salafis at the time," he said.

But now he was critical of Arab preachers who had started to flock to the country in the last years of the Soviet Union and challenge the traditional Central Asian way of practicing Islam, thus causing a split among the Uzbek clergy and Muslims. "They taught hadiths and ayahs, but they did not teach how to apply those things in life. If you come to someone who for seventy years has been a Communist and tell him to grow a beard—would that not be ignorance in itself? A beard is considered good in religion, but it is not the basis of it. You cannot all of a sudden tell someone who knows nothing about religion or about the Prophet to grow a beard," Usmon said.

"And the way the Prophet taught was gradual: at first he taught that there is only one God; then he taught how to pray and so on. Everything was step by step, and the ayahs came gradually.

"For example, concerning wine, everyone drank it at first. Then there came an ayah saying that wine can do both good and harm; then there came an ayah saying that one should not pray after drinking. And only later was it said that drinking in general was not good.

"The Koran is meant to bring light to people. But those Arabs, even though they meant well, it was not all good that they brought. They did not teach people how to use hadiths in life. They came, and—boom!—they threw everything at people in one go, and that sparked differences. It was a big sin. There is no forcing in religion."

In Usmon's opinion, those new ideas were bound to find many zealous followers among new enthusiastic Uzbek Muslims because of the general lack of religious knowledge and points of reference. And a clash between the old and new Muslims was inevitable in a society now intoxicated with a sudden sense of apparent freedom but used to the domination of a monoideology and with no experience of pluralism.

"It does not matter how you pray, but they [Soviet people] are so used to doing everything like everyone else, together, collectively. They are not used to hearing different opinions and seeing that there are various ways of living.

"There were some who understood religion very narrowly—they were branded Wahhabis. These were people who had serious gaps in their education," Usmon said.

"The most important thing in that period was to teach people to love God. That is the basis of religion. First people have to understand what God is and who the Prophet was.

"But they caused a split. And that was inevitable. In those days, anyone could get hold of a microphone and say anything they wanted into it, anything they had on their minds."

And it was also inevitable that Uzbekistan would turn into a dictatorship, Usmon said. "Our people are afraid of everything. People are used to keeping quiet. 'Better an empty stomach than an earful' is their favorite saying. We won't have any government overthrow in the next hundred years," he said.

"Every man is a dictator in Uzbekistan. That's why we always have problems. For any Uzbek his boss is God. They are used to obeying someone, to having someone above them who will give them orders. And everyone wants to be a dictator. If a man cannot be a dictator at work, he is a dictator at home. Uzbekistan has become a piece of hell that has fallen on earth," he said.

I wanted to know his thoughts about what happened to Rukhitdin.

Usmon said his brother was "yet another victim" of Karimov's government. "He wanted to speak about his religion, to preach his religion to those who wanted to listen, because people need it, because our hearts long for spirituality. He is very religious. I saw only good coming from him. He was against jihadists; he said the time of jihad was gone; he said it was time for education, that only through preaching could anyone spread religion now."

Usmon said that he would hang in Tashkent's main square all the policemen who torture detainees and inmates in Uzbek jails. Probably he saw the perplexity in my eyes and smiled. "Do you think I'm no better than the Taliban?" he asked.

I hoped those were just the emotions of someone whose brother was given seventeen years in jail on fabricated charges. My hope was strengthened with Usmon's next words. He said that to become a better place, his homeland needed a just political system. "If everyone gets a voice, if there is equality and freedom, then we will have democracy and justice," he said.

But what Usmon was most bitter about when he spoke about his homeland was what he described as the loss of dignity and morale among his fellow countrymen. "A people is about its qualities; if there is no nobility in them, then they're just a group of animals. If such qualities disappear, a people disappears too. Then there is no use for such a people. If they have no morals, they are only bodies without souls. A people that does not work on itself will never develop."

He said the longer he lived, the more he understood "that father was right, that he was always right" in the way he brought them up. "He taught us to be optimists, to think about doing good for people around us, or else, he would say, our lives would be useless. That has become my main principle in life."

Usmon's wife, Malika, kept to the kitchen most of the time. Their marriage was arranged by other members of the Stromsund-Bracke Uzbek refugee community. She had been blacklisted by the Uzbek authorities for taking part in antigovernment protests in Tashkent in the 1990s in support of persecuted Muslims. She was a student at the time. Like many other such activists, she then spent years in hiding to avoid arrest, until finding a way to cross to Kazakhstan and then getting asylum in Europe through the UNHCR.

We ended our conversation and went to sleep at around two a.m.

* * *

The next morning, as I waited for Usmon to finish his prayers, I looked out of the window and watched a snow-clearing vehicle at work. The town was so small that I could see its edges, beyond which were snowy plains and pine forests—a landscape in such contrast to the sun-soaked deserts and valleys of Uzbekistan.

After breakfast I asked Usmon to help me translate from the Uzbek Rukhitdin's poem that he had written in prison, dedicated to their parents. Usmon eagerly agreed—maybe because it could offer him a glimpse of what was in his elder brother's heart.

"We always keep losing one another," Usmon said of their relationship.

Usmon sat beside me in front of my laptop, and we began reading. It turned out to be a painful exercise for Usmon. The reading and translating process was frequently interrupted by Usmon's emotional comments.

At the beginning he was dismissive of his brother's poetic ability altogether. "What kind of words did he use? It doesn't make sense! It's unreadable! What kind of language is this?" Usmon exploded after reading almost every line.

Then he calmed down until we came to the lines in which Rukhitdin expressed repentance for causing pain to his parents. "Aha, now he is saying it! Now he's understood!" he exclaimed.

Usmon's reaction to Rukhitdin's poem bared the deep resentment and anger that Rukhitdin's brothers and sisters were feeling inside—but keeping to themselves—about the choices he made in his life and which have consequently filled with pain and shattered, in one way or another, the lives of every member of their family.

Rukhitdin's poem was given to me by Fazlitdin aka, during one of our conversations in their home in Tashkent. He brought it, printed on several sheets of A4 paper, out of his bedroom; he put his reading glasses on and read it out for me—his hands and voice were trembling, and he was hardly able to hold back his tears.

Rukhitdin's poem (written in 2006):

> May every deed be in the name of Allah,
> May Allah be blessed endlessly—
> In the footsteps of the Prophet I found the path of truth.
> I am your son who belongs to Mohammad's tribe,
> I am your son who's been thrown into jail.
>
> In the repressive 1930s came the Soviets
> And destroyed the faithful ones.
> But my grandparents named you
> "The dignity of religion."[3]
> I am your son who is proud of your name,
> I am your son who's been thrown into jail.
>
> Since my young years you've encouraged me to study,
> You wanted me to be physically strong.
> You asked God that I should grow up a noble man.
> I am your son raised by you this way,
> I am your son who's been thrown into jail.
>
> I've loved and respected you since my early days,
> You've been the greatest man for me.
> I was afraid I would lose you one day—
> Maybe that's made my hair turn gray so soon.
> I am your son who's been thrown into jail.
>
> I am a son for whom you were a role model—
> The way you dressed and lived,
> The way you treated the old and the young,
> The way you cared about those you love.
> I am your son who's been thrown into jail.
>
> I have mastered secular knowledge
> As much as I could.
> I've also acquired religious knowledge.
> Don't know how many books I've read—
> I read them all for you.
> I am your son who's been thrown into jail.

Some people respect me as a man of knowledge.
I wish it were true, but it is not—
I am a student still.
I am your son who knows so little,
I am your son who's been thrown into jail.

Some people call me an enemy
And put hurdles in my way.
They want to incarcerate my soul—
This way the evil ones want to cover up their crimes.
I am your son who is far from rebellious thoughts,
I am your son who's been thrown into jail.

O Father, all I know is
That I cannot repay my dues to you.
My soul is grieving—
What will I say on Judgment Day?
I am a son begging for your blessing,
I am your son who's been thrown into jail.

I'd like to remind you of Jacob's story:
He lost his son Joseph and his youngest one,
But one day Allah reunited them all.
I am a son who wishes you Jacob's patience,
I am your son who's been thrown into jail.

I know it's been very hard for you, dear Father—
Your sons are away from you.
But one day all five of us will stand by your side.
I am your son, who sees Joseph's dreams,
I am your son who's been thrown into jail.

Father is one's gate to paradise.
Enter this gate if you can,
If not, you are at a loss, O ignorant son.
I am your son who's read such hadiths,
I am your son who's been thrown into jail.

I want to find that gate,
I'd do anything to make you happy,
But I know not if I have the time.
I miss being by your side,
I am your son who's been thrown into jail.

Mother, I have words for you from my heart.
I miss your pure and kind words,
You care about me most after Allah.

I am a son who knew it far too late,
I am your son who's been thrown into jail.

At night you sang me a lullaby,
Gently stroking my face.
You washed my clothes
As I was gaining my strength.
I am a son who can't pay back your kindness,
I am your son who's been thrown into jail.

When I was sick you knew no rest,
You could give your life for me any time.
It is my turn to be by your side,
But I can't even ask, "How are you?"
I am your son who's been thrown into jail.

I never had to worry about food and clothing,
I knew I had a mother to provide that.
My children come to visit me in jail.
I am a son who cannot visit his mother,
I am your son who's been thrown into jail.

I wish I could take your hands
And feel your fingers' touch on my eyes.
I wish I could wipe the tears from your face.
I see your clear eyes in my dreams,
I am your son who says, "Don't grieve, it's Allah's land."
I am your son who's been thrown into jail.

I often recall my last meeting with you,
How I spoke with tears in my eyes.
Did my heart know separation was near?
I am your son who always thinks of you,
I am your son who's been thrown into jail.

If it were possible to worship a human being,
I would kiss your feet,
Because paradise is at a mother's feet.
I am a son who has not paid his dues,
I am a son who's been thrown into jail.

If you call me, I'll interrupt my prayer that moment.
"Take your parents' blessing before it's too late,
Or else you'll never enter paradise," the Prophet said.
I am a son who needs your prayers,
I am your son who's been thrown into jail.

Here is my prayer:
May Allah save my parents' souls;
I'd give anything for that.
I am your son whose soul will be sacrificed for you,
I am your son who's been thrown into jail.

* * *

I asked Usmon if he still held a grievance against Rukhitdin for choosing to preach Salafism in defiance of the official policy.

"Everyone makes their own choices. I cannot judge anyone. Maybe he made mistakes, but maybe everything he did was right. The story is not over yet," Usmon said. "I love and respect him. He has suffered a lot. He was living for other people, for his students, his followers, his religion. Sometimes I begin to have doubts—maybe he was wrong? But I stop myself, saying: It is not for you to judge; Allah will judge him."

Usmon suggested that his brother's views on Islam might have changed with time. "Maybe he's started to change. Life changes everyone."

Usmon told me about the evolution of his own understanding of Islam and faith in general. His Salafi belief had first been shaken at Al Iman, where for the first time he encountered the diversity of Islam.

"They did not teach Salafism. They are tolerant to everyone there. There were Sufis, Salafis, Shiites, others there, and everyone was treated equally by teachers.

"I spent time with Sufis. I liked being with them; they were good people. I changed my opinion about it [Salafism]. It is wrong to divide people into different groups. It's better to be just a simple man, just a believer. What's wrong with being nobody, not belonging to any group?

"It is more important to know yourself, to make this world a better place, to understand things in the right way. It is more important than to belong to some group," Usmon said.

It explained why Usmon was critical of Imam Nazarov and his followers. He said he was resisting their attempts to make him part of their community, which would mean attending their regular gatherings and recognizing Nazarov without question as their spiritual leader. Usmon wanted to keep his freedom of consciousness.

I asked Usmon why he thought Allah was giving him so much pain and suffering.

He half smiled and after a moment of consideration said, pausing after almost every word, as if still searching for an answer: "Because he loves me. Probably he does not want me to go to hell. He wants me to pay for all my sins already in this life," he said.

"What sins?" I asked.

He smiled. Then he looked down and, thinking for a few moments, said, looking me in the eye: "I don't want to go to hell. I am afraid of hell. You know how hell is described in the Koran: 'And they will give you lashes until your skin comes off. And after a new skin grows on you, they will lash you again until your new skin comes off.' And so on and so on."

He was quoting this passage from the Koran:

Those who have disbelieved in Our signs—
We will burn them in fire.
As often as their skins are roasted through,
We will exchange them for other skins so that they may taste the punishment.
Indeed, Allah is Exalted in Power, Wise.[4]

Notes

1. The girl's name is not used to protect her identity.
2. Steven Erlanger, "At Yemen College, Scholarship and Jihadist Ideas," *New York Times*, January 18, 2010; Kareem Fahim, "Yemen's Opposition May Be Caught by Its Own Double Game," *New York Times*, December 2, 2011.
3. The meaning of Fazlitdin aka's name.
4. Surah an-Nisa, 4:56.

AFTERWORD

As a Soviet schoolchild, I remember feeling enormously lucky to have been born in the Soviet Union, where, I believed, there was no discrimination toward anybody on any grounds, no war, and no rich and no poor. I imagined with horror that, had I been so unfortunate and lived in a capitalist country, I would have probably suffered from racial abuse, been poor, and lived in a cardboard box.

History was one of my favorite subjects. I absolutely loved our history teacher, Tamara Popova—we called her, using her patronymic, Tamara Vasilyevna. She was strict, but her strictness commanded respect, not just obedience. She was an excellent storyteller—our class would listen to her accounts of historical events as if mesmerized, in complete silence.

She styled her short, light-brown hair with curlers, like almost every Soviet Russian woman, but she had her own strict dress code: when it was cold, every single day she would wear a dark-blue medium-length skirt and a black turtleneck; when it was warm, she would change between two or three simple short-sleeved dresses. I am not sure what motivated her dress style—most other teachers seemed to like dressing up—but I took it as humility and discipline, and I respected her for that. Now, many years on, it is easy for me to picture her in my head in her dark-blue skirt and black turtleneck, slowly walking between the rows of desks, softly running her hand over them and telling us about past kingdoms, empires, wars, and revolutions.

I still remember Tamara Vasilyevna's classes fondly despite knowing that she taught us an ideologically twisted and Russia-centered version of history. Essentially, for me those were stories about right and wrong, about good people, or ideas, fighting against bad people, or ideas, and it did not really matter what each side was called.

What had a real impact on me, stirred questions, and, I believe, shaped me internally was literature. Our house was a five-minute walk from the Republican Children's Library. Going there, returning books I'd finished reading, spending time choosing new ones from the rows of shelves in a spacious quiet room, which felt like a sacred place, and then carrying them back home was a special ritual that filled me with joy and anticipation of new words and stories to absorb.

The very first piece of literature that shook me to the core was a short story I read when I was eight years old. The story called "The Red Shoes" was in our school reading book. It was about a little black girl in America who dreamed about getting a pair of beautiful red shoes—her old ones were worn out beyond repair. Her mother had to work extra hours as a dishwasher to earn enough money to pay for those shoes. Finally, they went to the shop. The shop owner, who was white, was rude and did not even want to believe they had the money to buy anything in his shop, so the woman had to show her wallet as proof. When the little girl tried a pair on, they turned out to be too tight, and her mother asked for another pair. The shop owner demanded that they still buy the pair the girl had tried on because nobody would want to have them after they had been tried on by a black girl. The eight-year-old me felt incredibly sorry for the girl. It was a big shock to discover that such injustice was possible somewhere in the world. I suspect that story contributed a lot to my sense of being lucky to live in the USSR.

I do not regret my Soviet childhood—there were good things about it, including free education, free health care, and free summer holidays by the Black Sea with my table tennis team. But I am glad that I did not have to live my adult life in the Soviet Union and endure any more ideological indoctrination. Fortunately, my last years of school, when I was beginning to form my own views, coincided with Gorbachev's perestroika. The Soviet ideological machine, as well as the country itself, was beginning to fall apart.

In the last days of the Soviet Union and early days of independence, thousands of my fellow countrywomen and men were rediscovering Islam to reconnect with their own cultural, ethnic, and spiritual identity. I too for the first time discovered in myself a yearning to understand the meaning of human life and how this life is to be lived.

The trigger was a thin book given to me to read by a neighborhood friend. It was called *Freedom from the Known* by the Indian spiritual teacher Jiddu Krishnamurti. It opened with these words:

> Man has throughout the ages been seeking something beyond himself, beyond material welfare—something we call truth of God or reality, a timeless state—something that cannot be distributed by circumstances, by thought or by human corruption. Man has always asked the question: what is it all about? Has life any meaning at all? He sees the enormous confusion of life, the brutalities, the revolts, the wars, the endless divisions of religion, ideology and nationality, and with a sense of deep abiding frustration he asks, what is one to do, what is this thing we call living, is there anything beyond it?[1]

I instantly knew that these were "my" questions and, moreover, that probably they were the most important questions. To answer them, Krishnamurti suggested an independent path of self-knowledge, and it sounded like my cup of tea as I always felt strongly against belonging to any group or following any leader.

I explored various religious and spiritual teachings in later years, not with the idea of adopting one but seeking to understand better what religion is in general. They have all left their mark on me and given me some knowledge and better understanding of myself. I look at them—and at any work of philosophy, literature, poetry, or art created by anybody anywhere in the world—as a heritage belonging to the whole of humankind, as our collective effort to understand ourselves.

Essentially, like people across the entire former Soviet Union after its collapse, on one or another level, that was what most people in Uzbekistan were trying to do—to know who we really were and which way we wanted to go. It was inevitable and natural that a variety of choices would be made from one individual to another, depending on their personal qualities, inclinations, level of education, and other circumstances.

But the most crucial choice about the Uzbek people's future was to be made by President Karimov. He chose tyranny. (It cannot be blamed solely on his being a product of the Soviet totalitarian system, because so were Gorbachev, Boris Yeltsin, and several other post-Soviet leaders, including in Central Asia, who chose more liberal paths.)

Karimov's choice decided what Uzbekistan's postindependence story would be about. It is not a story about religious radicalism. It is a story about an inhumane, tyrannical regime.

Of all the Uzbeks who were killed, jailed, tortured, abducted, or forced to flee their homeland for alleged religious extremism under Karimov's rule, only a small minority might have had something to answer for before the law, and even they did not get, or would not have gotten, a fair trial.

The absolute majority and their families suffered for nothing. Thousands are still languishing in jail, which means continued suffering for them and their loved ones.

* * *

On February 22, 2012, Imam Nazarov was shot in the head at the bottom of the stairs of his apartment block in the Swedish town of Stromsund, which had become his place of refuge. For over two years he remained in a coma. He is now able to talk again. He remains in Sweden, but his whereabouts are kept secret.

His followers are sure that the assassination attempt was contracted by the Uzbek government. In 2014 a suspect with dual Uzbek-Russian citizenship, a man called Yuri Zhukovskiy, was detained in Russia over the attack. He was extradited to Sweden, where in 2016 a court sentenced him to life in prison for his crime. Zhukovskiy is also suspected of murdering Fuad Rustamkhojayev, one of the founders of an Uzbek opposition movement in exile, in Russia in 2011.

In my conversations with him, Nazarov maintained he was an adherent of Hanafi Islam, traditional for Central Asia, and that was what he taught his followers. My contacts with Nazarov have left me with an impression that he was not someone who could lie. Radicals do not and cannot hide their radical ideas because they are completely possessed by them.

I also saw that Nazarov genuinely felt responsible for the suffering his students and family members endured because of their being linked to him. It was clearly something that lay heavily on his heart.

His students, all mostly from an urban background, left me with the impression that they were educated, intelligent, and determined to live virtuously. The fact that under official pressure—instead of going to Afghanistan or the Middle East to join militant groups—they chose a life in hiding, in constant danger of arrest, still doing their best to provide for and look after their families, and then sought asylum in Europe, is further evidence that Nazarov did not preach violent jihadism to them.

Regarding Rukhitdin, Imam Nazarov told me that, as far as he could tell, he had at least once had contact with more radically inclined Uzbek Muslims. He had been sought out by them as a reference point because of his proper Islamic training. They wanted to know his opinion on militant jihad. Rukhitdin turned to Nazarov for advice. Nazarov's advice, he said, was to tell them that they should abandon such ideas.

Rukhitdin himself was not one of them. But if any of those radically minded Uzbeks were later arrested, they would, under torture, name Rukhitdin and provide whatever incriminating testimony against him that the government had fabricated. There are serious grounds to suggest that the government was behind the rape of his daughter to make him sign confession papers. And it speaks volumes about the validity of their accusations against him. As a popular independent preacher, he was doomed to be blacklisted.

When he was captured, Rukhitdin lived in the hope that soon the authorities would realize their mistake and see that he was not the "terrorist" they were after and let him go. That did not happen. As I write these lines in 2017, he has been imprisoned for twelve years.

He is dreaming of doing gardening when he is released. There is a fellow inmate who is a gardener, and he has told him all the secrets—what soil is good for what plant, what different plants like. He wants to grow a fruit garden and flowers. He is also planning to keep sheep. He asks his family to bring him newspapers and books, mostly Russian classics like Tolstoy and Pushkin.

Zukhra's husband, Farrukh, as another independent preacher, was doomed too. With him the authorities chose a particularly callous and shocking method, abduction, to psychologically pressure his wife's family to cooperate with the authorities in hunting down Rukhitdin. Imam Nazarov's son Khusnutdin was "disappeared" for a similar reason, to pressure his family to give away the imam's hiding place.

The story of Rukhitdin's youngest brother, Usmon, stands out as a good illustration that, had Uzbeks who adopted Salafism (or any other new teaching that was around at the time of Uzbekistan's Islamic revival) been given time and a chance to learn more about Islam and other schools and interpretations within it, they might have had a change of heart. Back then, Salafism happened to be on offer—with help from Saudi Arabia, which promotes and sponsors its spread across the Muslim world—as an alternative to the old Soviet ideology and officially controlled religious practice. What also should be remembered is that practicing Salafism does not automatically lead to violent jihadism—becoming a militant or suicide bomber is an altogether separate choice.

Usmon came to religion out of a rejection of Soviet ideology and out of his dissatisfaction with the moral and spiritual state of Uzbek society. I saw the same motivation, not always clearly and eloquently articulated, in many other Uzbeks who turned to Islam after the Soviet collapse. Karimov's regime was the exact opposite of what they wanted their society to be. It is their aspirations for a fairer and more moral society that Karimov sought to crush.

* * *

Karimov suffered a stroke in late August 2016 and died a few days later at the age of seventy-eight. In his twenty-six-year rule he was guided by nothing but fear of losing power, contempt for his people and their human rights, and suspicion of the outside world.

He turned the secret service, the police, the prosecutors, and judges into a monstrous repressive machine. Karimov himself and the entire country became hostages to that machine. The people who did the system's dirty work were allowed to unleash their lowest instincts and commit atrocities against other human beings with full impunity and turn breaking and taking other people's lives into their daily job and source of income.

Without using torture, the Uzbek law-enforcement and justice system would not have been able to provide Karimov with regular reports about how it had uncovered and locked up more and more alleged Islamists allegedly plotting to overthrow him. Karimov depended on such reports to feel that his power was secure.

Describing the Stalinist system in his book *The Rise and Fall of the Soviet Empire*, the historian Dmitri Volkogonov says that for that system to function, "for it to achieve its economic, social and political goals, permanent purge was a necessity." Similar constant terrorizing of citizens was necessary for Karimov's regime to go on.[2] It is hard to exaggerate how degrading and destructive Karimov's rule, during which police and security cells were turned into torture chambers, has been for the Uzbek nation.

Fyodor Dostoyevsky in *Zapiski iz Mertvogo Doma* (*The House of the Dead*) passes a profoundly harsh verdict on a society that allows the total physical abuse of its own citizens:

> Someone who has tasted this kind of power, this unlimited power over flesh, blood and soul of another man like himself . . . he cannot help losing control over himself. Tyranny is a habit; it can grow on you, it can eventually grow into a disease. . . . Blood and power intoxicate people: they grow callous, perverted; the mind and senses begin to accept and, eventually, crave the most abnormal things. Human being and citizen die in a tyrant forever, while return to human dignity, to repentance, to revival becomes almost impossible for him. . . . A society that indifferently watches such a phenomenon, is already

contaminated at its very core. In a word, the right of physical punishment given to one person over another, is one of the social ills, one of the most powerful ways of destroying in it any embryo, any attempt at civil society and a sure condition for its inevitable and unavoidable decay.[3]

Another way in which Karimov denied human dignity to his citizens was through economic deprivation, despite Uzbekistan's significant economic potential. His regime stifled the national economy through restrictions on trade and currency exchange, and closure of major Soviet-era industrial enterprises. Millions of Uzbeks have been forced to go to Russia as guest laborers, so they can feed their families, despite facing official abuse and racist attacks there.

Economic deprivation might even have been a deliberate government policy. An Uzbek economist told me once that the government's economic policy was based on the assumption that Uzbek people are so industrious that even if completely abandoned by the state—given no jobs, no decent wages, no economic rights—they will still figure out how to survive. The ordinary people's complete absence of rights left them open to abuse by absolutely anyone with any amount of power—traffic policemen, tax inspectors, and so on.

This is what caused the emergence of the group behind the Andijan uprising. It was an attempt to escape and create an alternative to the soulless, hopeless, and grim reality of Karimov's Uzbekistan. They were made to pay a very high price for it.

* * *

Karimov's regime blatantly exploited an exaggerated threat of religious extremism to restrict citizens' rights—to free speech, civic and political activity, and to openly and freely practice a religion of their choice. (Christians, other than the officially supported Russian Orthodox Church, and other religious groups faced persecution too.)

There is an assumption promoted by the media and experts and accepted by the general public, in much of the former Soviet Union—notably in its less free parts, including Russia—that Karimov's harsh rule saved Central Asia from the spread of violent religious extremism. The fact is that during Karimov's rule, violence and illegality were predominantly perpetrated by the government itself—by its policemen, security officers, soldiers, judges, investigators, prosecutors, and prison wardens. No religious or political group was ever allowed to operate at all.

There are complex reasons behind modern-day extremism—historical, political, social, geopolitical, psychological, and technological. A December 2015 report by the security intelligence firm Soufan Group linked the rise in extremism in the Middle East in the past few years to the Syrian war and the post-US invasion chaos in Iraq. When it comes to foreigners going to fight in Syria, most of them did so for personal, not political, reasons, it said. In a further report in October 2017 the group said many joined in reaction "to local conditions of poor governance and social stagnation."

Soufan Group's 2017 report put the number of Uzbek fighters in Syria at 1,500. But the other Central Asian nations contributed too: 1,300 went from Tajikistan, 500 from Kyrgyzstan, the same number from Kazakhstan, and another 400 from Turkmenistan. Relative to each country's population (as of 2017 Uzbekistan had 32 million people; Kazakhstan, 18 million; Tajikistan, 9 million; and Kyrgyzstan and Turkmenistan, about 6 million each), the region's biggest contributor of fighters for the IS group was Tajikistan, followed by Turkmenistan, then Kyrgyzstan, and only after that Uzbekistan. The report said that overall the IS group attracted more than 40,000 fighters from more than 110 countries around the world, including some 3,400 from Russia (mainly from the northern Caucasus) and more than 5,700 from Western Europe. This bigger picture helps to show that claims that Uzbekistan is, or is prone to becoming, a breeding ground of radical Islamism are seriously exaggerated.

Karimov's oppressive rule did create textbook conditions for citizens to get radicalized, but compared to the numbers of Uzbeks who ended up with militant groups, incomparably larger numbers chose instead to leave in search of better economic opportunities. As of January 2016, about 1.8 million Uzbek labor migrants were in Russia, according to official Russian figures. Thousands have gone looking for a living to Kazakhstan, South Korea, the United Arab Emirates, and other countries or migrated to the West.

Political, social, and other factors do play a role, but fundamentally the violent ideology that jihadist groups promote appeals to only a very limited number of people who are first and foremost inclined toward violence rather than being driven by ideas of justice or being especially pious. According to Islamic State records of more than 4,000 foreign fighters, 70 percent of them say they have only basic knowledge of Islam, the French scholar on Islam Olivier Roy wrote in an article in the British newspaper *The Guardian* on April 13, 2017.

Roy said that his study of the backgrounds of all perpetrators of terror attacks in France and Belgium in the past twenty years led him to the conclusion that they represented a wider nihilist youth culture, or movement, "constructed independently of parental religion and culture." Almost all of them had histories of petty crime, time in jail, and dysfunctional families. Almost all were newly converted Muslims, and the main attraction for them was not Islam, not religion, but Islamist groups' radical violent agenda.

"The caliphate is a fantasy," Roy wrote. Jihadism had a very narrow social and political base and could only draw in those on the fringe—"the disturbed, the vulnerable, the rebels without a cause"—by offering "a narrative framework" to vent their anger, he added.

Sayfullo Saipov, an Uzbek national who on October 31, 2017, drove a pickup truck into people in New York, killing eight, seems to have done just that: vented his anger over his personal failures. My former AP colleague Mansur Mirovalev, now a freelance journalist based in Moscow, has visited and interviewed Saipov's family and neighbors in Tashkent (on an assignment for CNN). Mirovalev found that Saipov came from a relatively secure family, but being the eldest child and only son meant he was under the pressure of heightened expectations. After graduating from the Tashkent Financial Institute, he worked as an accountant but harbored bigger ambitions. When in 2010, he suddenly won the US green card lottery, he took it as his big chance. But his attempts to start his own business in the United States failed, and he ended up as an Uber driver. He considered going back to Uzbekistan, but returning with nothing to show for himself seemed too much for his ego. His neighbors in the United States, according to media reports, said that in the months leading to the New York attack, Saipov had become increasingly psychopathic and antisocial.

Those who argue that Central Asia faces the danger of religious extremism also often cite its geographical proximity to Afghanistan. This perceived danger is an especially popular idea with the Russian government, as a way of convincing the regional governments that they need Russian military support.

But the number of Central Asian fighters in Afghanistan is not significant enough (the largest estimates I have ever heard from experts and governments is around two thousand) to represent a serious military threat. The Uzbek-Afghan border is short and well protected, and Uzbekistan's army is the most powerful in the region. The Tajik-Afghan border goes through the Pamir mountain range—with an average altitude of 6,100 meters it is one of the highest in the world. And mountains cover 90 percent of Tajikistan. The Turkmen border is more penetrable, but much of the country's territory is a sparsely populated desert. As for the Afghan Taliban, they have their own agenda—to fight the foreign military presence, not to capture foreign territory. Most importantly, society in Central Asia is predominantly secular, and a highly repressive theocracy is not what the majority of Uzbeks and Central Asians, or their ruling elites, want.

* * *

My last visit to Uzbekistan was in 2011. When I flew to Tashkent again the following year, from London, where I now live, I was prohibited from entering the country and deported after being kept in the airport's transit area for twenty-three hours. I was not given any reason, only told that I was now banned from visiting for the next five years. My mum was waiting for me at the airport, but I never showed up at the arrivals gate. We were in the same building but never saw each other. She was in tears and worried that I had probably been arrested.

Because of that five-year entry ban, I was not able to come to Tashkent in the summer of 2016, when Mum was dying. I tried talking to her on the phone on the day she died. She could only say my name; her voice sounded like she was already being sucked into nothingness.

That was the cruelest thing done personally to me by Karimov's regime—an experience that left me feeling angry and helpless against a ruthless system that at will breaks into your life and takes away from you and your nearest and dearest anything it wants. The experience also allowed me to feel for myself a tiny fraction of what Zukhra and her family and many other Uzbek families must have felt when the state literally crushed their lives.

In our conversations, Zukhra often spoke about the time before the start of Karimov's all-out crackdown on dissident Muslims as "peacetime" and the time after as "war." For her, psychologically, what she went through—a violent and sudden disruption of her life, the agony of losing her husband and not knowing what had happened to him—amounted to war, something that probably all human beings would name as the worst and most terrifying thing that could happen in their lives.

Zukhra is still in Tashkent. Her son, Abdullo, is a student majoring in computer technology. Her father, Fazlitdin aka, died, just weeks after my mum and just weeks before Karimov.

* * *

Uzbekistan now has a new leader, Shavkat Mirziyoyev, Karimov's prime minister for thirteen years. He has taken some encouraging steps: a few political prisoners have been released; a few thousand people have been removed from the blacklist of suspected radical Islamists; international human rights organizations have been invited back; and steps have been taken to seemingly reduce the influence of the security service, the main enforcer of Karimov's repressive policies. I began hearing from family and friends in Uzbekistan that there was significantly less tension in the air, that people were feeling hopeful. But then in September and October 2017 the authorities arrested two independent journalists, dampening hopes for any further relaxation of political control.

It seems at this point that Mirziyoyev's ambitions are limited to advancing the country economically, and in the spheres of politics and human rights he is only going to go as far as is necessary to improve the country's image so that foreign investors can invest without fear of being accused of doing business with a particularly notorious regime.

It is clear that Mirziyoyev wants to gloss over Karimov's dark legacy: Tashkent's airport has already been named after Karimov, a big mausoleum is being built for him in his home city Samarkand, and monuments to him are being erected.

There are too many people from the old regime still in positions of power, although the security chief, Rustam Inoyatov, was fired in January 2018. There are others in the law-enforcement and judicial organs who under Karimov directly, on a daily basis, participated in the arbitrary prosecution of their fellow citizens and violation of their fundamental rights. Should the truth be revealed about those abuses, these officials would have to be brought to account, those unfairly jailed would have to be released, and the deaths by torture and forced disappearances would have to be investigated.

I do not know if the victims of Karimov's regime will ever get that kind of official justice, for it would require a leadership with a lot of moral courage, the dismantling of the current system of power based on nepotism and corruption, and a strong civil society. It might take a long time before all these things are in place in Uzbekistan.

But there is another kind of power that can already be used to vindicate them today—the power of words. "For, while the tale of how we suffer, and how we are delighted, and how we may triumph is never new, it always must be heard. There isn't any other tale to tell, it's the only light we've got in all this darkness."[4]

Notes

1. Jiddu Krishnamurti, *Freedom from the Known* (New York: Harper One, 2009), 9.

2. Dmitri Volkogonov, *The Rise and Fall of the Soviet Empire* (London: HarperCollins, 1999), 109.

3. Fyodor Dostoyevsky, *Zapiski iz Mertvogo Doma* [*The House of the Dead*] (St. Petersburg: Lenizdat, 2013), 253.

4. James Baldwin, "Sonny's Blues," in *The Jazz Fiction Anthology,* ed. Sascha Feinstein and David Rife (Bloomington: Indiana University Press, 2009), 47.

GLOSSARY

Terms are Uzbek, including Arabic words in common usage in Uzbek, unless otherwise stated.

ada—father, father-in-law.

Adolat—justice; one of the vigilante groups that emerged in the Fergana Valley in the 1980s.

aka—elder brother.

Assalomu Alaykum—Arabic greeting; "Peace be upon you."

ayah—sign, evidence in Arabic; used to name Koranic paragraphs or verses.

Basmachi—armed resistance against the Bolsheviks in Central Asia after the Russian Revolution of 1917.

birodar—brother.

birodarlar—plural of *birodar*; what members of the group behind the 2005 Andijan revolt called themselves.

Bismillohir Rahmonir Rahim—"In the Name of God the Compassionate and Merciful" (Arabic).

Detskiy Mir—Children's World (Russian); used to describe the neighborhood in Tashkent where Zukhra and I grew up; so named because of the children's department store beneath our apartment block.

Eid—major Islamic holiday, celebrated twice a year—at the end of the yearly pilgrimage to Mecca (Eid al-Adha) and after the holy fasting month of Ramadan (Eid al-Fitr).

fetwa—an edict issued by an Islamic scholar.

GUVD—City Police Department (Russian abbreviation).

glasnost—openness in Russian; a policy that was part of Gorbachev's perestroika.

hadith—canonized sayings of the Prophet Mohammad.

hoja—families believed to be descendants of the Rightly Guided Caliphs.

hijra—the Prophet Mohammad's flight from Mecca to Medina to escape assassination.

hujra—a system of underground religious teaching.

hujum—Bolshevik campaign to unveil women of Central Asia.

inorodtsy—aliens (Russian); how Central Asians were categorized by the colonial Russian government.

inshallah—God willing.

ishans—families who believe they are direct descendants of Mohammad's daughter Fatima and her husband Ali.

Islom Lashkarlari—Warriors of Islam, a vigilante group set up by Tohir Yuldosh, the future leader of the militant Islamic Movement of Uzbekistan.

221

jadid—a promoter or supporter of Jadidism.

Jadidism—a progressive reformist movement in the late nineteenth/early twentieth centuries in the Muslim parts of Tsarist Russia.

jamoat—groups, society.

"jon" as an ending—means soul; added to one's name as a sign of affection and love.

jonginam—my little soul.

jonim—"my soul" used to address loved ones;

Khlopkovoye Delo—The Cotton Case (Russian); a large-scale corruption investigation against Uzbek Soviet officials in the 1980s.

kolkhoz—short for collective farm (Russian).

Komsomol—the Soviet Communist Party's youth wing (Russian).

kulak—a wealthy peasant (Russian).

madhhab—a school of Islamic jurisprudence, of which there are four main ones in Sunni Islam.

madrasah—religious school.

mahallya—neighborhood.

maktab—school.

mojaheddin—those struggling on the path of jihad.

Muallimus Soniy—*Second Teacher*, a thin booklet sold in Uzbekistan which explains to non-Arab speakers the Arabic alphabet and helps them read the Koran.

muezzin—a person in a mosque who sings the call to prayer.

*mujaddidiya, (*singular—*mujaddid)*—renovators.

*mushriklar (*singular—*mushrik)*—polytheists.

MVD—Ministry of Internal Affairs (Russian abbreviation).

namoz—prayer.

ona—mother.

onajon—dear mother.

opa—elder sister.

osh—Uzbek rice and carrot dish.

ota—father.

otajon—dear father.

otin—female religious teacher, usually in communities.

oyi—aunt.

perestroika—liberal reforms started by Mikhail Gorbachev in the late 1980s that led to the disintegration of the Soviet Union (Russian).

qazi—an Islamic judge.

qori—someone who knows the Koran.

qozhi—someone who has done pilgrimage to Mecca.

Ramadan—a holy month of fasting in Islam.

Raskulachivaniye—(Russian) the Bolshevik campaign to nationalize the property of wealthy peasants (*kulaks*).

RUVD—District Police Department (Russian abbreviation).

Salafism—an ultra-conservative ideology that rejects the entire Islamic theology and jurisprudence and calls for a return to the "pure" Islam of the time of the Prophet Mohammad and the use as reference only of the Koran and hadiths. Salafism has roots in some medieval movements within Islam, but its modern forms really started in the eighteenth and nineteenth centuries. As a widespread and "most dissatisfied" form of modern Islam, it only emerged in the 1980s.

Sangorod—abbreviation of the Russian *Sanitarnyy Gorod*, Sanitary Town; prison hospital in Tashkent.

sheikh—Islamic scholar.

SNB—The Uzbek National Security Service.

Sunnah—the Prophet Mohammad's way of life.

Sura—a Koranic verse.

tafsir—commentary, interpretation of the Koran.

TashGU—The Tashkent State University (Russian abbreviation).

TashMI—The Tashkent Medical Institute (Russian abbreviation).

uka—younger brother.

Ummah—Islamic community.

UVD—Interior Department (Russian abbreviation).

voronok—a van for transporting detainees, convicts, defendants, inmates (Russian).

Vostfak—short for Russian *Vostochnyy Fakultet*, the Oriental Studies Department.

Wahhabism—the Saudi name for Salafism. Wahhabism is so called after its founder Abd al Wahhab (d. 1792), who was expelled from his native Iraq but found popularity with Saudi Arabian tribes. He supported the Saudi royal family's coming to power and they in exchange made his ideas official ideology. The Salafis find the term Wahhabi derogatory as it links them not to the Prophet but to a mortal human.

waqfs—Islamic property endowments used for funding schools or hospitals.

zhanoza—funeral prayer.

BIBLIOGRAPHY

Abashin, Sergey. *Ferganskaya dolina: etnichnost, etnicheskiye protsessy, etnicheskiye konflikty.* Moscow: Nauka, 2004.

———. "The Logic of Islamic Practice: A Religious Conflict in Central Asia." *Central Asian Survey* 25, no. 3 (2006): 267–86.

Abdirashidov, Zaynabidin. *Ismail Gasprinskiy i Turkestan v nachale XX veka: svyazi-otnosheniya-vliyanie.* Tashkent: Akademnashr, 2011.

Ahmed, Shahab. *What Is Islam? The Importance of Being Islamic.* Princeton, NJ: Princeton University Press, 2016.

Armstrong, Karen. *The Battle for God: A History of Fundamentalism.* New York: Random House, 2001.

———. *Islam: A Short History.* London: Phoenix Press, 2001.

Atkin, Muriel. "The Rhetoric of Islamophobia." *Central Asia and the Caucasus* 1 (2000). http://www.ca-c.org/journal/2000/journal_eng/eng01_2000/16.atkin.shtml.

Babajanov, Bakhtiyar. "O 'pravilnykh' i 'nepravilnykh' pravovernykh." *Centrasia.ru,* February 17, 2008. http://www.centrasia.ru/newsA.php?st=1203198720.

Babajanov, Bakhtiyar, Ashirbek Muminov, and Anke von Kugelgen. *Disputy musulmanskikh religioznykh avtoritetov v Tsentralnoy Azii v 20 veke.* Almaty, Kazakhstan: Daik-Press, 2007.

Babajanov, Bakhtiyar, Ashirbek Muminov, and Martha Brill Olcott. "Muhammadjan Hindustani (1892–1989) and the Religious Environment of His Era (Preliminary Reflections on Formation of 'Soviet Islam' in Central Asia." *Vostok (Oriens)* 5 (2004): 43–59.

Bailey, F. M. *Mission to Tashkent.* Oxford: Oxford University Press, 1992

Baran, Zeyno. *Hizb ut-Tahrir: Islam's Political Insurgency.* Washington, DC: Nixon Center, 2004. http://www.bits.de/public/documents/US_Terrorist_Attacks/Hizbut -ahrirIslam'sPoliticalInsurgency.pdf.

Bartold, Vasily. *Raboty po istorii islama i arabskogo khalifata.* Vol. 6 of *Sochineniya.* Moscow: Nauka, 1966.

Bekjan, Safar. *U vkhoda na tot svet. Kak ya sidel v Tashtyurme.* https://www.neweurasia.info /archive/Uzbeks_book/index.html.

Bisenbayev, Asylbek. *Mify drevnikh tyurkov.* Almaty: Fond Dizayn, 2007. http://www.kyrgyz .ru/articles/library/ak_bisenbaev_mify_drevnih_tyurkov/1/.

Bogaturov, A. D., Ye. G. Kapustyan, V. G. Korgun, K. V. Pleshakov, V. P. Safronov, and M. A. Khrustalev. *Krizis i voyna: mezhdunarodnyye otnosheniya v tsentre i na pereferii mirovoy sistemy v 30-40kh godakh.* Moscow: Voyennaya Literatura, 1998.

Dwivedi, Ramakant. "Religious Extremism in Ferghana Valley." *Strategic Analysis* 30, no. 2 (2006). http://www.idsa.in/strategicanalysis/Religious%20Extremism%20in%20 Ferghana%20Valley_rdwivedi_0406.

Ezgulik. "Doklad posvyashchennyy godovshchine andizhanskikh sobytiy 13–14 Maya 2005." *Mutabar.org,* May 14, 2006. https://mutabar.org/ru/2006/05/11784.

Fitrat, Abdurauf. *Rasskazy indiyskogo puteshestvennika (Bukhara kak ona yest)*. Translated by N. Kondratyeva, edited by D. A. Alimova. Tashkent: Patent Press, 2007.

Golden, Peter. *Central Asia in World History*. New York: Oxford University Press, 2011.

Gorbachev, Mikhail. *Memoirs*. London: Doubleday, 1996.

Haaj, Shaykh Murabtal. "Fatwa on Following One of the Four Accepted Madhhabs." Translated by Hamza Yusuf Hanson. http://www.masud.co.uk/ISLAM/misc/mhfatwa .htm.

Hiro, Dilip. *Between Marx and Muhammad*. London: HarperCollins Publishers, 1995.

Hopkirk, Peter. *The Great Game: On Secret Service in High Asia*. London: John Murray, 2006.

Human Rights Society of Uzbekistan. "Andijan Refugees Speak Out." November 2010. http:// en.hrsu.org/archives/836.

Human Rights Watch. "The Andijan Massacre: One Year Later, Still No Justice." May 11, 2006. https://www.hrw.org/legacy/backgrounder/eca/uzbekistan0506/uzbekistan0506 .pdf.

———. "Bullets Were Falling Like Rain: The Andijan Massacre, May 13, 2005." 17-5(D) (2005). https://www.hrw.org/report/2005/06/06/bullets-were-falling-rain/andijan-massacre -may-13-2005.

———. "Burying the Truth: Uzbekistan Rewrites the Story of the Andijan Massacre." 17-6(D) (2005). https://www.hrw.org/report/2005/09/18/burying-truth/uzbekistan-rewrites -story-andijan-massacre.

International Crisis Group. "Central Asia: Islam and the State." Asia Report no. 59, Brussels, 2003.

———. "Central Asia: Islamist Mobilisation and Regional Security." Asia Report no. 14, Brussels, 2001.

———. "Radical Islam in Central Asia: Responding to Hizb-ut-Tahrir." Asia Report no. 58, Brussels, 2003.

———. "Uzbekistan: The Andijon Uprising." Asia Briefing no. 38, Brussels, May 25, 2005.

International Historical and Educational Charity and Human Rights Society. "Bezhentsy iz Uzbekistana v stranakh SNG: ugrozy bezopasnosti." October 11, 2006. http://old .memo.ru/uploads/files/283.pdf.

———. "Ivanovskiye uzbeki budut osvobozhdeny." Memorial, March 2007. https://memohrc .org/ru/news/ivanovskie-uzbeki-budut-osvobozhdeny-0.

———. "A List of People Prosecuted for Political Reasons, the Republic of Uzbekistan, the 1990s." Memorial (website). http://www.memo.ru/hr/politpr/lists1/uzb1.htm.

———. "Political Repressions in Uzbekistan in 2009-2010." http://www.nhc.no/filestore /Dokumenter/Land/Uzbekistan/Repression_inUz_RUS.pdf.

———. "Uzbekistan: Fight against Terrorism and Human Rights," Memorial (website), December 23, 2008. http://memohrc.org/news/uzbekistan-borba-s-terrorizmom-i-prava -cheloveka.

———. "Uzbekistan: A Review of Events in the Sphere of Human Rights in December 2002." Memorial (website). http://memohrc.org/specials/uzbekistan-obzor-sobytiy-v-oblasti -prav-cheloveka-za-dekabr-2002-goda.

Islam, identichnost i politika v post-sovetskom prostranstve. Papers presented at the international conference Islam, Identity and Politics in Post-Soviet Space: Comparative Analysis of Central Asia and Russia's European Part (Kazan, Russia, April 1-2, 2004). In *Kazan Federalist* 1, no. 13 (special edition, 2005).

Johnsen, Gregory D. "Yemen's Al-Iman University: A Pipeline for Fundamentalists?" *Terrorism Monitor* 4-22. Washington: The Jamestown Foundation, 2006.

Kadyrbayev, Aleksandr, A. Chudodeyev, and V. Novikov. "Tyubeteyka Rossiyskoy imperii." *Itogi* 30, no. 894 (2013): 26–29.

Kaligulayev, Mir. *Doroga k smerti bolshe chem smert.* Wolverhampton, UK: Black Quadrat, 2005.

Kamp, Marianne. "Where Did the Mullahs Go? Oral Histories from Rural Uzbekistan." *Welt des Islams* 50 (2010): 503–31.

Karagiannis, Emmanuel. "Political Islam in Uzbekistan: Hizb ut-Tahrir al-Islami." *Europe-Asia Studies* 58, no. 2 (2006): 261–80.

Kasymov, Farkhod, and Bakhodir Ergashev. "Bukharskaya revolyutsiya." *Rodina* 11 (1989). http://greylib.align.ru/735/buxarskaya-revolyuciya-zhurnal-rodina-1989-11.html.

Keller, Nuh Ha Mim. "What Is a Madhab? Why Is It Necessary to Follow One?" *Q News* (2000). http://www.masud.co.uk/ISLAM/nuh/madhhab.htm.

———. "Who or What Is a Salafi? Is His Approach Valid?" *Q News* (1995). http://www.masud.co.uk/ISLAM/nuh/salafi.htm.

Keller, Shoshana. *To Moscow, Not Mecca: The Soviet Campaign against Islam in Central Asia, 1917–1941.* Westport, CT: Praeger Publishers, 2001.

Khalid, Adeeb. *Islam after Communism: Religion and Politics in Central Asia.* Berkeley: University of California Press, 2007.

———. *Making Uzbekistan: Nation, Empire, and Revolution in the Early USSR.* Ithaca, NY: Cornell University Press, 2015.

———. "A Secular Islam: Nation, State and Religion in Uzbekistan." *International Journal of Middle East Studies* 35 (2003): 573–98.

Kulchik, Yuri. "Respublika Uzbekistan v seredine 90-kh." *Applied and Imperative Ethnology Studies* 90. Moscow: The Institute of Ethnography and Anthropology of the Russian Academy of Sciences, 1995. http://static.iea.ras.ru//neotlozhka/90-Kulchik.pdf.

Krishnamurti, Jiddu. *Freedom from the Known.* New York: Harper One, 2009.

Lenin, Vladimir. "Sotsializm i religiya." *Revolyutsiya* newspaper online library, 1905. http://revolucia.ru/soc_relg.htm.

The Library of the Congress (Federal Research Division). *The Country Studies Series: Uzbekistan,* 1988–99.

Mahmudov, Abdulaziz. "Istoriya zhizni uzbekskogo imama Abdullazhona Utayeva." Human Rights Society of Uzbekistan, March 8, 2013. http://ru.hrsu.org/archives/4331.

McGregor, Andrew. "Prosecuting Terrorism: Yemen's War on Islamist Militancy." *Terrorism Monitor* 4, no. 9 (2006). http://www.jamestown.org/single/?tx_ttnews%5Btt_news%5D=759&no_cache=1#.V2k2brgrKoo.

———. "Yemeni Sheikh al-Zindani's New Role as a Healer." *Terrorism Focus* 4, no. 8 (2007). http://www.jamestown.org/single/?tx_ttnews%5Btt_news%5D=4057#.V2kjxrgrKoo.

Mourad, Suleiman. *The Mosaic of Islam: A Conversation with Perry Anderson.* London: Verso, 2016.

Muminov, Ashirbek. "Traditional and Modern Religious Theological Schools in Central Asia." In *Political Islam and Conflicts in Russia and Central Asia,* edited by Lena Jonson and Murad Esenov, 101–11. Stockholm: Utrikespolitiska Institutet, 1999.

Murad, Abdal Hakim (Timothy John Winter). *Understanding the Four Madhabs.* Cambridge: Muslim Academic Trust, 1999.

Nourzhanov, Kirill, and Christian Bleuer. *Tajikistan: A Political and Social History.* Canberra: Australian National University E Press, 2013.

"Obrashcheniye Ko Vsem Musulmanam Rossii I Vostoka." *Russian Perspectives on Islam.* Accessed April 3, 2017. http://islamperspectives.org/rpi/items/show/11587.

Olcott, Martha Brill. *In the Whirlwind of Jihad.* Washington, DC: Brookings Institution Press, 2012.

———. "The Roots of Radical Islam in Central Asia." Carnegie Endowment for International Peace, January 2007. http://carnegieendowment.org/files/olcottroots.pdf.

Olcott, Martha Brill, and Diora Ziyaeva. "Islam in Uzbekistan: Religious Education and State Ideology." *Russia and Eurasia Program* no. 91, Carnegie Endowment for International Peace, July 2008. http://carnegieendowment.org/files/cp91_islam_uzbek_final.pdf.

Olimov, Muzaffar. "V. V. Bartold o natsionalnom razmezhevanii v Sredney Azii; zapiska Akademika Bartolda po voprosu ob istoricheskikh vzaimootnosheniyakh turetskikh i iranskikh narodnostey Sredney Azii." *Vostok (Oriens)* 5 (1991). http://www.ca-c.org/datarus/st_13_olimov.shtml.

Olimov, Muzaffar, and Saodat Olimova. "Political Islam in Modern Tajikistan, Islam in the Post-Soviet Space: A View from Inside." In *Collection of Academic Papers*, revised by Alexey Malashenko and Martha Brill Olcott. Moscow: Moscow Carnegie Centre, 2001. http://podelise.ru/docs/index-24877094-1.html?page=25.

Panova, Vera, and Yuriy Vakhtin. *Zhizn Muhammada.* Moscow: Politizdat, 1990.

Platonov, Andrei. *Jan.* http://thelib.ru/books/platonov_andrey_platonovich/dzhan-read.html.

Rasanayagam, Johan. *Islam in Post-Soviet Uzbekistan: The Morality of Experience.* New York: Cambridge University Press, 2010.

Rashid, Ahmed. *Descent into Chaos: The U.S. and the Disaster in Pakistan, Afghanistan, and Central Asia.* London: Penguin Books, 2009.

———. *Jihad: The Rise of Militant Islam in Central Asia.* New Haven, CT: Yale University Press, 2002.

de Rubruck, William. *The Journal of William de Rubruck: Account of the Mongol.* United Kingdom: Amazon, 2017.

Sadykova, Bakhyt. *Mustafa Choqai v emigratsii,* 2011. http://bibliotekar.kz/chitat-knigu-onlain-mustafa-chokai-v-yem.

Scheuer, Michael. "Saudi Salafism a Stronger Force in Islamist Militancy Than Recanting Clerics." *Terrorism Focus* 5, no. 26 (2008). http://www.jamestown.org/programs/tm/single/?tx_ttnews%5Btt_news%5D=5057&tx_ttnews%5BbackPid%5D=246&no_cache=1#.V2k3RLgrKoo.

Shmulevich, Avraam. "Will Central Asia Become Islamist? Social Conditions for the Growth of Islamism." *Russian Journal,* January 2007. http://www.russ.ru/layout/set/print/pole/Stanet-li-Central-naya-Aziya-islamistskoj-Stat-ya-tret-ya.

Volkogonov, Dmitri. *The Rise and Fall of the Soviet Empire.* London: HarperCollins Publishers, 1999.

Whitlock, Monica. *Beyond the Oxus: The Central Asians.* London: John Murray, 2002.

Wintle, Justin. *History of Islam.* London: Rough Guides, 2003.

Yuldoshev, Akrom. "Ymonga yol." http://www.liveinternet.ru/users/4799013/post361298367/. Russian translation: http://www.portal-credo.ru/site/index.php?act=news&type=archive&day=16&month=5&year=2005&id=33436ж.

Zaidi, Syed Manzar Abbas. "Uzbek Militancy in Pakistan." *Centre for International and Strategic Analysis (SISA)*, report 1 (2013). http://strategiskanalyse.no/publikasjoner%20 2013/2013-02-04_SISA1_Uzbek_Militancy_in_Pakistan_-_Syed_Manzar_Abbas _Zaidi.pdf.
Zemskov, Viktor. "GULAG (istoriko-sotsiologicheskiy aspect)." *Sotsiologicheskiye Issledovaniya*, no. 6–7 (1991). http://www.hrono.ru/statii/2001/zemskov.php.

Websites

Fergananews.com (Moscow-based independent news and comments on Central Asia)
Ozodlik.org (Prague-based Radio Liberty Uzbek Service)
Uznews.org (now defunct Germany-based independent news on Uzbekistan)
Uzxalqharakati.com (Uzbek opposition)

BAGILA BUKHARBAYEVA is a former Central Asia correspondent for the Associated Press. She is a winner of the Paul Klebnikov Courage in Journalism Award.

www.ingramcontent.com/pod-product-compliance
Lightning Source LLC
Chambersburg PA
CBHW052000270326
41929CB00015B/2723